toddler
healthy
eating
planner

mitchell beazley

toddler
healthy
eating
planner

the new way to feed
your toddler a balanced
diet every day, featuring
more than 250 recipes

amanda grant

Toddler Healthy Eating Planner
by Amanda Grant

First published in Great Britain in 2004 by Mitchell Beazley, an imprint of
Octopus Publishing Group Limited,
2–4 Heron Quays, London E14 4JP.
© Octopus Publishing Group Limited 2004
Text © Amanda Grant 2004

Commissioning Editor: Rebecca Spry
Executive Art Editor: Yasia Williams
Art Editor: Tim Pattinson
Design: Miranda Harvey
Editor: Diona Gregory
Consultant Nutritionist: Tanya Carr
Special Photography: Francesca Yorke
Front Jacket Photographs: Francesca Yorke and Ariel Skelley/CORBIS
Stylist: Juliet Harvey
Home Economy Assistant: Sibilla Whitehead
Production: Alexis Coogan and Gilbert Francourt
Proof-reader: Julie Tolley
Index: John Noble

Typeset in Praxis
Printed and bound by Toppan Printing Company in China

Acknowledgements
Thank you to the paediatric dieticians, health visitors, midwives and nutritionists for their invaluable contributions to this book – especially to Victoria Morris (paediatric dietician), Tanya Carr (registered dietician and consultant nutritionist), Fiona Hunter (nutritionist) and Wendy Robertson RGNRM.
     Thank you to Billy, who helped me throughout with research, testing recipes and lots of support. Thanks to Francesca for being so patient and creative with all the children; the photographs are wonderful. Miranda, you have done it again, the book looks totally fabulous, and thanks for all the gorgeous styling Juliet. A huge thank you to Diona for editing another of my books; with my usual pregnancy brain this is always a challenging a role and you have done it brilliantly! Thanks again to Becca, whose creativity and brilliant vision for this book has helped it all come to fruition. Thanks also to all my friends, especially Annie, and all the beautiful children who modelled for the book.

Library picture acknowledgements: page 32 Photodisc

To Finley, who was delivered the day after the manuscript.

information about this book

recipe symbols:
● The symbols used for each nutrient are for visual identification only; they do not imply that your toddler can eat the food shown in that symbol.
● The "also rich in" symbol (see page 6) indicates that a portion of a dish contains more than 25 per cent of your toddler's daily requirement of the listed nutrients.

recipes:
● All toddler portion sizes are approximate, based on the age group of the chapter, and the points listed are based on the stated portion size. However, all toddlers appetites are different.
● Wash all fruit and vegetables that have not been peeled.

points system:
● The points system is only intended to be a guide.
● If you are still breastfeeding, assume as a guide that your toddler is consuming the same number of points of each nutrient as is provided by the recommended amount of milk.

nutrition:
● The "most recently published recommended nutrient intakes" refer to the British Government's Reference Nutrient Intakes (RNIs).

Note: Most of the recipes in this book are suitable for the whole family and many of the fresh dishes will make enough to feed a family of four. The frozen recipes are often suitable for freezing in small individual portions so that you can have ready meals to hand.

contents

6   **how to use this book**

8   **toddler nutrition**
10   why nutrition matters
12   nutrition for development
22   milk
25   vegetarian toddlers
26   special toddler diets
27   food purity
30   foods to eat and foods to avoid

34   **toddler kitchen**
36   toddlers in the kitchen
37   toddlers at the table
40   toddler storecupboard
44   toddler storecupboard recipes

46   **1-2 years**
48   what's happening to your
      toddler
49   which nutrients are key

50   your toddler's routine
51   troubleshooting
52   sample 1-2 year meal planners
54   fresh breakfasts
58   quick bites: breakfasts
60   fresh lunches
64   quick bites: lunches
66   lunches to freeze
70   quick bites: snacks
72   fresh suppers
78   quick bites: suppers
80   suppers to freeze
84   fresh and frozen puddings
88   quick bites: puddings
90   celebration food

94   **2-3 years**
96   what's happening to your toddler
97   which nutrients are key
98   your toddler's routine
99   troubleshooting
100   sample 2-3 year meal planners
102   fresh breakfasts
106   quick bites: breakfasts
108   fresh lunches
112   quick bites: lunches
114   lunches to freeze
118   quick bites: snacks
120   fresh suppers
126   quick bites: suppers
128   suppers to freeze
132   fresh and frozen puddings
136   quick bites: puddings
138   celebration food

142   **3-4 years**
144   what's happening to your toddler
145   which nutrients are key
146   your toddler's routine
147   troubleshooting
148   sample 3-4 year meal planners
150   fresh breakfasts
154   quick bites: breakfasts
156   fresh lunches
160   quick bites: lunches
162   lunches to freeze
166   quick bites: snacks
168   fresh suppers
174   quick bites: suppers
176   suppers to freeze
180   fresh and frozen puddings
184   quick bites: puddings
186   celebration foods

190   further reading/glossary
191   index

How to use the charts and symbols

For one-, two- and three-year-olds, over 30 nutrients that are essential to health must be obtained from food and drink. However, five nutrients are particularly important in this age group: protein, iron, zinc, calcium and vitamin C. The "nutrients required per day" chart opposite illustrates how I have converted the most recently published recommended nutrient intakes (see "nutrition" on page 4), which are usually measured in grams (g), milligrams (mg) or micrograms (mcg), into points for each of these nutrients. Where the recommended daily nutrient intake does not convert exactly to points, I have rounded it up to the nearest half point. All my recipes have icons illustrating how many points of each of these nutrients a single portion of the dish contains. So, using the "nutrients required per day" chart as easy reference, you can count up the points for each nutrient that you've fed your toddler in a day to check that he is getting the required amount.

Of course, you must also ensure that your toddler has a sufficient intake of the other important nutrients, in particular saturated and unsaturated fats, carbohydrates (starch and sugar), vitamins A, D, E, and B group, and the mineral phosphorous. However, as long as he's enjoying a varied diet, he's likely to be getting enough of all of these nutrients. On pages 12-21 you'll find a guide to how much of each of these nutrients your toddler needs, as well as lists of which foods contain them. Recipes that are rich in one or more of these nutrients (apart from fats and carbohydrate) feature a symbol (see below and "recipe symbols", page 4).

how to
use this book

The most important thing to remember is that this points system is designed to be used as a guide. Keep in mind, however, that many toddlers will need less than the recommended nutrient intake that the "nutrients required per day" chart refers to, but a small minority will need slightly more; if in doubt, ask your health visitor. Some days your toddler will exceed the recommended nutrient intake for a particular nutrient and other days he'll fall short, but it's his average intake over weeks that's important. If you are ever in doubt about your toddler's nutritional intake, always ask your family doctor or registered dietician for advice.

symbols

Each recipe in this book features a selection of these nutrient symbols. Each represents a nutrient and is accompanied by a number to show how many points of that nutrient a portion of the dish contains. The tick symbol shows that a portion of the dish gives more than 25 per cent of the recommended daily requirement of the nutrient listed alongside it.

 protein

 iron

 zinc

 calcium

 vitamin C

 rich in listed nutrient/s

nutrients required per day

This chart shows how many points of each key nutrient your toddler needs. Although the nutritional requirements of babies increases regularly throughout the first year because of the rapid development of their organs and brain, the guideline remains static for toddlers aged one to three (inclusive). I have based the figures on age rather than weight, but weight may have an impact on nutritional requirements; if you are concerned, speak to your family doctor or registered dietician.

	protein 1 point = 1.5g	iron 1 point = 1.5mg	zinc 1 point = 1mg	calcium 1 point = 105mg	vitamin C 1 point = 5mg
1-3 years (inclusive)					
total points recommended	10 (14.5g)	5 (6.9mg)	5 (5mg)	3½ (350mg)	6 (30mg)
350ml milk provides	7 (10.5g)	0 (0.21mg)	1½ (1.4mg)	4 (400mg)	0 (0mg)
points required from food	3	5	3½	0	6

how to build a daily meal plan for your toddler

This shows how to ensure your toddler gets enough nutrients by adding up the points in his daily food. It doesn't matter if the points requirement is exceeded, but it is not recommended that you excessively exceed the iron intake on a regular basis.

time	food and milk	protein	iron	zinc	calcium	vitamin C
breakfast	150ml full-fat cow's milk	3	0	½	1½	0
	1 portion fruit salad with yogurt sauce	2	½	½	1	10½
mid-am	muesli with blueberries	6	1½	1½	1½	2
lunch	1 portion onion and potato tortilla	9½	1½	1½	1½	1
mid-pm	drink	0	0	0	0	0
supper	1 portion sausage stew	7½	1½	1	½	½
	1 portion apple and blackberry crumble	2½	½	½	½	1
bedtime	200ml full-fat cow's milk	4	0	1	2	0
	total points	34½	5½	6½	8½	15

Good nutrition is vital to help your toddler's body to function, grow efficiently and repair itself, and to promote good health throughout her life. As toddlers have small appetites, they need small, frequent meals made up of nutrient-dense foods, with healthy snacks in-between. This will ensure energy levels are maintained, which is crucial for energetic and inquisitive toddlers. All foods provide a mixture of nutrients, but no single food provides them all. Try to include a broad range of fresh, unrefined foods. A good mixture of foods will also help keep her interested at mealtimes, and your goal during these three years should be to feed your toddler the same foods as the rest of the family.

toddler
nutrition

why nutrition
matters

There is an abundance of information on healthy eating and nutrition, and most parents have a fair idea of what constitutes a healthy diet. Nevertheless, the newspapers regularly carry stories about diet-related disorders among toddlers and food-related health problems among people of all ages. We are just beginning to see more clearly how a diet that is heavily dependant on processed foods and high in sugar, fat and salt is affecting the next generation.

Good nutrition may not only benefit your child's health, but also her behaviour and emotional wellbeing. What your toddler eats during her formative years will have a significant impact on her future health, and good eating habits formed now are likely to last a lifetime. As much as possible your toddler should be eating the same sorts of foods as the rest of the family and at the same times. Of course, this is assuming that the family as a whole is eating a well-balanced and varied diet. If not, having a toddler around is a great opportunity to pay more attention to what the whole family eats. It is important to remember, however, that healthy eating guidelines intended for adults do not fully apply to pre-school children (age one to five years). Diets that are high in fibre or low in fat are not suitable for toddlers.

Your toddler will develop and grow at an amazing rate. Her new-found independence will spur her on to explore and test her world. All this increased activity and inquisitiveness requires fuel. Regular meals are particularly important for toddlers. They should have three meals a day, with two small, healthy snacks in-between. This ensures that they get enough calories, but also enables you to give a wide range of foods in the space of a day.

Breakfast really is the most important meal for toddlers because they have gone through the night without eating. A good breakfast, including carbohydrate (eg porridge) with some protein (eg milk), will set them up for the day. Lunch should ideally include some protein (eg egg, chicken, pulses), where the fat supply in the foods can help with an energy boost for afternoon activities and where the protein can help with growth, development and repair. Carbohydrate foods such as pasta or rice are especially important at supper time because they will help make your toddler feel full throughout the night, helping her to sleep more soundly.

Snacks should be as nutritious as possible, ideally fruit, vegetables or other healthy nibbles – sometimes, if your child had a late breakfast or lunch, just a drink of diluted fruit juice will be enough. Sugary snacks should only be given occasionally, preferably relatively soon after a meal to help prevent a blood sugar rush. Encourage your toddler to drink lots during the day – particularly water, with some milk (preferably organic) or very dilute fruit juice.

Good nutrition is not just about a well-balanced diet, it is also about your whole approach to food and eating. If your family embraces the idea that food is something to be enjoyed and shared, your toddler is likely to have this attitude too. While healthy eating should be your goal, try not to place too much emphasis on so-called "good" or "bad" foods. Inevitably toddlers are drawn towards processed foods, particularly because of their packaging. It is unrealistic to try to exclude them, and you may run the risk of exaggerating their desirability. It is far better to have the attitude that there are no "good" or "bad" foods, just that everything can be eaten in moderation.

food allergies and intolerances

Until recently special diets for children were relatively unusual, but research has indicated that many disorders, such as asthma, may be treated by restricting certain foods. Similarly, some disorders are linked to certain foods – for instance, some E numbers in processed foods have been connected to hyperactivity. These kinds of allergies and intolerances are being reported with greater frequency.

When foods that are normally harmless to most of us (eg cow's milk, nuts or wheat) are perceived to be foreign by the immune system, an allergic reaction can be triggered. Some of the reactions may simply cause mild discomfort (eg a rash), whereas others can be life-threatening (eg anaphylactic shock). A serious allergy will generally become apparent a few minutes after your toddler has eaten a particular food. If you suspect an allergic reaction, speak to your family doctor immediately. If there is any family history of food allergies, avoid giving any sort of nuts or nut products before the age of three. Foods that have traditionally caused an allergic reaction in the family may need to be avoided, but your doctor or dietician can advise about this. Food intolerances are less serious and may not be as immediately apparent. They are often indicated by milder symptoms, such as tummy ache, diarrhoea, asthma, eczema or poor growth. Both allergies and intolerances can be treated by changing the diet, but always seek the advice of your family doctor or registered dietician before excluding any food (see pages 30-33 on foods to avoid) to ensure that your child continues to get all the nutrients she needs and that you are not cutting out foods or nutrients unnecessarily.

the points system

To help make your life easier, I have chosen five of the key nutrients your toddler needs (see page 6) and designed a points system around them. This is intended to help you easily get used to feeding your toddler a balanced diet. At the same time, it will reassure you that she is eating the recommended amount of each of these nutrients on a daily basis. There are, however, other nutrients that are also very important during your toddler's life. To find out how to ensure a healthy intake of all the key nutrients, see pages 12–21.

nutrition for growth
and development

key protein foods

These foods may not all be suitable for all toddlers in all age groups. See relevant chapters for specific advice.

Protein foods providing all the essential amino acids include:
- Meat, such as chicken and lamb
- Fish, such as salmon and tuna
- Dairy products, particularly milk, cheese, eggs and yogurt
- Soya beans and soya products, such as tofu, soya cheese and soya milk.

Good vegetarian protein sources (other than the soya products mentioned above) include:
These do not contain all the essential amino acids. However, in combination they can, for instance, vegetable burgers served with rice.
- Beans and pulses, such as chickpeas, beans, lentils and butter beans
- Cereals and grain foods, such as rice, pasta, oats and muesli (with finely chopped nuts – do not give nuts or seeds to toddlers under the age of three if there is a family history of food allergies)
- Ground nuts, such as hazelnuts and almonds, and smooth nut butters (see warning above)
- Ground seeds, such as sunflower seeds and sesame seeds (see warning above).

protein

Protein consists of building blocks called amino acids. There are two types of amino acids: essential and non-essential. Essential amino acids must be obtained directly from food, while the body can produce non-essential amino acids. Therefore you need to make sure that your toddler's diet contains enough essential amino acids (see "key protein foods", left).

why your toddler needs it

Protein is one of the most important nutrients for helping the body to build and repair muscles, tissues, hair and organs, and maintain an effective immune and hormonal system.

how to make sure your toddler gets it

An adequate intake of protein in particular should be ensured. This will be easy to achieve if you aim to feed your toddler a diverse diet. "Infants in the UK, whose diets rapidly diversify and who by the age of nine months are regularly consuming meat, fish, eggs or reasonable quantities of milk, are unlikely to be protein deficient," according to the UK Department of Health.

However, if you are feeding your toddler a vegetarian or vegan diet you must make sure that she gets a good combination of protein-rich foods. Most plant foods are low in protein compared with foods of animal origin (with the exception of soya products such as tofu and soya milk), the proteins from any single plant, unlike animal protein, do not contain all the essential amino acids. This is why it is important to feed your toddler a mixture of plant foods to help make sure that the complete range of essential amino acids is provided (see vegetarian toddlers, page 25). Mothers wishing to offer their toddler a vegan diet should seek specialist advice from a registered dietician.

Whole nuts are not recommended for children under five.

iron

There are two main types of iron in food: haem iron from lean red meat and non-haem iron from plant sources, such as vegetables, dried fruits and finely chopped or ground nuts (do not give nuts to toddlers under the age of three if there is a family history of food allergies).

why your toddler needs it

Iron is needed for healthy blood and muscles. A lack of iron can lead to a common form of anaemia. Toddlers who are poor eaters, or on restricted diets, are most at risk. Normally toddlers who are affected by anaemia can seem listless and lethargic and have a general a lack of appetite or interest in their food. However, the symptoms are not always so obvious. It is important to prevent iron-deficiency anaemia because it has been linked to poorer health, slower development and specifically poor mental development. Studies into iron deficiency and anaemia in toddlers show that they are common among 2 year olds in the UK, but become less common the older the child gets. If you have any concerns about your toddler's iron intake, speak to your family doctor or state-registered dietician. Iron-deficiency anaemia is relatively easy to treat by changes to diet and with iron supplements.

how to make sure your toddler gets it

Iron-rich foods form a vital part of a healthy diet. You can help to increase iron absorption by giving your toddler certain combinations of foods at the same meal. Foods rich in vitamin C, particularly citrus fruits and some green vegetables, significantly help the absorption of iron. For example, serve red meat with green vegetables or fresh fruit juice with breakfast cereals. Similarly, meat and fish help to increase iron absorption from non-animal foods, such as pulses and vegetables. Fortified foods can also help to increase iron intake from the diet. Some foods, particularly those containing tannin or caffeine, such as tea or chocolate, or foods high in fibre, such as bran, can hinder iron absorption. You should avoid giving your toddler large quantities of these foods. These points are particularly relevant if you are feeding your toddler a vegetarian or vegan diet (see page 25).

key iron foods

These foods may not all be suitable for all toddlers in all age groups. See relevant chapters for specific advice.
- Red meat
- Eggs
- Beans, including baked beans
- Tofu
- Oily fish, eg tuna and mackerel
- Dried fruits, eg unsulphured apricots, raisins and prunes
- Wholegrain cereals and bread
- Nuts – finely chopped or ground (do not give nuts to toddlers under the age of three if there is a family history of food allergies).
- Certain fortified foods, eg breakfast cereals
- Green vegetables.

calcium

Calcium is a mineral needed for strong, healthy bones and teeth.

why your toddler needs it

99 per cent of the body's calcium is found in bones and teeth, with 1 per cent in blood plasma and soft tissues. During her formative years your toddler needs calcium to help with the normal function of all cells as well as for bone and teeth development. Lack of calcium has been linked to the development of osteoporosis. Although this is rare in children, a diet that meets calcium requirements in childhood will help ensure healthy bones in adulthood.

how to make sure your toddler gets it

Your toddler can get sufficient calcium quite easily if she eats a good range of dairy produce and other calcium-rich foods. Products made from fortified white flour provide useful sources of calcium. Ensuring vegan toddlers, or those on restricted diets, have enough calcium is more challenging (see page 25).

zinc

The mineral zinc has many functions in your toddler's body. These include maintaining healthy blood function and an efficient immune system and helping wounds to heal.

why your toddler needs it

The most recent information from the British Food Standards Agency shows that around 14 per cent of children under four years old have average intakes of zinc below recommended levels. In extreme cases the symptoms of zinc deficiency can include a lack of appetite, skin problems and poor healing of wounds. Zinc deficiency can lead to poor growth.

how to make sure your toddler gets it

A toddler given a diet that includes plenty of meat, fish and dairy products, is unlikely to be zinc deficient. Vegetables and other plant foods, such as pulses, are not such good sources of zinc, so you need to give your vegetarian or vegan toddler a wide variety of these foods (see page 25).

vitamin C

Vital for growth and healthy gums, teeth, bones and skin, vitamin C is particularly important for the healing of wounds. It is also needed to aid the absorption of iron. Vitamin C is also one of the best-known antioxidant vitamins, which also helps to boost the immune system and in particular helps to prevent common colds.

why your toddler needs it

It is important to give your toddler foods that contain vitamin C every day. Vitamin C is a water-soluble vitamin and the body cannot store excess amounts, it just uses what it needs. Severe vitamin C deficiency is characterized by several symptoms, including poor wound healing and swollen or inflamed gums. However, if you are giving your toddler a wide range of fruits and vegetables, it is very unlikely that she will become vitamin C deficient.

how to make sure your toddler gets it

It is important that your toddler's diet provides a good combination of both raw and cooked fruits and vegetables. Vitamin C is very easily destroyed by heat and light, so include raw or very lightly cooked foods, such as steamed vegetables, in your toddler's diet as much as possible. Chunks of raw, soft fruits and vegetables make great snacks, but until she is confident with chewing and eating crunchier foods always stay with her while she is eating them.

key vitamin C foods

These foods may not all be suitable for all toddlers in all age groups. See relevant chapters for specific advice.
- Kiwi fruit
- Strawberries and raspberries
- Oranges and other citrus fruits
- Mango and melon
- Blackcurrants
- Red, yellow and orange peppers
- Broccoli
- Nectarines
- Cabbage
- Peas
- Grapefruit
- Cauliflower
- Peaches
- Spinach
- Potatoes and sweet potatoes
- Swede.

fats

Fats and oils are made up of molecules of three types of fatty acids and glycerol. Depending on which type of fatty acid is present in the largest proportion, a fat is said to be saturated, for example butter; mono-unsaturated, for example olive oil, or polyunsaturated, for example sunflower oil.

why your toddler needs them

Many parents are concerned about the amount of fat in their toddler's diet, but it is essential to include some fat, both saturated and unsaturated. Fat is an energy-dense food and allows your toddler to obtain her energy requirement from a manageable amount of food. This is particularly helpful because your toddler has such a small stomach capacity. Fats also contain the fat-soluble vitamins A, D, E and K, all of which are vital for her healthy development. Low-fat products and low-fat diets are not suitable for your toddler, although semi-skimmed milk can be given to toddlers from two years as long as they are following a healthy balanced diet.

how to make sure your toddler gets them

Give your toddler a healthy, balanced diet, which includes both saturated and unsaturated fats.

carbohydrates

There are two types of carbohydrates: simple (sugars) and complex (starches and fibre). Both can be found in a natural form or they can be refined. Carbohydrates are the body's primary source of energy.

why your toddler needs them

Your toddler needs a good source of carbohydrates to provide her with energy to get through each day but also to fuel her growth and development. It is very important that she gets the right balance of carbohydrates. Too much refined carbohydrate, such as sugar and honey, including cakes and biscuits which contain them, can lead to dental or weight problems. Similarly, too much fibre in unrefined carbohydrates, such as brown rice or wholewheat pasta, can inhibit the absorption of other nutrients and the release of energy.

how to make sure your toddler gets them

Sugars provide energy but have little nutritive value. Your toddler should find fruit and milk-based products sweet enough without extra sugar, because they contain natural sugars. Other foods containing sugars, including cakes and biscuits, should only be given in moderation. You should aim to give your toddler a variety of complex carbohydrates, such as cereals, vegetables, pasta and pulses, every day.

key starch foods

These foods may not all be suitable for all toddlers in all age groups. See relevant chapters for specific advice.

Refined starch foods:
- Breakfast cereals such as Weetabix and porridge
- White flour and white bread
- Biscuits and cakes
- Baby rice.

Natural starch foods:
- Potatoes and bread
- Breakfast cereals
- Sweetcorn
- Root vegetables, eg parsnips
- Nuts – finely chopped or ground (do not give nuts to toddlers under the age of three if there is a family history of food allergies)
- Chickpeas
- Bananas.

key sugar foods

These foods may not all be suitable for all toddlers in all age groups. See relevant chapters for specific advice.

Natural sugar foods:
- Fruit and vegetables
- Breast milk and full-fat milk.

Refined sugar foods:
- White and brown-coloured sugar
- Biscuits, cakes and jellies.

vitamin A

Vitamin A is found in animal products. Beta-carotene is a substance found in plant foods and converted by the body into vitamin A.

why your toddler needs it

Vitamin A is needed for growth, development, healthy skin and hair, and good colour and night vision. It also helps the development of healthy teeth.

how to make sure your toddler gets it

If your toddler is being given a healthy well-balanced diet she should get all the vitamin A or beta-carotene she needs. Always speak to your family doctor or state-registered dietician before giving a vitamin A supplement, as too much vitamin A can be detrimental to your toddler's health.

vitamin B group

The vitamin B complex comprises vitamin B1 (thiamine), B2 (riboflavin), B3 (niacin), folic acid, B5 (pantothenic acid), B6 (pyridoxine), and B12 (cyanocobalamin).

why your toddler needs them

The B vitamins play many roles: they are essential for your toddler's metabolism and for helping with the conversion of carbohydrate into energy. They are also vital for the maintenance of healthy nervous and immune systems, mucous membranes and a healthy brain. They assist in the production of red blood cells, skin and hair.

how to make sure your toddler gets them

Some foods, such as red meat, contain all the B vitamins. If your toddler is being fed a well-balanced diet she should get all the B vitamins she needs. However, if she is being fed a restricted diet, she may need supplements (see page 25) – toddlers following a vegan diet will need supplements. All the B vitamins are water-soluble, so where you can, give your toddler raw or uncooked fruit and vegetables, bread and cheese to maximize her B vitamin intake. Chunks of raw, soft fruits and vegetables make great snacks, but until she is confident with chewing and eating crunchier foods always stay with her while she is eating them.

key vitamin B foods

These foods may not all be suitable for all toddlers in all age groups. See relevant chapters for specific advice.

B_1:
- Brazil nuts and peanuts – finely chopped or ground (do not give nuts to toddlers under the age of three if there is a family history of food allergies)
- Potatoes
- Bacon and red meat
- Bread and cereal products
- Full-fat milk.

B_2:
- Liver and red meat
- Full-fat milk and cheese
- Fortified cereals and eggs.

B_3:
- Meat
- Potatoes, bread and cereal products
- Dried fruit
- nuts – finely chopped or ground (see warning above).

Folic acid:
- Green leafy vegetables
- Oranges
- Yeast extract
- Cereal products and bread fortified with folic acid
- Nuts – finely chopped or ground (see warning above).

B_6:
- Red meat and liver
- Fish and eggs
- Bananas and avocados
- Cereal products.

B_{12}:
- Meat
- Full-fat milk products.

vitamin D

Vitamin D is essential for the absorption of calcium and the growth and development of strong bones and teeth. It also plays a role in maintaining a healthy immune system.

how to make sure your toddler gets it

Vitamin D is naturally present in only a few foods, and these are all of animal origin. Some products, such as breakfast cereals and margarine, are fortified with vitamin D and should be included in your toddler's diet. However, vitamin D is mainly made by the skin in the presence of sunlight, hence its nickname the "sunshine vitamin". For this reason all toddlers should spend at least 30 minutes outdoors each day – if this is not possible your toddler may need a supplement: speak to your family doctor or state-registered dietician.

vitamin E

Vitamin E is an antioxidant that is thought to play an important role in reducing the risk of diseases such as cancer and heart disease.

why your toddler needs it

Vitamin E is needed to help develop and maintain strong healthy cells, especially in the blood and nervous system.

how to make sure your toddler gets it

If your toddler is being given a balanced diet she should get all the vitamin E she needs.

phosphorus

Phosphorus is a mineral that works in a way similar to calcium.

why your toddler needs it

Phosphorus is vital for energy production. It helps to build and maintain healthy bones and teeth. It also aids the absorption and transport of many other nutrients.

how to make sure your toddler gets it

About half your toddler's phosphorus will come from milk. Phosphorus is present in nearly all foods.

key phosphorous foods

These foods may not all be suitable for all toddlers in all age groups. See relevant chapters for specific advice.
- Breast milk or full-fat dairy products
- Bread and cereal products
- Red meat and poultry
- Fish
- Eggs
- Pulses, eg chickpeas
- Potatoes
- Yeast extract
- Pumpkin seeds
- Fruit and vegetables
- Nuts – finely chopped or ground (do not give nuts to toddlers under the age of three if there is a family history of food allergies).

supplements

Current British Government guidelines recommend that all children between six months and five years should be considered for receiving vitamin A, C and D drops. If your toddler is a good eater and being given a healthy, well-balanced diet, including a wide range of foods, she will probably not need any drops. However, problem eaters, those who were born prematurely, those on restricted diets such as vegans (see page 25), or toddlers with little chance of being outside in the sunlight, may need them. Always speak to your family doctor or registered dietician before giving any supplements to your toddler. Vitamin drops may be available free of charge to certain families, but this does vary from area to area.

milk

Milk, whether breast, formula or cow's, makes a vital contribution to your toddler's nutrition. Breast milk is a naturally nutrient-rich food that is easily digested by your toddler, and if you wish you can continue to breast-feed a toddler up to two years. La Leche League, a voluntary organization that promotes breastfeeding, believes that antibody production in breast milk increases after one year of breastfeeding, which helps boost your child's immune system. Breast milk is also free!

From the age of one it is possible to make the transition from breast or formula milk to pasteurized full-fat cow's milk (not semi-skimmed or skimmed). Infant formula is normally based on cow's milk and is the main alternative to breast milk in the first six months of your baby's life. After six months you can introduce "follow-on" milks – these are similar to formula, but with different nutritional qualities (however, if your baby is getting a broad range of foods as she is being weaned, ordinary formula will be just as good). After one year there is generally no reason to continue giving formula or follow-on milk, as cow's milk can now be given as a drink.

cow's milk

From the age of six months, cow's milk can be used in dishes, but it should not be given as a drink until your baby is at least one year old.

Toddlers over one year need a minimum of approximately 350ml full-fat milk a day, inclusive of milk used in food. Most toddlers need up to 565ml full-fat milk per day, with approximately 350ml of that being given as a drink. Milk makes an important contribution to a toddler's diet, providing a substantial proportion of their daily intake of protein, fat, zinc, calcium and B vitamins, particularly riboflavin. Often, at this stage, growth may slow down and your toddler's appetite may slacken off. Giving milk will help to ensure that your child is receiving many essential nutrients in one hit.

When you are giving cow's milk as a drink to toddlers under the age of two, always make sure it is full fat. The fat content of milk is an important source of energy for one to two year olds. Also, the vitamins A, D and E are found mainly in the milk's cream.

Toddlers aged two to four are generally eating a wider range of foods, so they do not need to rely on cow's milk so much. At this stage, as long as your toddler is a good eater, with a varied diet that provides sufficient good fats, semi-skimmed milk can be introduced. Skimmed milk should not be given to children under the age of five.

Cow's milk contains all essential nutrients. However, the concentrations of several of these nutrients are different in cow's milk from in breast milk and formula. For example, full-fat cow's milk contains less iron and is a poor source of vitamin D compared to breast milk. Most toddlers will be consuming sufficient amounts of these nutrients from other foods and, in the case of vitamin D, through the action of sunlight on the skin, so there is no cause for concern. In a few cases where your toddler's diet is restricted or she cannot make enough vitamin D because she is not getting enough exposure to sunlight, your family doctor may recommend continuing formula feeding and giving vitamin supplements.

milk intolerance

A small number of young children may not be able to tolerate cows' milk. This may be for one of two reasons. Cows' milk contains the milk sugar lactose, and some people may be intolerant to this as they may lack or have an insufficient amount of the enzyme lactase in the gut to help digest this sugar. Symptoms include digestive problems such as stomach pain and diarrhoea. Cows' milk also contains cows' milk protein, which a small percentage of young children may be allergic to. This means their immune system views this protein as something foreign and reacts against it, resulting in various symptoms such as asthma and eczema. Most children grow out of both of these intolerances. In both cases, a dairy-free diet may be recommended by the doctor or dietician. Some toddlers who are lactose-intolerant may be able to tolerate a small amount of diary foods, whereas with cows' milk protein allergy, a dairy-free diet will certainly be recommended until the child grows out of it.

milk alternatives

When cows' milk is not an option, breast milk should ideally be promoted, depending on the age of the child. If that is not possible, soya products enriched with calcium are suggested as the next option. This is because they have a high-quality protein equivalent to cows' milk and because the calcium is as equally well absorbed as that from dairy. If a child cannot tolerate soya, some other alternatives such as pasteurised goats' and sheeps' milk may be suggested. However, both of these are low in iron and vitamin D. Goats' milk is also deficient in folic acid. When these are recommended by health professionals, vitamin drops are also suggested.

organic

Milk is one of the biggest organic sellers in supermarkets. Organic milk is different from ordinary milk because the cows feed on organic pastures, hay and silage. The other feeds they are given are vegetable based and so will not contain animal by-products, such as fishmeal. This is one of the main reasons why organic milk has, in my opinion, a noticeably better flavour than non-organic milk. Organic milk is guaranteed to be free from antibiotics, as the routine use of antibiotics is prohibited in organic farming. Organic goat's and sheep's milk are also becoming more widely available.

soya drink

Regular calcium-enriched soya drinks and yoghurt alternatives can be given to young children as part of a healthy balanced diet, but not as the main source of milk under two years of age. If your toddler has an intolerance to cow's milk, or you have chosen to give her a vegan diet, you will need an alternative milk source. The Government recommends breast milk as the best main drink for your toddler so, if you can, continue to breastfeed. It is important, where there is an allergy or intolerance, or if you choose a cow's, breast or formula milk alternative, to seek advice from family doctor or registered dietician, who may recommend a hydrolysed cow's milk formula or soya infant formula.

bottle, breast or beaker

By nine months, bottle-fed babies should be drinking all of their water, diluted juice and most of their milk feeds from a beaker. By the age of one, all drinks, with the exception of breast milk (unless you are expressing), should now be given in a beaker or cup.

Having reached this stage, the transition from formula milk to cow's milk will be only a matter of taste. I feel that because formula is based on cow's milk, which you will have been using in cooking, the change is relatively easy. If you are switching from beaker-fed breast milk, you may need to make the change more gradually.

However, if you have managed to breastfeed into your toddler's first year, you may want to wean her from the breast during her second year. This will require more careful planning, because it is a far more emotional transition. For each breastfeed that you are giving your baby, you need to allow five to seven days to drop it. In my experience the night-time feed is the most difficult to drop, so leave that one until last. Start by reducing each feed by around five minutes, topping up with cow's milk given in a beaker. This will also help your body to adjust to the change, preventing blocked milk ducts, which can lead to sore and painful breasts.

vegetarian
toddlers

Vegetarians do not eat meat or fish, but they do eat dairy produce, eggs and honey. A varied and balanced vegetarian diet provides all the nutrients for healthy growth and development, but a diet that keeps an adult vegetarian in good health is not necessarily appropriate for a toddler. A toddler's rapid growth and development means that she needs energy- and nutrient-dense foods daily, such as milk, cheese, pulses and nut butters.

A vegan diet excludes all animal-derived produce, including honey. You should talk to your family doctor, health visitor or registered dietician before you begin feeding your toddler such a diet.

For vegetarian and vegan diets you need to pay particular attention to the following nutrients (see pages 12-21 for more information).

Protein: Milk and milk products are rich in protein, as are pulses, soya products, nuts, nut butters and seeds (do not feed seeds or nuts or their products to toddlers under the age of three if there is any family history of food allergies). Bread and cereal-based products (eg pasta, noodles, rice) and potatoes are useful sources. As plant sources of protein (except for soya) do not contain all the essential amino acids, it is important to feed your toddler a variety of plant foods (eg noodles with peanut sauce or baked beans on toast).

Iron: Good sources include eggs, green vegetables, dried fruit, beans and tofu. Foods containing vitamin C (eg citrus fruits), will aid iron absorption. Avoid high-fibre foods (eg bran) or any containing tannin or caffeine (ie tea and coffee), as they inhibit iron absorption.

Calcium: Milk and milk products are the best sources for vegetarians. Other sources include leafy green vegetables, fortified white bread and breakfast cereals, dried fruit (eg apricots), nuts and tahini (see warning above), calcium-fortified soya drink, tofu and miso.

Zinc: Good sources include oats, wholemeal bread, nuts (see warning above), rice, pulses, soya products including tofu and miso, parsley and bean sprouts.

Vitamin D: Milk is the best source for vegetarians. Other sources include fortified breakfast cereals and margarine. However, vitamin D is mainly made by the skin in sunlight. It is important for your toddler to be outside for at least 30 minutes daily between the months of March and October in the Northern Hemisphere or they may need a supplement (see page 20).

Vitamin B$_{12}$: Milk and milk products are good sources for vegetarians. Also fortified breakfast cereals and yeast extract. Vegans are likely to need a supplement (see page 19).

Riboflavin (vitamin B$_2$): Milk, fortified breakfast cereals, eggs and some fortified soya drinks provide vitamin B$_2$. Vegans are likely to need a supplement (see page 19).

Fibre: Potentially, vegetarian and vegan diets have a high fibre content. With a wide variety of foods, your toddler's fibre intake will be adequate. Avoid bran, which can impair the absorption of minerals, particularly calcium and zinc.

special toddler
diets

Diabetes and obesity are two of the main food-related disorders in toddlers.

diabetes

Type one diabetes is a condition where the body does not produce enough insulin, which is needed to process glucose into energy. A toddler suffering from diabetes often experiences drastic swings in energy levels as her blood sugar fluctuates. Untreated diabetes can be fatal. About one in 500 children have this kind of diabetes. It can develop suddenly, with the child often feeling unwell for a couple of weeks, feeling thirsty and going to the toilet frequently. If you notice these sorts of symptoms speak to your family doctor – a simple urine test can provide a quick diagnosis. This type of diabetes can be managed through a combination of monitoring blood sugar levels, insulin injections and a well-balanced diet. Type two diabetes usually develops later in life – its onset has been linked to excess weight and obesity, where eating a high-fat and high-sugar diet has contributed to this.

obesity

An obese toddler weighs 20 per cent or more above her ideal weight. While your child's weight and shape is partially predetermined by genetics, their diet and lifestyle plays an important role, and it is this that we can control. The fat and sugar content of toddlers' diets has increased significantly recently, particularly in "children's" foods. Today's toddlers are also less active than they were a generation ago. Obesity at a young age can be detrimental to your child's health as an obese child is predisposed to obesity later in life. If you are concerned, take her to see your health visitor or family doctor to check her growth. However, many toddlers may look plump, or just be larger than average. If your child is over-weight or obese, the first approach in young children is to maintain weight so that as they grow their weight levels itself out with the child's increased height. The best course is to give your toddler a healthy, well-balanced diet with regular mealtimes. Take time to read labels if you are buying processed foods and find out what your child is eating if and when they are out of your care. Don't offer food as comfort. And encourage her to enjoy active play and to walk as much as possible. After the age of four, an obese child is likely to remain fat, so it is important to address the causes of obesity during this stage of toddlerhood.

coeliac disease

This is a condition in which the lining of the gut is damaged by gluten, a protein found in wheat and rye. Coeliacs are also affected by similar proteins present in barley and possibly oats. The damage that occurs significantly reduces the absorption of nutrients from the gut, causing weight loss, diarrhoea and poor growth if not treated. It is easily treated by excluding gluten from the child's diet. Advice should be given by your doctor and registered dietician.

organic food

With recent health scares, particularly BSE, there has been an increased public awareness of issues surrounding food production. The Soil Association, a UK-based registered charity and organic certifying body, describes organic farming as a "safe, sustainable farming system, producing healthy crops and livestock without damage to the environment". Sustainability is at the heart of organic food production. Organic food is produced without the use of synthetic pesticides, fungicides, fertilizers and growth hormones. It is the residues of these chemicals in non-organic foods that cause concern – although they have been used in food production for many years, we still don't know the health impacts of long-term exposure to them.

Buying certified organic produce is a guarantee that your toddler's food has been grown and produced according to strict standards, set out in law to prohibit the use of certain chemicals. These stringent regulations must be followed, not only by food producers and growers, but also by food manufacturers, processors, packers and importers. As organic farming is more labour intensive than conventional farming, organic food can cost more to produce and so can be more expensive to buy than non-organic. Buying organic food in season will help to keep costs down, as will buying food from markets, farm shops or local producers. In my opinion it is wise to buy as many organic foods as you can afford, even if it is just basics such as milk, bread, apples and potatoes.

genetically modified foods

Throughout history different crops and animals have been bred specifically to produce certain desirable qualities, for example cross-breeding potatoes to produce a crop that will keep better. Genetic modification (GM) permits scientists to move DNA from one plant or animal species to another. This means that a vegetable may contain a small part of an animal gene, which has the effect of making it resistant to a certain herbicide or antibiotic. There has been little research into the long-term effects of such foods on the environment and on human health. All foods containing GM products are now required by British law to be clearly labelled.

food
purity

additives and preservatives

Food additives come in the form of preservatives, antioxidants, artificial colourings, artificial flavourings, artificial sweeteners, stabilizers and thickeners. Additives all play different roles in factory-produced food and are often used to make poor-quality and over-processed foods more palatable. Although some additives help to make some food safe to eat, most have no health benefits. In fact, additives have been connected to certain reactions in children, such as asthma or eczema, as well as some behavioural problems. Few additives are known to be completely safe, and the quantity of additives toddlers consume can be large. According to the Food Commission, by the time children have reached the age of 17 they have typically consumed their own weight in food additives.

Additives that have been approved for food use in the EU are allocated an "E-number": so far there are more than 900 approved E-numbers. Artificial colours and sweeteners have been banned in baby food and toddler foods in the EU, but they may be present in family food that you feed your toddler. It should be noted that some foods, including some biscuits, crisps, chicken nuggets etc, may not be regarded by manufacturers as "children's foods" and so may contain higher quantities of additives and salt.

Some additives are permitted in certain foods, usually because they have a specific role, such as stopping a product going rancid – but crucially these are all additives that have been fully reviewed by the EU, approved and given an E-number. The Food Commission has found that some "E-numbers" may adversely affect one in four toddlers. Read labels carefully. All food labels in the UK must list all E numbers or the actual name of the additives contained in the product in the ingredients list.

freshness

Fresh homemade food is the best choice for your toddler. It will maximize her intake of essential nutrients, especially if the food is served raw when appropriate or cooked for the shortest time possible. Steaming is a particularly good method of cooking, because many water-soluble nutrients are retained. Always stay with your toddler when she's eating, particularly when she's eating lightly cooked or raw foods, until she is fully confident with chewing. Fresh foods often look, smell and taste better than processed foods. Giving them to your toddler, especially when you eat them yourself, will help her to develop an appreciation for fresh, unprocessed foods, which will hopefully last a lifetime.

labels

Checking the label is the best way to prevent your toddler from eating large quantities of additives. Look out for salt, which is often listed as sodium. To convert sodium to salt, multiply the sodium figure by 2.5 (ie 1g of sodium per 100g is the same as 2.5g of salt). For one to three year olds the RNI is 500mg per day. Sugar present in food may be listed as sucrose, dextrose, glucose, fructose, lactose, maltose, honey or invert sugar syrup. Meat or vegetable extracts, hydrolyzed vegetable protein or yeast in savoury foods often indicate over-processing. Processed starches, including modified cornflour, maltodextrin, rice starch and wheat starch are often used to counteract the overuse of water; they are low-nutrient fillers that dull the flavour of food and take up the space of more nutritious ingredients. Their presence often means the food will need flavouring or added sugar or salt to make it taste better. It is difficult to avoid giving you toddler some processed food (eg baked beans), but I find the best way to counteract this is to at least serve them with some fresh food, such as adding some chopped fresh ripe tomatoes to beans on toast.

"children's foods"

Many parents assume that their children need to be cooked for separately, rather than eating what the adults eat. Parents also find themselves under pressure from their toddler who, influenced by her peers, wants foods that are not good for her. Many parents rely on pre-packaged foods – specifically marketed as "children's foods" or "convenience" foods – and it can be a hard habit to get out of. For example, a little cartoon-covered pot of brightly coloured yogurt will be irresistible to most toddlers, and there is a staggering range of these kinds of foods available. If the whole family has a healthy diet, you can feed your toddler what the rest of the family eats – just simplify it or chop it up as appropriate. The recipes in this book are designed for the whole family. Inevitably, it will be almost impossible to avoid junk food altogether, and being too prohibitive will only make the issue more contentious, just keep it to a minimum (see page 30).

foods to eat and
foods to avoid

salt

Every toddler needs a little salt in her diet in order to stay healthy. Many children are consuming far more salt than is necessary, which can be detrimental to their health. Too much salt in early life can lead to a marked taste for salty food that can be difficult to overcome. Excessive salt consumption has also been linked to high blood pressure later in life. Generally, there is enough salt naturally present in food to meet the recommended daily amounts for your toddler. There is no need to season food with salt for toddlers, just put salt on the table for the rest of the family. If you are worried about food being bland, season with freshly ground black pepper, herbs and spices – cinnamon, ginger and milder herbs, such as sage and parsley, are almost always popular with toddlers. Avoid giving your child savoury snacks that are high in salt and always check labels if you are buying pre-packaged food – salt is often referred to as sodium (see page 29).

sugar and artificial sweeteners

Sugar is one of the most common ingredients in processed foods, particularly those aimed at children. Even if you think your toddler's diet is healthy, you may be surprised by her real sugar intake – sugar is listed on food labels under other names such as sucrose, maltose, dextrose, glucose, fructose, honey or invert sugar syrup. These may sound healthier, but they are all sugars and – if given in excess – they can be bad for your child's dental and general health. There can be quite a lot of sugar in baked beans, peanut butter, ready-made pasta sauces and even chips. Sugar is cheap, it is a good preservative and helps to improve the texture and flavour of cheap food.

Sugar is a major factor in the cause of tooth decay, and too much at this stage can also lead to unhealthy cravings later in life. A diet high in sugar contributes to the causes of diabetes. Sugar contains empty calories – a lot of energy but few nutrients – so food high in sugar will induce a burst of energy that will drop off suddenly, making her feel lethargic. For this reason, a diet high in sugar has been linked to hyperactivity in children. Too much sugar has been noted as being addictive for some children and can affect your toddler's appetite for savoury foods.

It is important to regulate the amount of sugar added to your toddler's diet to sweeten other foods, such as breakfast cereals or stewed fruits. Try using chopped dried or fresh fruit or vanilla to sweeten tart foods. It is a good idea to give unsweetened foods from time to time, such as full-fat natural yogurt. Try not to encourage the idea that anything sweet is a treat. If you prepare home-cooked food you can control how much sugar is added. I would not advise ever giving your toddler artificial sweeteners instead of sugar. There are many still-unanswered questions about the safety of sweeteners. Studies have linked sweeteners to headaches, mood swings and epilepsy in children. Many processed foods also contain sweeteners instead of sugar, so check labels. Names for sweeteners include: Mannitol, sorbitol, xylitol, hydrogenated glucose syrup, aspartame, saccharin, thaumatin.

caffeine and tannins

Tea, coffee, chocolate and soft drinks, such as cola, contain high quantities of caffeine, a stimulant that may cause edginess and hyperactivity in certain toddlers. Tea also contains tannins, which can inhibit the absorption of certain nutrients, particularly iron and magnesium.

burgers, chicken nuggets, fish fingers...

Many toddlers become interested in processed foods, such as nuggets, through advertising and peer pressure and because such foods are often served at nurseries and schools. They are usually made from the cheapest forms of meat and often contain lots of saturated fat and additives to make them taste better, making them some of the least healthy foods to give to children. Their "convenience" may come at a high price – they can even be more expensive than the homemade equivalent.

It is far better to buy burgers from a good butcher, or to make your own using good quality lean mince, and freeze them. Choose sausages with a meat content of at least 70 per cent. Re-formed foods, such as chicken nuggets, can be substituted with grilled pieces of chicken breast or fish fillet (100 per cent cod fish fingers are fine occasionally). Try making chicken or fish kebabs or fish cakes. If you do buy shop-bought versions, check the labels – organic are often better quality and have fewer additives. It might not always be possible to avoid ready-made convenience foods, and this is acceptable so long as they do not feature as a main or regular item on your child's menu.

soft drinks

Most drinks marketed for children are high in sugar, additives and often caffeine. Excessive sugar is bad for milk teeth. The best way to pre-empt your toddler's requests for fizzy/flavoured drinks is to encourage her to drink water from an early age, particularly between meals. Alternatively, try fruit smoothies; diluted fruit juice or low-sugar cordials, occasionally mixed with sparkling water; iced fruit tea mixed with ice, chopped fruit and mint; or for hot drinks try herbal tea or weak cocoa.

breakfast cereals

Many breakfast cereals contain a lot of sugar and sometimes salt. Aim to buy cereals with no added sugar, such as muesli, Weetabix and Shredded Wheat, or make your own museli or granola. To make breakfasts more interesting, simply try adding chopped fresh or dried fruit or full-fat natural yogurt.

chips

Try not to make chips a routine staple. Bought, precut, precooked chips are often high in fat with few nutrients, especially if they are made from reconstituted potato. Have some good quality frozen chips as a freezer stand-by, otherwise try making home-made chips or crispy potato wedges.

Serve them with a chunky vegetable salsa rather than lashings of sweet or fatty processed sauces. Make mash too; if the lumps put your toddler off, try investing in a potato ricer for lump-free mash.

tinned baked beans
Tinned beans have some useful fibre, protein and some beneficial vitamins but they also contain a surprising amount of sugar and salt. They are now available in low-sugar varieties, but are best kept as a storecupboard stand-by. Try using other varieties of tinned beans, such as butterbeans, and serve them with a home-made tomato sauce.

pizza
Bought pizza can contain overly sweet tomato purées and highly processed cheeses and meats. Home-made pizza is quick to make, or use good bought pizza bases and add healthy toppings.

sweets and chocolate
Most sweets and chocolates aimed at children are very unhealthy blends of hardened fats and sugar, with vast amounts of additives. They are bad for health, particularly the teeth, when eaten in-between meals. The best way to avoid confrontations is not to keep them in the house. For sweets, try substituting snacks of dried fruits. For chocolate, give small quantities of really good quality chocolate – one with 70 per cent cocoa and cocoa butter and milk instead of vegetable fats and flavourings. It would be unrealistic to ban sweets and chocolates altogether, just offer them occasionally without making a fuss that is likely to increase their desirability.

biscuits and cakes
Most bought biscuits and cakes are little more than mixes of highly refined flour, sugar and hardened fats and flavourings. Almost any home-made alternative, such as fruit teabreads, muffins or flapjacks, is bound to taste better and will be more healthy. If you do buy ready-made biscuits and cakes, look for simpler varieties, such as shortbread, that are made with unprocessed, simple ingredients. Check labels and bear in mind that products made with butter or oil are better than those made with hydrogenated vegetable fat (this is vegetable fat whose structure has been changed in the manufacturing process so that it becomes like saturated fat and similar to animal fat) or margarine.

crisps
Crisps are high in saturated fat, even brands labelled "low-fat" can contain up to 20 per cent fat. Crisps also contain high quantities of salt: sometimes over 1g per 34.5g packet, which far exceeds the recommended daily allowance for a child. Surprisingly, some crisps also contain sugar and, if

they are flavoured, large quantities of additives, too. If you do buy crisps, look for natural potatoes (rather than reconstituted ones) that have been fried in oil with no added salt, or bags of crisps that contain little blue packets of salt that need not be added. Healthier snacks include low-salt corn or tortilla chips, puffed rice crackers and breadsticks.

ice-cream
Many cheap, bought ice-creams are made with synthetic ingredients and a lot of air. Air makes ice-cream cheaper to produce but dilutes its flavour, which is enhanced with additives and sugar. It is better to buy premium ice-cream occasionally, or make your own ice-cream or fruit lollies.

yogurt and fromage frais
Shop-bought yogurt and fromage frais, especially those aimed at children, are often high in sugar, sometimes containing as much as 14.5g in a 100g pot. They can also be high in artificial sweeteners, thickeners, preservatives, flavours and colours. Look instead for brands flavoured with fruit purée and natural sugar. Alternatively, mix natural full-fat yogurt with fresh fruit, honey or vanilla.

nuts and seeds
If there is any history of allergy in your family, avoid giving toddlers under three nuts and seeds, their products or foods containing them, and seek professional advice from your doctor or registered dietician. Whole nuts, including peanuts, should never be given to children under the age of five as there is a risk of choking.

shellfish
Shellfish can occasionally trigger an allergic reaction in some toddlers when first introduced. The best thing is to introduce one kind at a time and look out for any adverse reaction.

unpasteurized cheeses
These contain the bacteria listeria. This thrives in the intestines of many healthy people with no adverse reactions. However, it can occasionally cause food poisoning, which for toddlers is more serious than for adults. It is best to avoid giving toddlers unpasteurized milk and cheeses.

hot and spicy foods
There is no reason not to gradually introduce herbs and spices to your toddler's diet, but be cautious with very hot ingredients such as chillies or fresh raw ginger.

The food that you give to your toddler and your attitude towards cooking and eating will greatly influence how she feels about food. While it is important to give your toddler a balanced diet, it is never a good idea to be precious about mealtimes or obsessive about healthy eating. Equally, to think of mealtimes merely as refuelling exercises is depressing for both of you. A wonderful gift that you can give to your child is the ability to enjoy eating and feel relaxed about food. A great way to achieve this is to get your toddler involved with the shopping and preparation of meals from an early age – encouraging her to help with simple tasks in the cooking and serving of the meal.

toddler
kitchen

toddlers
in the kitchen

Your toddler is far more likely to be interested in what is being served at mealtimes if he has had some involvement in the food's preparation and knows something about how it's grown or where it comes from.

Many parents dread grocery shopping with toddlers, but this can be a great time to teach them about different ingredients, especially if you ever get the chance to go to a farmer's market or farm shop. When you take your toddler shopping, try simple tricks to keep his interest, such as asking him to choose one vegetable to include in that night's supper. Better still, at a market or local shop, ask if he can taste things, such as cheese or fresh fruit juices; most stallholders will be happy to oblige and chat to children.

As soon as your toddler is old enough, let him sit and watch you cook. I actively encourage my girls to taste things and to help with simple tasks, such as mixing foods and crushing garlic, which need not involve too much mess. Even something as simple as getting them to smell fresh herbs can capture their imagination. My daughter Ella is captivated when I whisk runny cream into thick soft peaks or egg whites into a meringue. Most toddlers will love to be given a small responsibility, even something as simple as pouring out drinks. Just make sure any potential hazards, such as sharp knives, are kept well out of reach.

At meals, talk about the food you are eating, ask your toddler questions, and encourage him to question you, too. Knowing how a food is grown or where it comes from can make toddlers more interested in their meals – this is particularly true if you are on holiday. If you have a garden or even a window box, try growing herbs or grow cress on a saucer. Above all, make meals a sharing experience, eat with your toddler as much as possible. It is important to give a child the idea that he can eat everything that you eat – your toddler's food needn't be different to yours. Making food more child-friendly, for example by cutting toast into soldiers, is fine, but I would avoid making food into over-complicated shapes or faces. Children should grow up loving good food, whatever its shape, colour or texture.

Now more than ever, when often both parents work and other family members (including toddlers) have busy social lives, trying to eat together can be challenging. Family mealtimes almost seem to be a thing of the past, and this makes it even harder than it used to be to encourage children to be interested in good food.

Establishing sensible mealtimes and routines and eating together as a family is one of the most important things that you can do for your toddler. Although children need to graze to a certain extent, making time for meals and viewing them as opportunities to talk and share experiences can help to create a real family bond; sharing food in this way is an important part of many cultures. Adults with fond memories of shared meals often have the most adventurous attitude towards food.

The structure created by these regular mealtimes will also be reassuring for toddlers. If time is an issue, remember that many fresh meals can be cooked quickly and simply and even prepared in advance.

On week nights many of my friends wonder when to eat – with their children early in the evening or with their partners later on. It is always far better for your children to eat something with them, because it enables you to lead by example. I often eat a small portion with them and have my main meal later with my husband, as I find it makes my girls far more interested in their food – it is more of a sociable and fun occasion. It is also important to remember that your toddler's attitude towards food will be learnt from you and that someone who has a bad relationship with food will often pass it on.

I find that involving my daughter Ella in the serving of meals, even if that means just talking her through what I am doing, helps to get her interested and at three she is now at the stage where she likes helping with little jobs that don't involve making too much mess, such as buttering bread or helping to lay the table. All this helps to create an air of expectation that the meal will be fun.

As well as the obvious three meals of breakfast, lunch and supper, it is a good idea to offer small healthy snacks occasionally to help maintain energy levels. I often keep these to fruit snacks, as my girls will have less of an appetite for their next meal if a snack is too filling. However, there are times when just fruit is not enough.

toddlers
at the table

Ideally, you should try to give your toddler a wide variety of fresh food without being overly prescriptive – try not to create the impression that there are "good" foods or "bad" foods. Healthy eating is just a question of balance.

Using positive words about the subject of food is important, but try to keep it general. This will also help to counteract the messages that toddlers get from the advertising that they see – usually for very sweet or processed foods. Similarly, try not to pre-empt your toddler by saying, "I won't give you this as you might not like it; it's for grown-ups". My daughter Ella tastes almost everything

restaurant menus

Many parents rarely take their children out to eat, expecting it to be difficult for all concerned – parents, children and restaurateurs. This is partly because a lot of restaurants are not prepared to deal with children. Many parents also feel that restaurant food is an indulgence that is wasted on children, or they are reluctant to spend money in a place where they are made to feel unwelcome.

Many restaurants have "child-friendly" menus, often of processed foods. While children may appear enthusiastic about these foods, the experience of eating them can be a let down and much of the food is left uneaten. In my experience, children are far more interested in eating what is on the adults' plates.

My advice is to always order from the main "adult" menu instead, but just choose a starter with a side order of vegetables, for example, which will often be no more expensive than the children's menu. Most restaurants will happily omit a sauce or dressing that you may feel is too rich. But even a few spoonfuls of something really delicious will give your toddler a more enlightened view of eating out.

To make your life easier it may be worth considering the following:
- Plan ahead and try to have the booking at a time when your toddler usually eats. If it is going to be much later, give a small snack a few hours before you go out.
- Make sure he is not tired; often lunchtimes are easier.
- If he is poorly, it is probably best to leave it to another time.
- Take a diversion for him to use while you wait for the food, eg crayons and paper.
- Choose an unpretentious but good restaurant. An independent, family-run business is always a good bet, somewhere with a biggish menu and lots of choice.
- Never insist your toddler eats everything – the idea is for the meal to be fun. Restaurant food often looks and smells fantastic, and the environment will make the whole experience very different from eating at home; try to make it a memorable and exciting adventure that he will want to repeat.

that we eat and she has a number of unexpected favourite foods, such as olives and raw green beans.

The main dilemma that parents face is what to do with a "picky eater" who starts to refuse foods on an apparently random basis. At around two years old this is quite common, as this is the stage at which toddlers begin to assert their independence – something most easily done at mealtimes. However, it can become a more deep-rooted problem. There are some foods that tend to make toddlers more suspicious than others: very rich or very spicy food, dishes that are overly complicated and include several ingredients or, in toddler-speak, things with lots of "bits". They usually like their food uncomplicated, especially if it is something new.

Don't give up on a food just because it has been rejected once – always try again a few days later. It is never a good idea to insist that a food is eaten or to offer substitutes, as the situation gets worse in the long run. If a toddler learns that what is on the menu is all that is being offered, he will soon realize that it is futile to make a fuss and wait for something else. If this means that your child goes hungry for a few days, don't panic – he won't starve. A little bargaining will be positively useful at times, but try to use activities such as helping with a train set as the reward for good behaviour, rather than sweet treats, as this just places an unhealthy emphasis on the desirability of almost all the foods you are trying to give in moderation!

toddler
storecupboard

There are lots of obvious storecupboard stand-bys for toddlers, such as baked beans and breadsticks, but there are several useful things that you may not have thought of. I have found the following items invaluable when planning and preparing meals for toddlers.

storecupboard

Passata: a ready-made purée of ripe tomatoes, usually sieved to remove the skin and pips, passata is packaged in jars or cartons with a long shelf-life. It is brilliant for making extra-quick pasta sauces or pizza toppings and makes a great base for lots of meat or vegetable stews. Avoid varieties with added herbs as they tend to have an unpleasant aftertaste and to be more expensive.

Pasta and noodles: there are hundreds of types of pasta, most of which children seem to love. One of my girls' favourites is rissoni, which is shaped like grains of rice and can be used in much the same way – served hot with a knob of butter and grated cheese as an accompaniment or cold as part of a salad. It is also a good thickener for soups.

Rice: red, wild, Basmati, Arborio – they are all easy to cook and eat. For extra flavour, add a little no- or low-salt vegetable stock or creamed coconut to the water during cooking. When you serve rice, add some chopped herbs or a little knob of butter. Most toddlers love the creamy texture of risottos and red and wild rice has a wonderful nutty texture that also goes down well.

Tinned fish: tuna is the most universally popular tinned fish, but try mackerel or sardines. Fish in oil is better than in brine. If you buy tinned fish in a sauce, check the label carefully, as they can be quite high in additives. Most tinned fish works well in salads, pasta dishes and baked potato fillings – try jazzing it up with lots of fresh parsley or spring onions.

Nuts: do not give nuts to toddlers under the age of three if there is any family history of food allergies. Chopped nuts make brilliant snacks for toddlers as long as the toddler knows how to chew them properly. I find cashews particularly popular. Always go for unflavoured and unsalted nuts. Add chopped nuts to pilaffs, salads, breakfast cereals and home-made muesli bars. If you are buying nuts loose from a health food store, make sure it has a good turnover as they can go stale quite quickly.

Dried fruit: there are many different varieties of dried fruits, all of which make excellent snacks for toddlers, but beware because too much can cause a tummy upset. Only give whole dried fruits to toddlers who are confident with chewing – otherwise always chop them up. The best dried fruit is unsweetened and unsulphured. Fruit without added sugar tends to be a little chewier, so try soaking it overnight in a little boiling water or warmed orange juice. Dried fruit is great to add to full-fat natural yogurts, cereals or meat stews.

Beans and pulses: baked beans are not the only tinned beans available. Other varieties, such as black-eyed beans, cannellini beans, butter beans and chick peas, are versatile and can be used in a wide range of dishes such as soups, hummus, salads and stews. Rinse and drain tinned beans thoroughly before using to help remove salt.

Creamed coconut: this is particularly good in mildly spiced soups, stews or chicken curries, which my girls love. It gives a wonderful flavour to plain rice, which can be served with chicken or fish or used in puddings such as rice pudding and custard. Do not give nuts to toddlers under the age of three if there is any family history of food allergies.

Couscous: it can be prepared in many ways, but the quickest is to just add boiling water or no- or low-salt vegetable stock. Serve with a stew, alongside a piece of chicken breast, or mixed into a chunky salad.

Tortillas: unopened tortillas keep for a few days. They make brilliantly quick pizza bases or lovely soft rolled sandwiches. They also make great snacks if spread with a little nut butter or hummus (do not give nuts to toddlers under the age of three if there is any family history of food allergies). They can be served plain to teething toddlers who need something to chew on.

Pesto: one of my girls' favourite meals is pesto, pasta, peas and bacon. Pesto is handy as a central ingredient, but it is also good as a marinade or added to soups, pasta sauces, dressings or risottos.

Full-fat cream cheese: this is ideal for spreading on bread or crackers for a quick lunch, but has the added advantage that it goes just as well with sweet things such as with mashed banana or ground cinnamon, as with savoury ingredients such as cooked ham. Add a few spoonfuls to sauces or soups to make them creamy.

Full-fat natural yogurt: get into the habit of keeping a large tub of yogurt in the refrigerator and add fruit, chopped nuts or honey to make quick puddings or use in sauces, marinades and cakes. Do not give nuts to toddlers under the age of three if there is any family history of food allergies.

Eggs: one of the main advantages of eggs, other than being a quick and easy source of protein, is their great shelf life of approximately three weeks. Always look for eggs stamped with the lion quality mark which guarantees that the eggs have been laid in Britain and come from hens vaccinated against salmonella.

Peanut butter: look for a good quality nut butter without added sugar. It can be used with noodles, as part of a marinade or in a quick peanut butter and banana sandwich. Do not give nuts to toddlers under the age of three if there is any family history of food allergies.

freezer

Vegetables: the most useful varieties include peas and sweetcorn. Peas are particularly good added to pasta, risottos and soups, while sweetcorn is great added to fish cakes, mashed potato and omelettes. Frozen spinach can be thawed and layered in lasagne, or added to cheese or tomato sauces for pasta.

Fruit: bags of mixed berries and homemade apple purée make brilliant stand-bys. Add to cereals and full-fat natural yogurt for breakfasts or to custard for a simple pudding. If you have the chance, look in the frozen section of your local farm shop, as they often have home-grown fruit available at sensible prices.

Sliced bread and part-baked loaves: instant bread is very useful – just pop a few slices straight from the freezer into the toaster. Also there are numerous things to do with toast, and part-baked loaves can be used in many ways, such as cut in half and filled with cheese or ham and baked or kept for times when you and your toddler fancy some warm bread quickly.

Fish fillets: a good source of protein, fish fillets can be added to dishes such as pasta or kedgeree, or baked or grilled either on their own or with a simple tomato or cream sauce.

Low-salt chicken stock: when you have cooked roast chicken, it is an excellent idea to put the carcass into a pan with water, vegetables and herbs, then cover and simmer for about 30 minutes. Cool, skim off the fat, then strain and freeze in small bags or freezerproof containers. You can add it thawed to soups and stews, or use it to cook couscous or rice for extra flavour.

toddler storecupboard
recipes

tomato sauce

makes: 500ml tomato sauce

storage: keep in the refrigerator for up to 3 days or freeze for up to 4 months

1tbsp olive oil
1 large onion, peeled and finely
   chopped
1 clove garlic, peeled and crushed
500ml passata (sieved tomato
   purée available in supermarkets)
2tbsp fresh herbs, eg thyme, basil,
   parsley, rosemary, chopped
freshly ground black pepper
milk to glaze

This is a versatile sauce that can be served with pasta, noodles, rice or polenta or as a topping on pizzas. To make it a bit more substantial try adding a small tin of flaked cooked tuna, chopped cooked ham or shredded cooked chicken and heat through thoroughly.

1 Heat the oil in a heavy-based saucepan and fry the onion until soft and pale golden – approximately 5 minutes. Add the garlic, stir and cook for 1 more minute.
2 Stir in the passata, herbs and a little freshly ground black pepper (if using) and simmer for 10 minutes.
3 Whiz with a hand-held blender (or in a food processor or blender) until smooth. Alternatively, you can leave the sauce slightly chunky. If freezing, leave to cool completely, pour into a freezerproof container and freeze.
4 Thaw thoroughly. Gently heat through until boiling hot. Cool before serving.

no-salt vegetable stock

makes: 1 litre stock

storage: keep in the refrigerator for up to 2 days or freeze for up to 6 months

50g unsalted butter
1 large onion, finely chopped
1 large carrot, finely chopped
1 celery stick, finely chopped
1 large leek, washed thoroughly and
   finely chopped
few parsley stalks
leaves of a thyme sprig or torn basil
   (optional)
freshly ground black pepper

Make sure that you chop all of the vegetables quite finely, as the flavour of the finished stock will be much better if you do. You can chop them in a food processor.

1 Melt the butter in large heavy-based saucepan. Add the chopped vegetables and cook over a low heat for 10–15 minutes, stirring occasionally.
2 Add the herbs and 1 litre cold water, bring to the boil and simmer for 15–20 minutes.
3 Strain and season to taste with freshly ground black pepper.
4 Leave to cool and then keep covered in the refrigerator or pour into freezer bags, label and freeze.
5 Thaw thoroughly before use.

white sauce

makes: approx 4–6 toddler portions
(approx 600ml white sauce)

storage: keep in the refrigerator
for up to 3 days or freeze for up to
3 months

40g unsalted butter
1 small onion, finely chopped
40g plain flour
600ml full-fat milk
freshly ground black pepper

for variations:
approx 50g Cheddar cheese, grated
  handful of fresh herbs, chopped
approx 3 slices freshly cooked ham
  or bacon, finely chopped
2 handfuls of sweetcorn
approx 100g tinned tuna in oil or
  water, drained and flaked
6 fried mushrooms, finely chopped
2 hard-boiled organic eggs and a
  handful of chives, finely chopped
1–2tsp mild curry powder

Make a plain white sauce and then add ingredients to jazz it up slightly for a complete meal.

1   Heat the butter in a heavy-based pan and fry the onion until soft.
2   Stir in the flour and cook for 1 minute, then gradually whisk in the milk, stirring constantly until you have a smooth sauce – approximately 5 minutes.
3   Add the other ingredients of your choice and heat through. Season to taste with freshly ground black pepper.
4   If freezing, leave to cool completely, pour into a freezerproof container and freeze.
5   Thaw thoroughly and gently heat through until boiling hot. Cool to serve.

stewed fruit compote

makes: approx 5 toddler portions

storage: keep in the refrigerator for up
to 3 days or freeze for up to 4 months

500g bag frozen fruits, eg summer
  berries, dark fruits
75ml water or orange juice
golden caster sugar, to taste

This can be added to yogurts, cereals and custards or used as a crumble base or under a sponge to make a pudding.

1   Put the frozen berries into a saucepan with the water or orange juice and sugar and bring up to a simmer. Cook for 5 minutes, until the fruits are just soft. Cool slightly.
2   Spoon half the berries into a jug and whiz to a purée with a hand-held blender (or in a food processor or blender).
3   Return to the pan and mix everything together.

During his second year, you will really begin to notice how fast your toddler is developing. One of the best things about his new-found self-awareness is that he will share experiences with you as he learns to gesture, talk and walk. This is often most obvious at mealtimes where, as he learns to feed himself, he will begin to express his likes and dislikes. Although this can be challenging at times, you can help him to become more sociable and to have an appreciation of good food by feeding him at the same time as the rest of the family eats. Most of the recipes in this book are both family- and toddler-friendly, making it easy to prepare the same meal for everyone.

1-2 years

what's happening to
your toddler

At this stage your toddler will be developing at an amazing rate. She will learn new things, however small, every day. For example, she will be constantly learning new words and by 18 months she will be able to say around 20 words, but will understand many more. It can be a challenging time for you as she becomes able to do more and more things for herself.

Your child will have been growing astonishingly fast, but at one to two years growth will level off to about 5–15cm per year, and she will gain approximately 25–50g a week. (Your health professional will keep a check on this.) She will look more in proportion and "adult". As her first-year growth spurt diminishes, you may also notice a natural waning of her appetite at around 18 months. This is often combined with a new level of self-awareness – she will begin to express preferences and wilful behaviour. However, she will find saying "no", especially when she is able to feed herself, an important way to assert her independence.

This behaviour is most common at mealtimes and it can sometimes seem like she is barely eating enough to keep a sparrow alive! However, your toddler will also be becoming more and more active, particularly as she learns to walk, scramble up and down stairs, and kick a ball. So energy-rich foods should be given at mealtimes and as little snacks. Because her appetite may be small, it is also vital to ensure that in the average week you have offered a wide range of foods, containing all the essential nutrients (see pages 12-21).

One of the delights of toddlerhood is being able to share experiences, as she learns to gesture and talk. This applies particularly to food because she can express likes or dislikes. Similarly, you can help to instil in her an interest in good food – this is especially important as eating requires her to sit still for more than two minutes! Make meals more relaxing by letting her learn to feed herself with her fingers or a spoon. At first, this may be a bit hit and miss, so it is a good idea to continue feeding her too until her co-ordination improves. Give her small portions in a shallow bowl; this is easier and more satisfying because she can finish them and ask for more.

A balanced diet will ensure that your toddler is getting all the nutrients she needs for healthy growth and development. This simply means a diet in which different amounts of a wide variety of foods from the five main food groups are eaten at different meals. The five main food groups are: bread, cereals and potatoes; fruit and vegetables; meat, fish and alternatives, such as tofu; foods containing fats and foods containing sugar; milk and dairy produce. A varied diet is essential because no single food provides all the nutrients your toddler needs, and it will also make mealtimes more interesting.

Just as adults have different nutritional needs at different stages of their lives, certain nutrients play a more central role in the diet as your toddler grows older. In particular, she will need plenty of energy. Energy-rich food should be given at breakfast time – slow-releasing carbohydrates, such as porridge with fresh fruit, are ideal because they will give your toddler a steady flow of energy until her next snack or meal. Healthy snacks make great energy boosters, but many processed, convenience foods, such as biscuits and crisps, only give short bursts of energy, often followed by a low in the form of a mood swing. The best way to ensure that your toddler is getting enough energy is to give her a good mix of protein, fat and carbohydrates throughout the day.

Protein is vital in toddlers' diets, as their bodies use it as building bricks for growth. Poultry, meat, fish, small amounts of dairy products and eggs are good sources of protein, but remember – whether your toddler is vegetarian or not – a mixture of beans, pulses, tofu, chopped nuts and grains will also provide a good source of protein. (Do not give nuts to toddlers under the age of three if there is any family history of food allergies.)

Your toddler may be vulnerable to iron deficiency during this year, which may cause anaemia. A toddler weaned on a broad range of foods is unlikely to be iron deficient (see page 13).

which nutrients
are key

your toddler's
routine

your toddler's feeds

During your baby's first year, it is likely that you will have established a good feeding routine. This needs to be continued during toddlerhood. Your toddler will be far more secure and confident about food if she knows she will be given meals regularly. Most toddlers are very active and need energy to avoid becoming over-tired and over-hungry, which, as every parent knows, can lead to fussy eating. Remember that a drink given just before a meal is likely to spoil your toddler's appetite. It is important for her to have a drink with her food, but get into the routine of giving it half way through the meal.

I follow the routine below for both my girls, making allowances for illnesses or holidays and I find that it works for all of us.

breakfast – around 7.30–8am
mid-morning snack – around 10am
lunch – around 12.30 –1pm
mid-afternoon snack – around 3pm
supper – 5–5.30pm
bed – 7–7.30pm

your toddler's sleeps

At the age of one, most toddlers are still having two sleeps during the day. During their second year this becomes less necessary, usually at around 15 months. Look out for signs that she does not want to sleep for as long as usual: it may take you longer to settle her for a day-time sleep, or she may wake up after only a short nap instead of the usual hour or so. With both of my girls it gradually became harder to settle them at night and they were waking up noticeably earlier in the morning. It is best to cut out one sleep at this stage because a sleep of up to an hour and a half, preferably after lunch, will be enough to recharge her batteries without affecting her night-time sleeps. Just make sure that she is awake before the middle of the afternoon so that she is tired at bedtime.

refusing to eat

The best thing you can do if your child refuses to eat her meal is not to get uptight about it. Whatever happens, try not to put any pressure on her to eat; just remove the plate and do not offer anything else until the next meal. The worst thing that you can do is to force the issue or become over-anxious. Toddlers pick up on this and can become uptight about eating. If she is hungry by the next meal, she should eat the food.

how long a toddler can go without food

At one to two years it is quite normal for your toddler's appetite to decrease as growth slows down. Often a baby between six months and one year will eat as much, and sometimes more, than a two year old. A toddler may go for a couple of days eating very little, but then make up for it by eating more later that week. A healthy child will not starve herself. However, it is important to make sure your child is eating a sensible amount to ensure she gets the nutrients she needs. If your toddler's appetite seems to have decreased dramatically and does not pick up over the week, contact your family doctor or state-registered dietician.

is good nutrition really important?

If a toddler does not eat a balanced diet, providing all the nutrients that she needs, she is less likely to achieve her potential in terms of growth, brain development, energy levels and moods. A poor diet may also have implications for her longer-term health. If your toddler will only eat a small range of foods and you suspect that she might not be getting a nutritionally balanced diet, try keeping a diary of what she eats and drinks for about two weeks. This may be a particularly useful exercise if your toddler eats away from home, for example, at a nursery or a relative's house. You may be pleasantly surprised by the true variety of her diet. If you are concerned about how to keep and make use of such a diary, talk to a state-registered dietician.

trouble
shooting

1-2 year meal planners

key to meal planners

portions: all servings are one portion
drink: preferably water, tap or bottled.
Alternatively very diluted fruit juice.
breakfast: 7.30-8am; **mid-am:** 10am;
lunch: 12.30-1pm; **mid-pm:** 3pm;
supper: 5-5.30pm; **bed:** 7-7.30pm.

Toddlers in this age group are increasingly active, and need plenty of energy-rich foods, particularly at breakfast. Toddlers over one year old need a minimum of 350ml full-fat milk per day, inclusive of milk used in food; most toddlers need up to 565ml, with about 350ml of that being given as a drink. Snacks are important to this age group, but try to give your toddler fresh food rather than shop-bought convenience products – a little fruit is fine.

	breakfast	mid-am	lunch	mid-pm	supper	bed
menu 1	150ml milk, bacon and parsley bread, drink	grapes filled with cream cheese, drink	minty chicken with vegetables, filo parcels, drink	pieces of fresh fruit; drink	baked rice with squash, baked custard, drink	200ml milk
menu 2	150ml milk, apple, pear and banana smoothie, drink	pieces of fresh fruit, drink	herb scones, drink	warm pitta bread with peanut dip, drink	cheesy pasta bake, drink	200ml milk
menu 3	150ml milk, grated apple honey and bread, drink	drink	buttered peas with spaghetti, drink	pieces of fresh fruit, drink	pineapple and ham pizza, drink	200ml milk
menu 4	150ml milk, bacon and egg scramble, drink	grapes, drink	couscous with salad and tuna, drink	bread sticks with dips, drink	jacket potato with coleslaw, almond rice, drink	200ml milk
menu 5	150ml milk, eggy raisin bread, drink	pieces of fresh fruit, drink	avocado and cream cheese dip, drink	pieces of banana, drink	minty mash with grilled lamb, rice pudding with pears, drink	200ml milk
menu 6	Ready Brek with prunes, drink	pieces of peeled pear, drink	creamy tomato soup, drink	yogurt with dried fruit compote, drink	baked chicken with rice, drink	200ml milk

	breakfast	mid-am	lunch	mid-pm	supper	bed
menu 7	150ml milk, ham omelette, drink	raisin toast with apple purée, drink	carrot and cheese sandwich, drink	pieces of peeled pear, drink	new potatoes wrapped in bacon, apple pie, drink	200ml milk
menu 8	150ml milk, raspberry muffins, drink	rice cakes with nut butter, drink	rice with chicken and bacon, drink	pieces of peeled pear, drink	tuna, butter bean, tomato and lettuce, rhubarb crisp with custard, drink	200ml milk
menu 9	150ml milk, mango and banana smoothie, drink	pieces of fresh fruit, drink	lamb kebabs with mango, drink	corn thins with avocado, drink	moussaka stuffed aubergine, fruit jelly with fresh fruits, drink	200ml milk
menu 10	150ml milk, porridge, drink	pieces of fresh fruit, drink	tuna and pesto baked potatoes, strawberries and mango toasted oats, drink	pieces of fresh fruit, drink	sausage and apple pastry, drink	200ml milk
menu 11	150ml milk, bagel with cream cheese and apricot, drink	segments of satsuma, drink	pesto chicken, drink	pieces of banana, drink	lasagne, drink	200ml milk
menu 12	150ml milk, scrambled eggs with Cheddar cheese, drink	pieces of fresh fruit, drink	bubble and squeak, drink	pinwheel sandwiches, drink	pumpkin stew, pear and sesame yogurt, drink	200ml milk
menu 13	150ml milk, bacon and cheese on toast, drink	pieces of peeled pear, drink	lamb with a minty sauce, drink	drink	quick sausage and beans, drink	200ml milk
menu 14	150ml milk, yogurt with dried fruit compote, drink	drink	rich mushroom stew, drink	drink	plaice with a tomato sauce, berrry compote with yogurt, drink	200ml milk

fresh breakfasts

bacon and parsley bread

makes: 10 toddler portions (approx 1kg loaf)

storage: best eaten fresh or keep in an airtight container for up to 3 days

400g plain white flour
400g wholemeal flour
100g Cheddar cheese, grated
6 rashers unsmoked back
  bacon (rind removed),
  grilled and finely chopped
25g sesame seeds (do not
  give seeds to toddlers
  under the age of three if
  there is a family history of
  food allergies)
handful fresh parsley,
  chopped
approx 360ml warm water
1tsp golden caster sugar
6g (1½ level tsp) dried yeast

vitamins B₁, B₆ –
phosphorous

This is brilliant for breakfast with scrambled eggs, but is also lovely to use for eggy bread or sandwiches.

1 Grease a 1kg loaf tin with butter. Sift the white and wholemeal flour into a large bowl and mix in the cheese, bacon, sesame seeds and parsley.
2 Put 100ml of the warm water into a measuring jug, stir in the sugar and yeast and leave for 10–15 minutes, until a froth has formed.
3 Make a well in the flour mixture and pour in the yeast mixture. Mix with a wooden spoon, gradually adding the rest of the warm water. Use your hands to mix it, adding a little more warm water if necessary, until you have a smooth dough that comes away from the edges of the bowl.
4 On a floured surface, knead the dough briefly for 3–4 minutes until it is smooth and soft. Shape into an oblong and drop into the prepared tin. Sprinkle the surface with flour, cover with a warm damp cloth and leave to rise in a warm place for 30–40 minutes. Preheat the oven to 200°C/400°F/ gas mark 6.
5 Bake the bread for 40 minutes, then remove from the tin and bake upside down on the shelf for 10–15 minutes to crisp up. When it is cooked, it will sound hollow when the bottom is tapped. Leave to cool on a wire rack.
6 Cut into thin slices, chop up each slice and serve.

mango and banana smoothie

makes: 6 toddler portions

storage: best eaten fresh or keep in the refrigerator for up to 24 hours

1 ripe medium mango
2 passion-fruit
1 ripe small banana, roughly
  chopped
250ml orange juice

vitamin B₆

If you like, try adding a little full-fat natural yogurt for a creamier taste. Serve with toast or cereal.

1 Peel the mango and cut the flesh away from the stone. Put into a blender (or food processor).
2 Cut the passion fruit in half and scoop the seeds straight into the blender. Add the orange juice and banana and whiz until smooth.

raspberry muffins

2½

½

1

in B₁₂

makes: 9 toddler portions
(9 mini muffins)

storage: best eaten fresh or
keep in an airtight container
for up to 2 days or in the
freezer for up to 3 months

185g plain flour
1½tsp baking powder
80g golden caster sugar
1 medium egg
125ml full-fat milk
½tsp vanilla extract
45g unsalted butter, melted
150g raspberries, fresh or
  frozen

Make these with any soft fruits that you have to hand. Muffins are really easy
to make so, if you have an older toddler, get her to help with the
preparation of these.

1 Preheat the oven 200°C/400°F/gas mark 6. Butter a mini-muffin tray or line
   with paper cases.
2 Sift the flour into a bowl with the baking powder. Stir in the sugar.
3 In a separate bowl, whisk the egg, milk, vanilla and melted butter together.
4 Make a well in the centre of the dry ingredients. Pour in the milk mixture
   and mix gently until you have a wet, lumpy batter. Stir in the raspberries.
5 Spoon the batter into the muffin cases and bake in the hot oven for
   10–12 minutes, until risen and golden. Cool on a wire rack.
6 If necessary, cut into smaller pieces before serving.

porridge

7½

1½

2

2

½

vitamins B₁, B₂, B₁₂, B₆
 – phosphorous

makes: 2 toddler portions

storage: best eaten fresh or
keep in the refrigerator for up
to 24 hours

350ml full-fat milk or
  calcium-enriched soya drink
100g porridge oats

There are so many ways to jazz up plain porridge, you may like to try adding
something to the mix before cooking, such as half a vanilla pod, split
lengthways, for a creamy vanilla porridge (remove pod before serving).
Alternatively, add one of the following to a bowl of porridge before serving:
1tbsp puréed dried fruit such as prunes or apricots; half a ripe small banana,
mashed; 1tsp soft brown sugar or runny honey.

1 Put all the ingredients into a heavy-based saucepan and gently simmer for
   5–10 minutes, stirring often, until the mixture has thickened.
2 Add a little more milk, soya drink or cooled boiled water to thin if necessary.

bacon and egg scramble

12

makes: 2 toddler portions

storage: best eaten fresh

1

small knob unsalted butter

2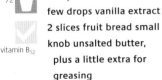

4 rashers unsmoked streaky
  bacon (rind removed), very
  finely chopped

½

3 medium eggs

4tbsp full-fat milk

1tbsp fresh parsley, finely
  chopped (optional)

vitamins B₁, B₆
– phosphorous

freshly ground black pepper

This is a quick and easy way to make scrambled eggs a bit more interesting –
especially if you add a little parsley, which toddlers seem to love. You could
use back bacon for this, but it's best to avoid smoked bacon, which can be
too salty for toddlers.

1 Melt the butter in a heavy-based frying pan and fry the bacon until crisp and
golden, approximately 5–10 minutes.

2 Meanwhile, whisk together in a bowl the eggs, milk, parsley and a little
freshly ground black pepper.

3 Pour off the fat from the bacon pan.

4 Place the pan with the bacon bits over a gentle heat. Add the egg mixture
and cook, stirring, until the eggs are scrambled and cooked through.
Serve immediately.

eggy raisin bread

4

makes: 2 toddler portions

storage: best eaten fresh

½

1tsp soft brown sugar

½

1 medium egg, slightly
  beaten

½

1tbsp full-fat milk

few drops vanilla extract

2 slices fruit bread small

vitamin B₁₂

knob unsalted butter,
  plus a little extra for
  greasing

This is an easy way to add a little extra protein to your toddler's diet. You
could just as easily make this without the sugar and use a savoury bread
instead of fruit bread.

1 Put the sugar, egg, milk and vanilla in a bowl and whisk together. Cut each
slice of fruit bread into 4 triangles.

2 Heat a frying pan over a medium heat and grease with a little butter. Dip
2 triangles of bread into the egg mixture and put into the hot frying pan.

3 Cook for 2 minutes on each side until golden and the egg is cooked through.
Repeat with the remaining bread. Serve immediately. If necessary, cut into
smaller pieces before serving.

quick bites breakfasts

Often it is a challenge to get everyone ready in the mornings, so quick breakfast ideas are essential.

All of the recipes make one toddler portion unless stated otherwise.

vitamins A, B₂, B₁₂, B₆ –
phosphorus

ham omelette

1 medium egg
small knob unsalted butter
1tsp olive oil
1 slice cooked ham, finely chopped

Break the egg into a bowl and lightly whisk. Melt the butter and oil in a frying pan over a medium heat. Swirl the fat around the pan, then pour in the egg to cover the base of the pan. Using a wooden spoon, draw the edges of the omelette into the centre. When the omelette is cooked and thee is no runny egg left in the pan, sprinkle over the ham and fold the omelette in half, then slide on to a plate. Chop into small pieces and serve. Try adding grated cheese, finely chopped cooked bacon, finely chopped herbs or finely chopped tomato.

Ready Brek with prunes

3 "ready to eat" prunes
75ml apple juice
30g Ready Brek
125ml full-fat milk

Prunes are high in fibre and minerals, particularly potassium and iron. Put the prunes into a bowl, add the apple juice and leave to soak for 10 minutes, then purée. Make the Ready Brek up according to the packet instructions, using the full-fat milk. Swirl the puréed prunes through the Ready Brek.

vitamins B₁, B₆ –
phosphorous

bacon and cheese on toast

2 rashers unsmoked streaky
bacon (rind removed)
1 slice white bread
15g Cheddar cheese, grated

Preheat the grill. Grill the bacon until cooked and slightly crisp. Cut into very small pieces. Grill the bread on one side, then scatter the bacon over the uncooked side. Top with the grated cheese and grill until slightly golden and bubbling. Cut into small pieces and serve.

vitamin B₆

apple, pear and banana smoothie

makes: 2 portions
1 eating apple, eg Cox's, peeled, cored
and chopped
1 ripe pear, peeled, cored and chopped
1 ripe medium banana, peeled, chopped,
or 2 ripe stoned plums, chopped
200ml apple juice

Put all of the ingredients into a jug and purée with a hand-held blender (or in a food processor or blender) until smooth.

stewed apple and blackberries

vitamins B₁, B₆ – phosphorous

1 eating apple, eg Cox's
2 handfuls of ripe blackberries (75–100g)
1tsp golden caster sugar, to taste
2tbsp natural full-fat yogurt
½ plain bagel, chopped into bite-size pieces

Peel, core and slice the apple and put into a small saucepan with 2tbsp water, the blackberries and sugar. Cook over a gentle heat until the apples are soft, then cool slightly. Purée with a hand-held blender (or in a food processor or blender) and return to the pan. Put into a bowl with the yogurt and serve with chunks of bagel.

bagel with cream cheese and apricot

1 plain bagel
2tbsp full-fat cream cheese
2 tinned breakfast apricots, drained

Breakfast apricots are different from ordinary tinned apricots as they have been dried and then soaked in juice, rather than syrup. When mashed, they make a less sugary alternative to marmalade or jam. Cut the bagel in half and spread each half with cream cheese. Mash the apricots well and spread them over the cream cheese. Cut into small pieces and serve.

fried bread with mushrooms

vitamin B₆

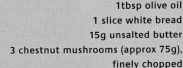

1tbsp olive oil
1 slice white bread
15g unsalted butter
3 chestnut mushrooms (approx 75g), finely chopped

Heat the oil in a frying pan. Fry the bread on each side until golden – about 1–2 minutes each side. Cut into pieces and put onto a plate. Melt the butter in the frying pan, add the mushrooms and fry until soft and lightly golden – approximately 3–4 minutes. Spoon the mushrooms onto the fried bread. A little fat, especially olive oil, is good for toddlers as they need it for energy. Cut into small pieces and serve. Only serve to toddlers who are confident with chewing.

strawberries and mango with toasted oats

vitamins A, B₁, B₆ – phosphorous

2tbsp porridge oats
1 handful of fresh strawberries (approx 50g), hulled and finely chopped
¼ small ripe mango, peeled and finely chopped
1tbsp full-fat natural yogurt

Dry-frying oats in a pan is a quick and easy way to make a crunchy topping for yogurt or fresh fruits. You can also toast chopped nuts and seeds in this way (do not give nuts to toddlers under the age of three if there is a family history of allergies). Heat a frying pan, add the oats and cook until lightly golden, stirring often. Cool. Put the chopped fruits into a bowl, top with the yogurt and sprinkle over the toasted oats.

scrambled egg with Cheddar cheese

     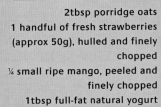

vitamins B₁, B₂, B₁₂, B₆, D – phosphorous

makes: 2 toddler portions
2 medium eggs
75ml full-fat milk
freshly ground black pepper
small knob unsalted butter
50g Cheddar cheese, grated
1tbsp fresh parsley, finely chopped (optional)
1 white or brown soft bun

Whisk the eggs and milk together with a little freshly ground black pepper. Melt the butter in a pan and add the egg mixture. Cook over a gentle heat, stirring with a wooden spoon, until the eggs begin to scramble. Sprinkle over the grated Cheddar and chopped parsley and continue to cook until the eggs are thoroughly cooked but not rubbery – approximately 3–4 minutes. Slice the bun in half and spoon the cheesy scrambled egg over the top. If necessary, cut into smaller pieces before serving.

fresh lunches

gnocchi, leeks and cheese sauce

3

1

½

½

1½ C

vitamins A, B₁, B₆
– folic acid –
phosphorus

makes: 4 toddler portions
storage: best eaten fresh

400g packet potato gnocchi
50g unsalted butter
2 small leeks, washed
  thoroughly, trimmed and
  very finely chopped
100ml no- or low-salt
  veg stock (see page 44)
100g peas, fresh or frozen
80g Boursin with herbs
2tbsp fresh parsley, chopped
freshly ground black pepper
2tbsp Cheddar, grated

Lunches that are as easy to make as this one are great. Add other soft vegetables too if you like; just chop them finely – courgettes or frozen sweetcorn would taste good.

1 Put a large pan of water on to boil, add the gnocchi and cook following the packet's instructions.
2 Meanwhile, melt the butter in a heavy-based pan and gently fry the leeks until soft and pale gold.
3 Add the stock, bring to the boil, then add the peas. Cook until the peas are done – approximately 2 minutes. Stir in the cheese and parsley and season with freshly ground black pepper.
4 Add the gnocchi and simmer for a few minutes. If necessary, cut into smaller pieces before serving and sprinkle with the grated Cheddar.

pesto chicken

14

½

1

1 C

vitamins B₂, B₆
– phosphorus

makes: 6 toddler portions
storage: best eaten fresh or
keep in the refrigerator for up
to 24 hours

4 chicken breasts
4tbsp pesto
50g unsalted butter,
  softened
juice of ½ lemon
freshly ground black pepper

This is an easy way of adding a little extra flavour to chicken breasts, and the pesto mixture helps to keep the breasts juicy and succulent during cooking. Serve with the vegetables of your choice and a little pasta or potato.

1 Cut a slit into the side of each chicken breast, open the breast out and lay flat on a board.
2 Cover with clingfilm or greaseproof paper and bash with a rolling pin to flatten slightly.
3 In a bowl, mix together the pesto, butter, lemon juice and freshly ground black pepper.
4 Preheat the grill to high. Grill the flattened chicken pieces on one side for 4–5 minutes. Turn the chicken over and spread each breast with the pesto mixture. Grill for another 4–5 minutes, until cooked through. Cut into small pieces before serving.

couscous salad with tuna

 7½

 1½

 ½

 1

 ½

vitamins B₁₂, B₆, D

makes: 4 toddler portions

storage: eat fresh or keep in the refrigerator for up to 3 days

200g couscous
400ml boiling no- or low-salt
 veg stock (see page 44)
150g feta cheese
8 ripe baby tomatoes
½ cucumber, peeled
198g tin tuna in oil or water,
 drained and flaked
1–2tbsp fresh basil, torn

Couscous is so quick to cook. By the time you have chopped up all the vegetables it will be ready. You can add pretty much any cooked vegetables that you have to hand to this dish; just be sure to chop them into small pieces for your toddler.

1 Put the couscous into a bowl, pour over the boiling stock, cover and leave for at least 10 minutes, or until the couscous has absorbed all of the liquid. Fluff up with a fork.

2 Meanwhile, cut the feta cheese, baby tomatoes and peeled cucumber into small pieces.

3 Add to the couscous with the drained tinned tuna and torn basil and mix together. If necessary, mash slightly before serving.

bubble and squeak

 3

½

½

½

4

vitamins B₁, B₆

makes: 4 toddler portions

storage: best eaten fresh

550g white potatoes, peeled
 and halved
50g unsalted butter
50ml full-fat milk
450g cooked vegetables,
 eg cabbage, onions, leeks,
 carrots or sprouts, well
 drained and finely chopped
1tbsp fresh parsley, finely
 chopped
freshly ground black pepper

You can add pretty much any cooked vegetables to this although leeks, cabbage or carrots seem to work best – nothing too watery is the rule. This would be delicious served with chopped cooked ham. Don't be too worried about flipping the bubble and squeak over; if it breaks, just turn over as many of the crispy bits as possible and cook the soft bits.

1 Bring a large pan of water to the boil and cook the potatoes until tender. Drain well and return to the pan.

2 Add half the butter and the milk and mash well.

3 Mix the cooked vegetables and parsley into the mash and season with freshly ground black pepper.

4 Melt the remaining butter in a heavy-based frying pan, then add the potato mixture, pressing it down well into the pan. Cook slowly over a low heat so a golden crust is formed on the bottom of the pan – approximately 5–10 minutes. Scrape up the bottom of the bubble and squeak and flip over to cook the other side for 5–10 minutes. Cut into small pieces before serving.

tuna and pesto baked potatoes

This makes a great weekend lunch for all the family. Once the potatoes are cooked, they take only minutes to prepare. Only serve raw vegatables to toddlers who are confident with chewing.

1 Preheat the oven to 180°C/350°F/gas mark 4. Bake the potatoes for 50 minutes, until crisp on the outside and soft and fluffy in the middle.

2 Cut the potatoes in half and scoop out the flesh. Mix the flesh thoroughly with the butter, pesto and tuna. Preheat the grill to high. Spoon the potato mixture back into the potato skins and sprinkle over the cheese. Grill for a few minutes, until the cheese is golden and bubbling.

3 Cut into smaller pieces before serving with steamed vegetable sticks. Only serve the skin to toddlers who are confident with chewing.

22 · **makes:** 4 toddler portions

1 · **storage:** best eaten fresh

1½ · **4 medium baking potatoes, scrubbed**

2 · **knob of unsalted butter**

2 · **3tbsp pesto**

400g tinned tuna in water, drained and flaked

100g Cheddar cheese, grated

handful of steamed sticks of carrot and courgette, to serve

vitamins B₁, B₁₂, B₆, D – phosphorous,

lamb with a minty sauce

It does not take long to grill a lamb chop, making this a speedy way to feed your toddler some protein at lunchtime.

1 Preheat the grill to high and cook the lamb chop for 3–4 minutes on each side, until cooked through.

2 Mix together the yogurt, mint and cucumber.

3 Cut the lamb chop into very small pieces and serve with the bread soldiers and minty yogurt.

5½ · **makes:** 1 toddler portion

½ · **storage:** best eaten fresh

1½ · **1 lamb chump chop, trimmed**

½ · **2tbsp natural Greek yogurt**

2 mint leaves, chopped

¼ cucumber, peeled and grated

1 slice white bread, toasted and cut into fingers

vitamins B₁, B₂, B₁₂, B₆ – phosphorous

quick bites lunches

All of the recipes make one toddler portion unless stated otherwise.

avocado and cream cheese dip

 ½ ½ ½ ½ 2½

½ ripe avocado, peeled, stoned and finely chopped
2tbsp full-fat cream cheese
squeeze of lemon juice
1 soft flour tortilla or 1 slice white toast, cut into strips
5cm piece of cucumber, peeled and cut into sticks

It's best not to make this too far in advance, or it will go brown. Put the avocado in a bowl and mash with a fork until smooth. Add the cream cheese and lemon juice and mix until smooth. Serve with the tortilla or toast strips and cucumber sticks. Alternatively, spread on warm white toast. If necessary, cut into smaller pieces before serving. Only give this to toddlers who are confident with chewing.

guacamole with ham

 1 1 ½ 4

vitamins B₁, B₆, B₁₂

2tbsp guacamole
½ ripe avocado, peeled and stoned
1 slice cooked ham, finely chopped
1 small plain bagel, halved and toasted

If you're buying the guacamole, check the label and avoid buying any with excessive added salt or sugar. It's best not to prepare this too far in advance, or it will go brown. Put the guacamole into a bowl with the avocado and mash together with a fork to form a rough purée. Stir in the finely chopped cooked ham. Spread onto the two halves of toasted bagel. If necessary, cut into smaller pieces before serving.

pasta with cheese and sweetcorn

 2 1 ½  7½

vitamins A B₂, B₆, B₁₂ – phosphorous

50g pasta
75g sweetcorn, fresh or frozen
50g full-fat Cheddar cheese, grated
15g unsalted butter
small pinch finely chopped fresh parsley (optional)

Bring a medium pan of water to the boil. Add the pasta and cook following the packet's instructions. Stir in the sweetcorn a few minutes before the end of the cooking time, bring back to the boil and cook until both are cooked. Drain and return to the pan. Add the Cheddar and butter, then stir everything together. You could also add some chopped fresh herbs. If necessary, cut into smaller pieces before serving.

pasta, avocado and tuna

 ½ 1 ½   8

vitamins B₁, B₆, B₁₂ – phosphorous

50g pasta
70g tinned tuna in oil or water
½ ripe avocado, peeled, stoned and chopped
1tbsp mayonnaise (optional)

Bring a medium pan of water to the boil and cook the pasta according to the packet's instructions. Drain. Drain and flake the tuna and then add it to the pasta with the avocado. Mix together. You could add a little mayonnaise to help bind everything together if you wish. If necessary, cut into smaller pieces before serving immediately.

pineapple and ham pizza

1 slice white bread
1 slice cooked ham
1 slice fresh ripe pineapple, peeled and chopped
25g Cheddar cheese, grated

Ham and pineapple is one of the most popular pizza toppings among children. Preheat a grill. Toast the bread on one side. Turn over, top with the ham, then the pineapple and finally the grated cheese. Grill until the cheese is bubbling and hot. Leave to cool slightly, cut into small pieces and serve.

rice with chicken and bacon

vitamins B_1, B_6 – phosphorous

50g white Basmati rice
1tbsp olive oil
2 rashers unsmoked streaky bacon, chopped
½ chicken breast, chopped
1tbsp raisins

Put the rice into a saucepan and add 100ml cold water. Cover and bring to the boil, reduce to a simmer, and cook for 11 minutes, still covered – or until the rice is cooked through. Remove from the heat and leave, still covered for another 10 minutes. Meanwhile, heat the oil in a frying pan, add the bacon and cook for a few minutes, then add the chicken breast and continue to cook, stirring occasionally, until it is just starting to turn golden and both the bacon and chicken are cooked through – approximately 10 minutes more. Add the raisins to the chicken with the cooked rice and mix everything together. If necessary, cut into smaller pieces before serving.

minty chicken with bite-size vegetables

vitamins A, B_1, B_6

1tsp mint sauce
1tbsp full-fat yogurt
2tsp mayonnaise
½ cooked chicken breast, chopped
5cm piece of cucumber, peeled and chopped into chunks
2 ripe tomatoes, chopped into bite-size pieces

Put the mint sauce, yogurt and mayonnaise into a bowl and mix together. Add the chicken and stir thoroughly. Tip into a bowl and serve with the cucumber and tomato chunks. If your toddler is used to more pungent flavours, try adding a teaspoon of mango chutney instead of the mint sauce, and serving the chicken with some chunks of fruit, such as mango, as well as the vegetables. If necessary, cut into smaller pieces before serving. Only serve chunks of raw vegetables to toddlers who are confident with chewing.

buttered peas with spaghetti

vitamins B_1, B_6 – phosphorous

75g spaghetti
75g frozen peas or petits pois
15g unsalted butter
3 leaves fresh mint or parsley, finely chopped (optional)
1tbsp Parmesan or Cheddar cheese, freshly grated (optional)

Bring a medium pan of water to the boil and cook the pasta according to the packet's instructions. 2 minutes before it is done, add the peas, bring back to the boil and cook for the remaining time. Drain and return to the pan. Add the butter and a little finely chopped mint or parsley. You could add some grated Parmesan or Cheddar cheese as well. Cut into smaller pieces before serving.

lunches to freeze

squash, carrot and orange soup

A true winter-warming soup with a slightly sweet flavour that is always popular with toddlers.

1½
½

½
3 C

vitamins A, B₆

makes: 8 toddler portions

storage: freeze for up to 3 months

25g unsalted butter
2tbsp olive oil
2 medium onions, chopped
2 medium carrots, peeled
   and cut into small chunks
2 sticks celery, finely chopped
1kg butternut squash, peeled,
   seeded and finely chopped
1 litre no- or low-salt veg
   stock (see page 44), boiling
juice of 1 orange
freshly ground black pepper

1 In a heavy-based pan, melt the butter with the oil. Add the onions and cook gently for about 10 minutes, until soft but not coloured.
2 Add the carrots, celery and squash and cook for another 10 minutes, stirring occasionally. Add the stock, bring to the boil and cook for 20 minutes, until the vegetables are soft.
3 Purée in a blender (or food processor), return to the pan to heat through, add the orange juice and season to taste with freshly ground black pepper. Leave to cool, pour into freezerproof containers or freezer bags and freeze.
4 Thaw thoroughly. Pour into a saucepan and reheat the soup gently until it is just boiling. Cool a little to serve.

creamy tomato soup

If your toddler likes the taste or texture of shop-bought soups, such as the classic Heinz tomato soup, this may be a big hit.

1½
½

½
2 C

vitamins A, B₆

makes: 10 toddler portions

storage: freeze for up to 3 months

10g unsalted butter
1 small red onion, chopped
1 garlic clove, crushed
1 small carrot, peeled and
   finely chopped
1 potato, peeled and chopped
1kg ripe tomatoes, chopped
2tbsp tomato purée
600ml no- or low-salt veg
   stock (see page 44)
ground black pepper
fresh basil leaves, torn
300ml full-fat milk

1 Melt the butter in a large saucepan. Add the onion, garlic and carrot and cook until soft and golden – approximately 5 minutes. Add the potato and cook for another 5 minutes, stirring occasionally.
2 Add the tomatoes, tomato purée, stock, a little freshly ground black pepper and basil. Stir and bring to the boil, then simmer for 8–10 minutes, until the potatoes are soft.
3 Whiz with a hand-held blender (or in a food processor or blender) until smooth, then pass through a nylon sieve. Leave to cool, pour into freezerproof containers or freezer bags and freeze.
4 Thaw thoroughly. Pour into a saucepan, stir in the milk and reheat gently until just boiling.

rich mushroom stew

makes: 5 toddler portions

storage: freeze for up to 4 months

vitamins B₂, B₆

25g dried porcini
2tbsp olive oil
4 shallots, peeled and finely
    chopped
2 garlic cloves, crushed
600g fresh mushrooms, eg
    field, oyster, brown caps etc
600ml no- or low-salt
    veg stock (see page 44)
2tbsp fresh parsley, chopped
freshly ground black pepper
boiled rice or mashed
    potatoes, to serve

You could add more flavour by cooking the rice in diluted no- or low-salt vegetable stock.

1   Cover the dried mushrooms with 150ml boiling water. Soak for 30 minutes. Drain, reserving the soaking liquid, and finely chop. Heat 1tbsp oil in a frying pan and cook the shallots and garlic until soft and pale gold. Tip onto a plate.
2   Finely chop the mushrooms. Heat the remaining oil in the frying pan and fry the fresh and dried mushrooms over a high heat, stirring often. When they begin to release their juices, add a little of the stock and bring to the boil. Add the remaining stock, shallots, garlic and porcini soaking liquid and simmer until the liquid has reduced and is syrupy – approximately 30 minutes.
3   Add the parsley and season well with freshly ground black pepper. Leave to cool completely, transfer to a freezerproof container, cover and freeze.
4   Thaw thoroughly. Transfer to a saucepan, heat through gently until just boiling. Serve with rice or mash.

lamb kebabs with mango

makes 8 toddler portions

storage freeze for up to 6 months

vitamins B₆, B₁₂

4tbsp olive oil
1tsp sesame oil
juice of ½ lemon
2 garlic cloves, peeled and
    finely chopped
2 shallots, peeled and finely
    chopped
2 large handfuls fresh
    coriander, finely chopped
550g lamb neck fillet, cut
    into small cubes
1 ripe large mango, peeled,
    stoned and cut into small
    pieces
wooden skewers
cooked Basmati rice, to serve

Freezing kebabs is an excellent way to have small portions ready to hand. Do not give nuts to toddlers under the age of three if there is any family history of food allergies. Remember – never refreeze raw meat that has already been frozen. Any pre-packaged meat will be labelled if it has already been frozen. Otherwise ask your butcher.

1   Mix the first 6 ingredients in a large freezerproof container.
2   Add the lamb, stir to coat thoroughly, then marinate for 15 minutes.
3   Thread the lamb onto skewers. Put back into the marinade, cover and freeze.
4   Thaw thoroughly. Preheat oven to 180°C/350°F/gas mark 4. Heat a griddle pan until hot, add a drop of olive oil and cook the kebabs for approximately 10 minutes, or until the lamb is cooked through, turning occasionally.
5   Remove the skewers, finely chop the lamb and serve with small pieces of mango and the rice.

herb scones

makes: 8 toddler portions (8 scones)

storage: freeze for up to 3 months

225g self-raising flour

1 level tsp baking powder

pinch of mustard

50g unsalted butter plus extra for greasing

75g Cheddar cheese, grated

1tbsp fresh parsley, finely chopped

150ml full-fat milk

vitamin B$_{12}$
phosphorus

You can try many variations of these scones using different herbs, chopped sundried tomatoes, cooked ham or cooked bacon.

1 Preheat the oven to 180°C/350°F/gas mark 4. Sift the flour into a bowl with the baking powder and mustard.

2 Rub in the butter with your fingertips, then stir in the parsley and all but 1tbsp of the cheese. Make a well and pour in the milk. Mix together to make a soft dough.

3 On a lightly floured surface, roll out to about 2.5cm thick and cut out 6cm rounds. Put the scones onto a greased baking sheet, sprinkle with the reserved cheese and bake in the moderate oven for 12–14 minutes until risen and golden. Serve warm or leave to cool and place in a freezerproof container or freezer bag and freeze.

4 Thaw completely and reheat in the oven at 180°C/350°F/gas mark 4 for 5 minutes or until warmed through.

lasagne

makes: 6 toddler portions

storage: freeze for up to 4 months

2tbsp olive oil

500g lean beef, minced

2 carrots, peeled

2 medium red onions

2 garlic cloves, crushed

100g button or chestnut mushrooms, sliced

200ml low-salt veg stock

2tbsp tomato purée

400g tin chopped tomatoes

1tbsp fresh parsley, chopped

40g unsalted butter

40g plain flour

600ml full-fat milk

100g Cheddar cheese, grated

200g ready-to-cook lasagne

50g Parmesan, grated

cooked peas or green salad, to serve

vitamins A, B$_1$,B$_2$, B$_{12}$, B$_6$ – phosphorous

This is a fantastic all-in-one meal, high in protein and carbohydrate – just serve it with some salad or peas.

1 Heat 1tbsp olive oil in a heavy-based pan and brown the mince, stirring to break it up. Remove from the pan and reserve.

2 Finely chop the carrots and onions. Heat the remaining olive oil and fry the onions, garlic, carrots and mushrooms until soft and pale golden – approximately 10 minutes.

3 Add the stock and bring to the boil. Stir in the tomato purée, tomatoes, parsley and mince and simmer for 30 minutes until the sauce is thick.

4 Meanwhile, melt the butter in another pan. Stir in the flour and cook for 1 minute. Remove from the heat and gradually whisk in the milk. Bring back to the boil, stirring constantly until the sauce is thick and smooth. Remove from the heat and stir in the Cheddar.

5 In an ovenproof and freezerproof dish, layer the meat sauce, lasagne sheets, then cheese sauce in turn until everything is used. End with a layer of cheese sauce sprinkled with Parmesan. Cool completely. Wrap in clingfilm and freeze.

6 Thaw thoroughly. Preheat the oven to 190°C/375°F/gas mark 5.

7 Cook in the oven for 30-35 minutes, until hot and golden. Cut into smaller pieces before serving.

quick bites snacks

Snacks play an important part in toddlers' diets, contributing to their nutritional requirements and helping them to keep going between meals. But, of course, this is only if the snacks that you give them are healthy! Generally, I give my girls fresh fruit and vegetables as snacks. However, there are times when their moods change as a result of a drop in their blood sugar levels, and they need to eat something more substantial to give them enough energy to keep going until the next meal. It is best not to give snacks too close to their next meal though.

All of the recipes make one toddler portion unless stated otherwise.

 1 1 1 6½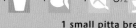

vitamins B₁, B₆

warm pitta bread with peanut butter

1 small pitta bread
1tbsp full-fat cream cheese
1tsp smooth peanut butter (do not give nuts to toddlers under the age of three if there is a family history of allergies)

Warm pitta is lovely and soft and a very comforting snack for toddlers to chew, especially if they are teething. Peanut butter can be quite salty, so look for brands with no added salt (or sugar). Warm the pitta in a moderate oven (180°C/350°F/gas 4) for 5 minutes. Meanwhile, mix the cream cheese and peanut butter together. Spread on the warm pitta before cutting into fingers.

vitamin B₆  ½ 2½

corn thins with mashed avocado

½ ripe small avocado, peeled and stoned
2 low-salt corn thins

Corn thins are available in most supermarkets, alongside the cheese biscuits. They are a little more chewy than rice cakes and a bit tastier. It's best not to prepare the mashed avocado too far in advance, or it will go brown. Mash the avocado flesh with a fork in a bowl. Spread the mashed avocado onto the corn thins or, if you prefer, break them into pieces and serve with the mashed avocado as a dip.

½ 1 1 5½

breadsticks and dips

2 breadsticks
3 level tbsp hummus or guacamole

Breadsticks are a great "occasional" snack either on their own or with dips. If you buy your dips, make sure you choose varieties with no (or very little) added salt or sugar, such as guacamole, salsa or hummus. You may find this snack a little messy to serve to one year olds. They are best off eating a little dip with a spoon, but as they get slightly older they tend to find dunking the breadsticks into the dips quite a novelty.

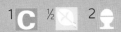

raisin toast with apple purée

1 slice raisin bread
3 level tbsp apple purée

Sweet, thick purées of mashed fruits or vegetables, such as banana or avocado, make a great alternative to sugar-laden jams. Simply toast the raisin bread and spread with the purée. Cut into fingers.

vitamins B₆, B₁₂

pineapple with ham

2 slices fresh ripe pineapple
1 slice cooked ham

If your toddler is not fantastic at eating fresh fruit and needs a little encouragement, you may find teaming fruit with meat helps. Peel the pineapple and cut 2 slices of the flesh into small chunks. Cut the ham into small pieces and thread a piece of ham and pineapple onto a blunt stick. Repeat with the rest of the fruits and ham. Help your toddler remove the sticks before she eats the ham and pineapple.

vitamin B₆

rice cakes with nut butter

1tbsp smooth nut butter, eg cashew nut butter (do not give nuts to toddlers under the age of three if there is a family history of allergies)
2 unsalted rice cakes

Look for nut butters from health food shops – they tend to have no added sugar or salt. There are so many other toppings that you could put onto rice cakes too, including low-salt yeast extract and honey. Spread the nut butter onto the rice cakes. If necessary, break into smaller pieces before serving.

yogurt with dried fruit compote

3tbsp natural full-fat yogurt
2tbsp dried fruit compote

Rather than rely on expensive little pots of fruit yogurts, that so often have a large amount of sugar added, make your own by adding fruit compotes or low-sugar jams to natural yogurt. Put the yogurt and dried fruit compote into a bowl and mix together.

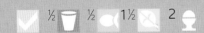

vitamin B₆

grapes filled with cream cheese

5 big black or green seedless grapes
1tbsp full-fat cream cheese

Most children love to eat grapes – which is a good thing as they are absolutely packed with energy as well as vitamins and minerals. Rather than just giving your toddler a bowlful of grapes, combine them with some cream cheese to make a more substantial snack. Simply cut the grapes in half and then spread each half with a little of the cream cheese before serving them to your toddler. Only serve to toddlers who are confident with chewing.

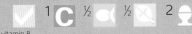

vitamin B₆

grated apple, honey and bread

1 small apple, eg Cox's
1tsp runny honey
1 slice wholemeal bread

Peel, core and grate the apple into a small bowl. Add the honey and mix together well. Spread onto the slice of bread and cut into fingers.

fresh **suppers**

sausage and apple pastry

4½

1

1

½

1

vitamin B$_6$

makes: 8 toddler portions

storage: best eaten fresh or keep in the refrigerator for up to 2 days and served cold

1tbsp olive oil

450g sausage meat

1 large onion, chopped

1 garlic clove, crushed

2 eating apples, grated

2 sprigs fresh thyme or pinch dried thyme

100ml apple juice

100ml no- or low-salt veg stock (see page 44)

freshly ground black pepper

450g ready-made puff pastry

full-fat milk, to glaze

Good-quality sausage meat with a high percentage of pork will taste better than the cheap stuff, and is also likely to have fewer chemical additives.

1 Preheat the oven to 220°C/425°F/gas mark 7. Heat the oil in a heavy-based pan and brown the sausage meat, stirring to break it up. Remove to a plate.

2 Add the onion and garlic to the pan and gently fry until the onion is soft, then add the apples and fry for a few minutes.

3 Return the meat to the pan with the thyme, apple juice, stock and some freshly ground black pepper, then simmer until all the liquid has gone. Cool.

4 On a floured surface, roll out the puff pastry into a rectangle about 2.5mm thick. Brush round the outside edge with milk, then lay on a baking sheet.

5 Spread the sausage mixture in the centre of the pastry, leaving a 2.5cm border all the way round. Fold the two short ends into the middle, overlapping slightly and pressing them together. Pinch the long sides together.

6 Brush the top with milk and bake for 15–20 minutes, then lower the heat to 180°C/350°F/gas mark 4 and cook for another 20 minutes, until golden and risen. Slice and serve warm. If necessary, cut into smaller pieces to serve.

corn pancakes

½

makes: 6 toddler portions (18 pancakes)

storage: best eaten fresh or keep uncooked batter in the refrigerator for up to 24 hours

200g tinned cooked sweetcorn

1 large egg

25g plain flour

5tbsp full-fat milk

unsalted butter, for frying

4 slices cooked ham, chopped

green salad, to serve

If you are using fresh sweetcorn for this recipe you will need to blanch it first. And remember to leave a couple of hours aside for chilling the batter. .

1 Drain the sweetcorn, then put half of it, the egg, plain flour and milk into a bowl and purée with a hand-held blender (or in a food processor or blender) to make a batter. Stir in the remaining sweetcorn. Cover and chill in the fridge for 2 hours.

2 Grease a heavy-based frying pan with a little butter and cook 2tbsp of the mixture at a time for about 2 minutes on each side. Both sides should be golden and the pancakes cooked through.

3 Add a little more butter to the pan as you cook the pancakes. Serve, chopped up if necessary, with a little chopped cooked ham and salad.

chicken with herbs and cheese

A simple stuffing of cream cheese, herbs and garlic helps keep the chicken breasts succulent during cooking. Mascarpone, a rich Italian cream cheese also works well.

10½

½

1

½

1½ C

vitamin B₁,
B₆ – phosphorous

makes: 6 toddler portions

storage: keep in the refrigerator for up to 2 days

225g full-fat cream cheese

2tbsp rosemary or mixture of fresh herbs, chopped

2 garlic cloves, peeled and crushed

zest of 1 unwaxed lemon

4 chicken breasts, skinless

cocktail sticks

750g new potatoes, scrubbed and halved

2tbsp olive oil

freshly ground black pepper

steamed spring vegetables, to serve

1 Preheat the oven to 200°C/400°F/gas mark 6. In a small bowl, mix together the cream cheese, herbs, garlic and lemon zest.

2 Cut a lengthways slit into the side of each chicken breast, to make a pocket. Stuff with the cheese mixture and seal with a cocktail stick. Cover and chill for 30 minutes. Remove the sticks.

3 Put the potatoes into a large roasting dish, drizzle with olive oil and season with freshly ground black pepper. Cook for 15 minutes in the hot oven, then push the potatoes to the one side and rest the chicken alongside, with the top of the breast faced downwards. Cook in the top of the oven for 20–25 minutes, or until cooked through. Remove the cocktail sticks.

4 Cut into small pieces before serving with steamed vegetables.

anything goes rice

I often give the girls rice with different things mixed in, such as cooked chopped lamb and little pieces of roasted butternut squash – both leftover from a Sunday roast. This recipe, a combination of chicken, chopped nuts and raisins, is always popular.

16½

2

2

2 C

vitamins B₁, B₆ –
phosphorous

makes: 2 toddler portions

storage: best eaten fresh or keep in the refrigerator for up to 24 hours and serve at room temperature (do not reheat rice)

100g Basmati rice

200ml water

2 handfuls frozen peas (approx 90g)

1 cooked chicken breast, shredded

handful of cashew nuts, finely chopped (do not give nuts to toddlers under the age of three if there is a family history of allergies)

handful of raisins

1 Put the rice and water into a medium pan, cover with a tightly fitting lid and bring to the boil. Reduce the heat and simmer for 11 minutes, still covered. Remove from the heat and leave to stand for another 14 minutes without taking off the lid.

2 Boil the peas for a few minutes until just cooked.

3 Add the chicken to the rice with the peas, chopped nuts and raisins. Stir everything together and serve.

plaice with a tomato sauce

14½

½

½

½

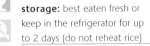
1½

vitamin B₁, B₁₂ B₆ –
phosphorous

makes: 4 toddler portions

storage: best eaten fresh

1tbsp olive oil

1 onion, peeled and finely
chopped

5 ripe tomatoes, chopped

freshly ground black pepper

handful of fresh parsley,
finely chopped

4 small plaice fillets, skinned

2–3tbsp crème fraîche

450g new potatoes,
scrubbed, to serve

200g sugar snap peas,
topped and tailed, to serve

This gorgeous fish dish is very easy to make and, thanks to the addition
of crème fraîche, the sauce has a creamy texture that toddlers seem to
absolutely love.

1 Heat the oil in a heavy-based saucepan. Add the onion and gently cook until
soft – approximately 5–10 minutes.

2 Add the tomatoes, freshly ground black pepper, finely chopped parsley
and fish, cover the pan and then simmer for 10 minutes, or until the fish is
cooked through.

3 Meanwhile, bring a pan of water to the boil, add the potatoes and cook until
tender – approximately 12–15 minutes. A few minutes before they are
cooked, add the sugar snap peas. Drain.

4 When the fish is cooked, stir in the crème fraîche and cook for a further
2 minutes.

5 Cut everything into small pieces before serving.

baked rice with squash

3½

1

½

3

vitamins A, B₆

makes: 8 toddler portions

storage: best eaten fresh or
keep in the refrigerator for up
to 2 days (do not reheat rice)

2tbsp olive oil

1 large red onion, finely
chopped

2 large leeks, washed
thoroughly and finely sliced

2 garlic cloves, peeled and
crushed

750g butternut squash,
peeled and chopped

400g white Basmati rice

800ml no- or low-salt
vegetable stock (see page
44), boiling

freshly ground black pepper

If you need to satisfy ardent carnivores, just add some cooked shredded
chicken to this dish.

1 Preheat the oven to 200°C/400°F/gas mark 6. Heat the olive oil in a large
heavy-based casserole. Add the onion, leeks and garlic, then sauté until really
soft – approximately 10 minutes.

2 Stir in the squash and rice and cook for 1 minute.

3 Pour over the boiling stock, cover with a tightly fitting lid or foil and bake in
the oven for 30–35 minutes, until the rice is tender and the stock absorbed.
Season to taste with freshly ground black pepper.

quick lemon fish with broccoli

 18

 ½

 1

 3

makes: 2 toddler portions

storage: best eaten fresh

1tbsp freshly grated
   unwaxed lemon zest
handful of fresh parsley,
   finely chopped
freshly ground black pepper
2 small fillets of white fish
1tbsp olive oil
4 broccoli florets

vitamins B₁₂, B₆ –
phosphorous

Most children enjoy fish, especially if it is served with a little coating of breadcrumbs. Another quick way of adding a little interest to white fish is to cover it in a mixture of herbs and lemon.

1 Put the lemon zest, finely chopped parsley and some freshly ground black pepper in a bowl and mix together.

2 Add the fish, using your hands to make sure that the mixture covers the fish.

3 Heat the olive oil in a large heavy-based frying pan until hot. Fry the fish for 2–4 minutes on each side, or until cooked.

4 Meanwhile, steam the broccoli over a small pan of boiling water until just tender – approximately 3–4 minutes.

5 Cut the fish into strips and chop up the broccoli to serve.

baked chicken with rice

 18½

 1½

 1½

 ½

 7

makes: 4 toddler portions

storage: best eaten fresh or keep in the refrigerator for up to 2 days and eat at room temperature (do not reheat rice)

3tbsp olive oil
8 small chicken pieces,
   eg thighs, drumsticks, or 4
   large pieces, eg breasts, legs
2 red or orange peppers,
   deseeded and finely chopped
1 large onion, chopped
2 garlic cloves, finely chopped
1tsp paprika
400g tinned cooked chickpeas,
   drained and rinsed
125g Kalamata olives, stoned
   (optional)
200g Basmati rice
400ml low-salt chicken or
   no- or low-salt veg stock
   (see page 44), boiling
handful of parsley, chopped

vitamins A, B₆
phosphorous

This easy-to-make dish has a lovely Mediterranean flavour. Served on its own, or with a lightly steamed green vegetable, it is perfect for the whole family.

1 Preheat the oven to 180°C/350°F/gas mark 4. Heat 2tbsp olive oil in a heavy-based casserole and quickly brown the chicken pieces in batches. Transfer to a plate.

2 Heat the remaining oil and gently fry the peppers, onion and garlic until soft – approximately 10 minutes.

3 Add the chickpeas, olives, rice and stock. Place the chicken on top and cover with a tightly fitting lid. Cook in the oven for 50–60 minutes, until the chicken is cooked through. Cut into smaller pieces before serving.

cheese frittata

10

1

1½

2½

vitamins B₂, B₆,
B₁₂ – phosphorus

makes: 2 toddler portions

storage: best eaten fresh or
keep for up to 24 hours in the
refrigerator and serve at room
temperature (do not reheat)

4 medium eggs
100ml full-fat milk
handful of fresh herbs,
 eg basil, chopped
125g grated Cheddar cheese
freshly ground black pepper
1tbsp olive oil

Frittatas are an easy way to serve eggs. Just add your toddler's favourite
foods, such as grated cheese, chopped cooked ham or chopped cooked
bacon and herbs, to give extra flavour.

1 Put the eggs, milk, herbs, cheese and freshly ground black pepper into a
 bowl and mix together well.
2 Preheat the grill. Heat the oil in a small heavy-based frying pan until hot,
 then add the egg mixture and cook over a medium heat for 4 minutes or
 until just set.
3 Put the frying pan under a hot grill for 1 minute, until the top of the frittata
 is golden. Turn out of the pan and cut into wedges. If necessary, cut into
 smaller pieces before serving.

tomato and chicken pasta

23½

2

3

2

4 C

vitamins B₁, B₆,
B₁₂ – phosphorus

makes: 2 toddler portions

storage: best eaten fresh or
store the sauce in the
refrigerator for up to 24 hours

200g dried pasta
1tbsp olive oil
1 small onion, finely
 chopped
1 garlic clove, finely
 chopped
400g tinned cherry tomatoes
handful of fresh basil, torn
1 chicken breast, finely
 sliced
freshly ground black pepper
pinch of light soft brown
 sugar
25g Parmesan or Cheddar
 cheese, grated (optional)

This is also good with a few handfuls of peas or sweetcorn thrown into the
pasta water a couple of minutes before the pasta has finished cooking.

1 Bring a large pan of water to boil and cook the pasta following the packet's
 instructions. Drain.
2 Heat the oil in heavy-based saucepan. Add the onion and garlic and sauté
 until just soft – approximately 10 minutes.
3 Add the tomatoes and cook for another 5 minutes before adding the basil
 and chicken. Simmer for a further 10-15 minutes, or until the chicken is
 thoroughly cooked. Season with freshly ground black pepper and a pinch of
 brown sugar.
4 Mix in the pasta, then spoon into bowls and top with a little grated cheese, if
 using. If necessary, cut into smaller pieces before serving.

quick bites

suppers

All of the recipes make one toddler portion unless stated otherwise.

 vitamin B₁₂ ½ 10½

grilled white fish with pesto

**1 small white fish fillet, eg sole
or plaice
1tsp fresh pesto
freshly ground black pepper
1 lemon wedge (optional)
mash or new potatoes, to serve**

Preheat the oven to 200°C/400°F/gas mark 6. Spread a little pesto onto each fish fillet. Season with a little freshly ground black pepper. Bake in the oven until the fish is cooked through – approximately 7 minutes. Squeeze a little lemon juice over (if that is your toddler's taste) and serve with mash or new potatoes. If necessary, cut the fish into smaller pieces before serving.

 vitamins A, B₁, B₂, B₆, B₁₂ – phosphorous ½ 3½

chicken breast stuffed with mushrooms

**makes: 2 toddler portions
2tbsp olive oil
½ small onion, peeled, finely chopped
3 chestnut mushrooms (approx 75g),
finely chopped
2tbsp full-fat cream cheese, eg
Boursin
freshly ground black pepper
1 chicken breast**

Heat the oil in a heavy-based pan and fry the onion until soft and pale gold. Add the mushrooms and cook gently until they release their juices and are soft. Remove from the heat and allow to cool, then stir in the cream cheese and season with freshly ground black pepper. Leave to cool completely. Preheat oven to 180°C/350°F/gas mark 4. Carefully cut a pocket lengthways down the side of the chicken breast and fill with the mushroom mixture. Bake in the oven for approximately 25 minutes, or until cooked through. Cut into smaller pieces before serving.

 ½ ½ ½ 6½
Vit B1

pitta bread with cottage cheese

**½ pitta bread
1 tbsp full-fat cottage cheese
1 chive stalk, finely chopped
(optional)**

Keep a packet of pittas in the freezer – you can slice and grill them almost as soon as you take them out. They are really handy for a quick snack or supper.

Grill the pitta bread half with the cut side facing uppermost. When it is ready, mix the cottage cheese with the chopped chives and spread on to the pitta. Cut into small strips.

 vitamins A, B₁, B₆ – folic acid 3 **C** 1

jacket potato with coleslaw

**1 small baking potato, scrubbed
1 medium carrot, peeled and grated
¼ small red cabbage, finely chopped
1tbsp fresh parsley, finely chopped
1tbsp raisins
1tbsp each of olive oil and lemon juice
knob unsalted butter**

Preheat the oven to 180°C/350°F/gas mark 4. Bake the potato for 1 hour until cooked. Meanwhile, mix the carrot, cabbage, parsley, raisins and olive oil together in a small bowl. Cut open the potato, top with the knob of butter and the coleslaw. Cut into smaller pieces before serving. Only serve the potato skins to toddlers who are confident with chewing.

new potatoes wrapped in bacon

vitamins B₁, B₆ –
phosphorus

6 small new potatoes
3 rashers unsmoked streaky
bacon (rind removed),
cut in half lengthways
50g cooked peas, to serve

Preheat the oven to 180°C/350°F/gas mark 4. Bring a medium pan of water to the boil and cook the potatoes for 20 minutes. Drain and cool slightly. Wrap each potato in a strip of bacon – secure with a cocktail stick, if needed – then roast for 30 minutes, until the bacon is crisp and golden. Remove the cocktail stick. If necessary, cut into smaller pieces before serving with the peas.

tuna, butter beans, tomato and lettuce

vitamins B₆, B₁₂ –
folic acid –
phosphorus

70g tinned tuna in oil or water,
drained and flaked
100g tinned cooked butter beans,
washed, drained and finely chopped
1 ripe tomato, halved and finely chopped
2–3 leaves iceberg lettuce, shredded into
tiny pieces
1tbsp fresh parsley, finely chopped

Mix all the ingredients together in a bowl. Cover and leave to stand at room temperature for 10 minutes before serving.

aubergine and chicken in tomato sauce

½ aubergine, cut into small cubes
½ chicken breast, cut into
bite-size pieces
1tbsp olive oil
freshly ground black pepper
½ quantity (250ml) storecupboard
tomato sauce (see page 44) or
250ml tomato passata
50g cooked pasta or cooked white
Basmati rice, to serve

Preheat the oven to 190°C/375°F/gas mark 6. Put the aubergine and chicken into a small roasting tin and pour over the oil. Season with freshly ground black pepper and mix everything together. Roast in the oven for 20 minutes, or until the chicken is cooked through. Pour over the tomato sauce, mix well and roast for another 10 minutes. Serve with cooked pasta or rice.

minty mash with grilled lamb

vitamins B₁, B₂,
B₆, B₁₂ –
phosphorus

1 medium floury potato, peeled
and cut into chunks
small knob unsalted butter
1tbsp full-fat milk
1tsp mint sauce
1 small lamb chop (75g), trimmed

Bring a medium pan of water to the boil and cook the potato until soft, drain. Preheat the grill. Add the butter, milk and mint sauce to the cooked potatoes and mash until fluffy. Keep warm. Grill the lamb chop for approximately 3–4 minutes on each side, until cooked through, and cut into small pieces. Serve the lamb chop chunks with the minty mash.

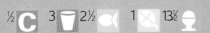

mushroom and ham sauce with pasta

50g macaroni
small knob unsalted butter
75g chestnut mushrooms, washed, sliced
½ slice of cooked ham, finely chopped
¼ quantity (150ml) storecupboard
white sauce (see page 45)

Bring a medium pan of water to the boil and cook the macaroni according to the packet's instructions. Drain and keep warm. Heat the butter in a frying pan and gently fry the mushrooms until soft and golden. Add the chopped ham and the white sauce and bring up to boiling point. Add the cooked macaroni and stir well. If necessary, chop into small pieces to serve.

suppers to freeze

moussaka stuffed aubergines

6½

½

1½

½

½

makes: 8 toddler portions

storage: freeze for up to 4 months

4 small aubergines
3tbsp olive oil
freshly ground black pepper
250g lean lamb, minced
2 medium red onions, finely chopped
4 garlic cloves, crushed
grating of fresh nutmeg
250ml low-salt lamb or no- or low-salt veg stock
200ml tomato passata
2tbsp fresh parsley, chopped
125ml natural Greek yogurt
75g buffalo mozzarella

vitamins B₁₂, B₆ – phosphorus

Never refreeze raw meat that has already been frozen.

1 Preheat the oven to 200°C/400°F/gas mark 6. Halve the aubergines, score the flesh with criss-cross lines, then drizzle over half the olive oil and season with pepper. Roast in the oven for about 20 minutes, until the flesh is cooked. Cool a little, then scoop out most of the flesh, leaving a 0.5cm layer.
2 Meanwhile, heat the remaining oil in a frying pan, then brown the mince. Transfer to a plate. In the same pan, sauté the onions and garlic until soft. Add the nutmeg, stock, passata, parsley and mince. Simmer for 20 minutes.
3 Mix the aubergine flesh into the mince and season with pepper. Cool.
4 Spoon the meat filling into the aubergine skins. Grate the mozzarella and mix with the yogurt, then spoon over the top. Wrap in foil and freeze.
5 Thaw thoroughly. Preheat the oven to 180°C/350°F/gas mark 4. Place the stuffed aubergines on a baking tray and cook in the oven for 20–25 minutes, until hot and slightly golden. Cut into smaller pieces before serving.

fish cakes

18½

½

½

½

1

makes: 6 toddler portions (approx 18 fish cakes)

storage: freeze for up to 4 months

900g fish, eg salmon, cod, tuna, all bones removed
approx 300ml full-fat milk
1kg potatoes, cooked, mashed
2tbsp fresh parsley, chopped
freshly ground black pepper
4tbsp plain flour, for dusting
2 medium eggs, beaten
150g fine breadcrumbs
olive oil, for frying

vitamins B₁₂, B₆ – phosphorus

Fish cakes' crisp outsides and soft centres seem to be perennially popular with children. Serve with a lightly steamed green vegetable or a salad.

1 Cut the fish into pieces and put in a pan with just enough milk to cover. Bring to a gentle simmer, remove from the heat, cover and leave the fish to cool in the milk. Flake the fish into the potato with just a little of the poaching milk. Mix in the parsley and some freshly ground black pepper.
2 Shape a large tbsp of the mixture into a cake. Dip into the flour, then the egg, then the breadcrumbs and rest on a plate. Repeat with remaining mixture.
3 Put into a freezerproof container, with greaseproof paper between the layers, cover and freeze. Thaw thoroughly. Heat a little oil in a frying pan and fry the cakes until golden – 3–4 minutes each side – then cook them on their edges for a minute, until they're cooked and golden. Rest on kitchen paper for a minute. If necessary, cut into small pieces before serving.

quick sausage and beans

11½

makes: 6 toddler portions

storage: freeze for up to
4 months

2½

2   **2tbsp olive oil**
6 good-quality pork sausages

½   **4 spring onions, sliced, or**
1 medium onion, chopped

2   **5 fresh tomatoes, chopped**
3 x 400g tinned cooked
   beans eg 1 x haricot, 1 x
   cannellini 1 x chopped butter,
   drained and rinsed

vitamins B₂, B₆, B₁₂ –
phosphorus

freshly ground black pepper
500ml tomato passata
1tbsp tomato purée
1tsp English mustard
pinch soft brown sugar
   (optional)

Generally, children love eating beans, and this is a great way to get them to eat varieties other than baked beans.

1   Preheat the oven to 180°C/350°F/gas mark 4. Heat 1tbsp olive oil in a heavy-based frying pan and fry the sausages until golden – approximately 5 minutes. Transfer to a heavy-based casserole.

2   Add the remaining olive oil to the frying pan and sauté the spring onions until soft. Add the fresh tomatoes and beans and season with freshly ground black pepper.

3   Cook for a couple of minutes, then stir in the passata, tomato purée, mustard and sugar, if using. Pour onto the sausages, stir, then cover and cook for 20–25 minutes in the oven, until the sausages are cooked and the sauce has thickened slightly.

4   Cool completely. Transfer to freezerproof containers and freeze.

5   Thaw thoroughly. Heat through in a pan until boiling. Cut into small pieces before serving.

pumpkin stew

2½

makes: 8 toddler portions

storage: freeze for up to
4 months

1½

½   **25g unsalted butter**
1tbsp olive oil

1½   **2 red onions, finely chopped**
1 sprig rosemary

10   **3 garlic cloves, thinly sliced**
3 red peppers, deseeded and
   cut into large dice

vitamins A, B₁, B₆
– phosphorus

1.4kg pumpkin or butternut
   squash, peeled and cubed
1 litre no- or low-salt veg
   stock (see page 44)
1tbsp tomato purée
2–3 sage leaves (optional)
freshly ground black pepper

Serve this mellow autumnal stew on its own for lunch or with mash and peas for a more substantial supper.

1   Heat the butter and olive oil in a heavy-based casserole, then fry the onions and rosemary for 5 minutes.

2   Add the garlic and peppers and cook over a low heat until the peppers are just soft – approximately 10 minutes.

3   Add the squash or pumpkin and cook for 5 minutes before adding the stock, tomato purée and sage, if using. Simmer for 35–45 minutes.

4   Remove the herbs and pour half of the stew into a bowl. Roughly purée with a hand-held blender (or in a food processor or blender). Return it to the casserole and season with black pepper to taste.

5   Cool completely. Transfer to freezerproof containers and freeze.

6   Thaw thoroughly. Heat gently in a saucepan until just boiling. Cool slightly before serving.

lamb with spices and apricots

makes: approx 8 toddler portions

storage: freeze for up to 4 months

50g dried unsulphured apricots, finely chopped

juice of 1 large orange

4tbsp olive oil

675g shoulder of lamb, in small cubes

vitamins B₆, B₁₂ – phosphorus

1 Spanish onion, finely chopped

3 garlic cloves, crushed

5cm root ginger, peeled, grated

2tbsp coriander seeds, toasted and ground

1tsp cumin seeds, toasted and ground

400g tin chopped tomatoes

900ml low-salt chicken stock

freshly ground black pepper

This lamb and apricot dish is delicious served with couscous – a real toddler favourite – which you can steam over the stew to give it more flavour.

1 Soak the apricots in the orange juice for approximately 15 minutes. Drain and purée.
2 Heat 3tbsp olive oil in a large heavy-based casserole and quickly brown the lamb. Transfer to a plate.
3 In the remaining oil, gently fry the onion, garlic and ginger for about 5 minutes until soft.
4 Add the coriander, cumin, tomatoes, stock, lamb and apricot purée, then season well with freshly ground black pepper. Bring to the boil, cover and simmer, stirring occasionally, for 1½ hours, or until the meat is tender. Cool completely.
5 Put into freezer bags or a freezerproof container and freeze.
6 Thaw thoroughly.
7 Reheat gently in a heavy-based casserole until just boiling. If necessary, cut into small pieces before serving.

cheesy pasta bake

makes: 4 toddler portions

storage: freeze for up to 4 months

few sprigs fresh thyme

1tbsp olive oil

2 red onions, finely chopped

freshly ground black pepper

25g unsalted butter

25g plain flour

300ml full-fat milk

300ml no- or low-salt veg stock (see page 44)

100g Cheddar cheese, grated

50g Parmesan cheese, grated

300g penne, cooked

2 thick slices white bread

handful of fresh parsley, finely chopped (optional)

vitamins B₆, B₁₂ – phosphorus

The perfect dish when the only shop open is the local corner shop.

1 Remove the leaves from the thyme. Heat the oil in a frying pan. Add the onions and thyme, then cover and sweat until soft. Season with freshly ground black pepper.
2 To make the cheese sauce, put the butter, flour, milk and stock into a saucepan and whisk over a gentle heat until the sauce is thick and smooth. Season with freshly ground black pepper. Stir in half the cheeses.
3 Stir the onion and cooked pasta together and spoon into an ovenproof and freezerproof dish. Pour over the cheese sauce.
4 Crumb the bread using a food processor. Mix together the remaining cheese, breadcrumbs and parsley and scatter over the pasta. Cool completely. Wrap in foil or clingfilm and freeze.
5 Thaw thoroughly. Bake in a preheated oven at 190°C/375°F/gas mark 5 for 25 minutes, until bubbling and golden. If necessary, cut into small pieces before serving.

fresh & frozen puddings

baked custard

6½

½

1

1½

vitamins B₂, B₆, B₁₂
– phosphorus

makes: 4 toddler portions

storage: best eaten fresh or keep in the refrigerator for up to 24 hours

3 medium eggs
1 medium egg yolk
50g golden caster sugar
½tsp vanilla extract
450ml full-fat milk
pinch grated nutmeg
berry compote, to serve
  (optional)

This is a really quick and nutritious pudding, high in protein and calcium. Try serving it with some stewed fruit (see page 45) or a little jam.

1 Preheat the oven to 170°C/325°F/gas mark 3. Whisk the eggs, egg yolk, sugar and vanilla together briefly in a bowl, then add the milk and whisk again lightly.
2 Pour the mixture through a sieve into 4 ramekins.
3 Sprinkle the tops with a little grated nutmeg. Put the dishes into a roasting pan half-filled with boiling water.
4 Bake in the moderately slow oven for approximately 30 minutes, until a skin has formed on the top and the custard is set in the middle. If desired, serve with some berry compote.

fresh fruit salad

2½ C

vitamin B₆

makes: 2 toddler portions

storage: best eaten fresh or keep in the refrigerator for up to 24 hours

¼ ripe small melon (approx 150g), eg Galia or Canteloupe
2 handfuls green or black seedless grapes (approx 100g)
2 handfuls blueberries (approx 100g)
50ml apple juice

Most toddlers of this age love fruit salad provided there aren't too many hard fruits. This is a lovely mixture of soft fruits with different textures.

1 Peel and chop the melon into bite-size pieces and put into a bowl.
2 Cut the grapes into quarters and add to the bowl along with the blueberries.
3 Pour over the apple juice. If necessary, mash before serving.

rice pudding with pears

makes: 6 toddler portions

storage: best eaten fresh or cold within 24 hours (do not reheat rice)

2 large knobs of unsalted butter (approx 30g), plus extra for greasing
75g pudding rice
1–2tbsp golden caster sugar
600ml full-fat milk
2 drops vanilla extract
pinch grated nutmeg
4 really ripe pears, peeled, cored and quartered

vitamin B₁₂

Make the most of the oven and cook some fruit alongside the pudding.

1 Preheat the oven to 110°C/225°F/gas mark ¼.

2 Butter an ovenproof dish.

3 Put the rice, sugar, milk and vanilla extract into the dish. Stir, then dot with a large knob of butter and sprinkle over grated nutmeg.

4 Bake in the very cool oven for 30 minutes, stir, and then continue to bake in the oven for another 1½ hours, until a brown skin forms and the rice is well cooked.

5 Meanwhile, put the pears in another buttered ovenproof dish. Dot with the remaining butter. Cook in the oven for 1½ hours. Cut into smaller pieces and serve with the rice pudding.

rhubarb crisp

makes: 6 toddler portions

storage: best eaten fresh or keep in the refrigerator for up to 3 days or in the freezer for up to 3 months

100g unsalted butter, diced and chilled, plus extra for greasing
165g plain flour plus 1tbsp
large pinch ground cinnamon
small pinch grated nutmeg
pinch salt
235g light soft brown sugar
750g rhubarb
juice and zest of 1 unwaxed orange

vitamin A

This is quite a sweet topping. You could always reduce the amount of sugar if you prefer, but as we hardly ever eat puddings I do not mind the sweetness, especially if it is on top of quite tart fruit such as rhubarb. As its name implies, the topping is a thin crisp layer rather than a thick layer of crumble.

1 Preheat oven to 180°C/350°F/gas mark 4. Butter a 1-litre ovenproof dish.

2 Sift 165g flour into a bowl with the cinnamon, nutmeg and salt.

3 Rub in the butter with your fingertips until the mixture resembles fine breadcrumbs. Stir in 175g light soft brown sugar.

4 Trim the rhubarb and cut into 2.5cm pieces. Put into the ovenproof dish with the remaining 1tbsp flour, 4tbsp sugar and the orange juice and zest. Mix everything together.

5 Sprinkle the crumble mixture over the fruit, making sure everything is covered. Bake in the oven for 25–30 minutes, until the top is crisp and golden and the fruit is tender.

apple pie

You may like to make a couple of these and pop one in the freezer. Serve with natural Greek yogurt or custard.

makes: 1 pie or 6 toddler portions

storage: best fresh or keep in the refrigerator for up to 3 days or freeze for up to 3 months

for the pastry:
175g plain flour
40g golden icing sugar
pinch salt
75g unsalted butter, diced and chilled
2–4tbsp water

vitamin B₆

for the filling:
675g cooking apples
225g eating apples, eg Cox's
juice and zest of 1 unwaxed lemon
40g golden caster sugar
½tsp ground cinnamon
good pinch grated nutmeg
full-fat milk, to glaze (optional)

1 Put the flour, icing sugar and salt into a food processor, quickly turn on and off to aerate the flour. Add the butter and process until the mixture resembles fine breadcrumbs. Gradually add the water, with the processor on, until the pastry just draws together.

2 Alternatively, sift the dry ingredients together in a large bowl. Rub in the butter with your fingertips until the mixture resembles fine breadcrumbs. Gradually stir in the water, until the pastry just draws together.

3 Wrap in clingfilm and chill for 30 minutes.

4 Preheat the oven to 180°C/350°F/gas mark 4. Peel the apples, core and cut into thick slices and mix together in a bowl with the lemon juice and zest, sugar and spices. Spoon into the pie dish.

5 On a lightly floured surface, roll out the pastry to 2.5mm thick and 1cm bigger than the pie dish. Cut a 1cm-wide strip of pastry and place on the dampened dish lip. Cover the pie with the pastry lid, and cut a small slit in the middle.

6 Trim the pie and crimp the edges together. Glaze with a little milk, if using.

7 Bake in the oven for 35–40 minutes, until the pastry is light brown. Leave to cool slightly. If necessary, cut the pastry into small pieces before serving.

banana scones

makes: 12 toddler portions (12 scones)

storage: best eaten fresh or keep in an airtight container for up to 3 days or in the freezer for up to 3 months

225g self-raising flour
1tsp baking powder
pinch ground cinnamon
50g unsalted butter, roughly chopped
2tbsp light soft brown sugar
150ml full-fat milk
1 ripe large banana, roughly mashed

Scones are very popular with toddlers, and particularly these banana ones, as they are very moist and easy to eat. They are lovely served with fresh fruit or just topped with some mashed banana or cream cheese.

1 Preheat the oven to 180°C/350°F/gas mark 4. Sift the flour, baking powder and cinnamon into a bowl.

2 Rub in the butter with your fingertips, then stir in the sugar and make a well in the middle. Pour in the milk, stirring with a knife, then add the banana and mix well.

3 Drop dessertspoonfuls onto a greased baking sheet and bake in the moderate oven for 12–14 minutes, until golden brown and cooked through. Serve straight away. If necessary, cut into smaller pieces.

quick bites puddings

Pieces of fresh fruit and yogurt make the best and easiest every day puddings for toddlers in this age group. But at the same time, all toddlers like to be treated to an extra special pudding occasionally, as do the rest of the family. So here are some simple ideas.

All of the recipes make one toddler portion unless stated otherwise.

vitamin B$_6$ 10 C ½ 1½

125g berries, frozen
2tbsp full-fat natural yogurt

berry compote with yogurt

For vegans, just serve the berry compote on its own. Put the berries into small saucepan and heat gently until soft. Take off the heat. Carefully transfer half the berries to a jug and purée with a hand-held blender (or in a food processor or blender). Return the puréed berries to the pan and mix everything together. Leave to cool, spoon into a bowl, and stir in the yogurt.

vitamin B$_6$ 4 C 1 ½ 2

handful fresh berries, eg raspberries,
strawberries, blueberries
1 scoop frozen natural yogurt

frozen yogurt with fresh fruit

On a hot day, a scoop of frozen yogurt with fresh berries scattered over the top can be just what is needed. Chop the berries and hull if necessary, then put into a bowl. Mash with a fork, then spoon a scoop of frozen yogurt on top.

1 C 1 1 1 2½

1 ripe pear
1 sesame snap (do not give nuts or seeds
to toddlers under the age of three if there
is a family history of allergies)
2tbsp full-fat natural yogurt

pear and sesame yogurt

Core the pear, peel and grate the flesh. Put the sesame snap into a plastic bag and bash into small pieces with a rolling pin. Mix the pear, sesame snap and yogurt together in a bowl, then leave for 5 minutes before serving.

3 C ½ 2

makes: 5 toddler portions
135g packet of fruit jelly
approx 200ml fruit juice
100g fruit (except kiwi or pawpaw),
fresh or frozen

fruit jelly with fresh fruits

When I tested this, I used raspberry jelly and frozen berries as the fruits – it went down a real treat! Make up the jelly following the packet's instructions, using fruit juice as well as water. Cut the fruit into small pieces and divide between 5 small jelly moulds or plastic cups. Pour the liquid jelly over the top and leave to set for at least 2 hours in a cool place.

filo parcels

3 1

2 sheets filo pastry
15g unsalted butter, melted
2 handfuls berries (approx 100g),
eg blueberries, hulled and chopped
strawberries, fresh or frozen
raspberries

Preheat the oven to 180°C/350°F/gas mark 4. Take 1 filo sheet and brush all over with some of the melted butter. Place the second filo sheet on top and brush with a little more butter. Cut the sheets in half to make approximately 17.5cm squares. Arrange the berries in the middle of the filo squares and then bring the sides of filo up and around the berries, scrunching the pastry together in the middle to make "a parcel". Brush with the remaining melted butter, put on a greased baking tray and bake in the medium oven until golden – 5–10 minutes. Cut into smaller pieces before serving and remove any hard bits of pastry. Only serve filo pastry to toddlers who are confident with chewing.

banana ice

2 ½

1 ripe small banana, peeled and halved
4 fresh raspberries (optional)

Put the banana into a freezerproof bag and freeze for at least 4 hours. Put the frozen banana into a blender and then whiz for a few seconds, until roughly puréed. Serve immediately, with or without fresh raspberries scattered over the top.

warm banana with yogurt

vitamin B₆ 2 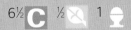 1

small knob unsalted butter
1 level tsp soft brown sugar
1 ripe small banana, peeled and sliced
1tbsp full-fat natural yogurt

This is a great pudding for a cold day or when your toddler is a little under the weather. There is something very comforting about warm bananas. Melt the butter and sugar in a small pan. Add the banana slices and cook gently until just soft around the edges. Serve with the yogurt. If necessary, lightly mash the banana slices before serving.

warm fruit compote

6½ C ½ 1

75g mixed berries, fresh
or frozen
pinch light soft brown sugar, or dash of
honey (optional)

Put the mixed berries in a pan with 1tbsp cold water and the sugar or honey, if needed. Heat the compote gently until the berries are soft and just begin to give up their juices.

almond rice

½ C 2 1 1 4½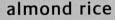

makes: 2 toddler portions
300ml full-fat milk
25g flaked rice
1tbsp ground almonds (do not give
nuts to toddlers under the age of
three if there is a family history of
allergies)
1tsp golden caster sugar

Put all of the ingredients into a heavy-based pan and bring to the boil. Reduce the heat and simmer gently for 10–12 minutes, until the rice is tender.

celebration **food**

Marmite and cheese straws

1

makes: 30 toddler portions (30 straws)

storage: best eaten fresh or keep in an airtight container for up to 3 days or in the freezer for up to 3 months

375g ready-rolled puff pastry
75g Cheddar cheese, grated
1tbsp Marmite
unsalted butter, for greasing

These are quick to make and very popular at children's parties – adults also seem to find them rather moreish! For younger ones, cut them into slightly shorter lengths.

1 Preheat the oven to 200°C/400°F/gas mark 6. Unroll the pastry and sprinkle over the grated cheese, then fold in half.
2 On a floured surface, roll the pastry out to its original size. Spread the surface evenly with the Marmite and fold in half again, with the long sides together. Press down firmly and then, using a sharp knife, cut into long, thin straws.
3 Twist each straw a few times and then put onto a greased baking tray.
4 Bake in the oven for 8–10 minutes, until risen and golden. Cool on a wire rack.

banana and date cake

3½
½
½
1

vitamins B₆, B₁₂

makes: 8 toddler portions

storage: best eaten fresh or keep in an airtight container for up to 3 days

3 medium eggs
175g soft brown sugar
200ml sunflower oil
175ml full-fat milk
125g plain flour
125g wholemeal flour
½tsp bicarbonate of soda
1tsp ground cinnamon
large pinch grated nutmeg
1tsp mixed spice
2 ripe bananas, mashed
250g dried dates, stoned, soaked and puréed
2tbsp runny honey (optional)

Both my daughters had this cake at their first birthday parties. They thoroughly enjoyed it and so did the adults. While toddlers are still pretty unaware of chocolate and sweet-covered cakes make the most of it – it's far less messy too!

1 Preheat the oven to 190°C/375°F/gas mark 5. Grease and lightly flour a 20cm round loose-bottomed cake tin.
2 Put all the ingredients into a bowl, except the bananas, dates and honey, and mix together.
3 Stir in the mashed bananas and dates and then spoon into the prepared tin.
4 Bake for 45–60 minutes, until a skewer inserted in the cake comes out clean. Turn out and cool on a wire rack.
5 Make holes in the cake with a fork and then drizzle over the honey, if using. If necessary, cut into small pieces before serving.

white chocolate krispie cakes

makes: 20 toddler portions
(20 krispie cakes)

storage: best eaten fresh or
keep in an airtight container
for up to 3 days

150g white chocolate,
  roughly chopped
50g unsalted butter, roughly
  chopped
2tbsp golden syrup
120g Rice Krispies

I made these for my daughter Jasmine's second birthday tea and every mum (OK, there were only four) asked for the recipe. They are rather sweet, it has to be said, but hey, we are celebrating.

1 Bring half a saucepan of water to simmering point, put the chocolate pieces, butter and syrup into a bowl and rest over (but not touching) the simmering water. Stir frequently, until the chocolate has melted. Remove from the heat.
2 Add the Rice Krispies and mix together well. Spoon into 20 paper cases. Leave to go completely cold.
3 Your toddler may be able to chew on one of these cakes quite happily, but if you are at all worried, break into small pieces before serving.

jam tarts

makes: 12 toddler portions
(12 jam tarts)

storage: best eaten fresh or
keep in an airtight container
for up to 3 days or in the
freezer for up to 3 months

180g plain flour
pinch salt
50g golden icing sugar
90g unsalted cold butter,
  cubed
1 medium egg yolk mixed
  with 2tbsp cold water
few drops vanilla extract
12–16 fresh berries, eg
  raspberries, blackcurrants,
  redcurrants
12–16tsp fruit compote
  (page 45)

If you are pressed for time, you could always use ready-made, sweet shortcrust pastry.

1 Chill a jam tart tin. Sift the flour, salt and golden icing sugar into a food processor and whiz for a few seconds.
2 Add the butter and process until the mixture resembles breadcrumbs. Add the yolk (mixed with the water) and vanilla extract and mix until a ball forms.
3 On a floured surface, roll out to 2.5mm thick, and cut out 12–16 circles with a fluted 6cm cutter, using them to line your tart tin. Chill for 15 minutes.
4 Preheat the oven to 180°C/350°F/gas mark 4. Bake the tarts for 10 minutes.
5 Spoon a berry into each pastry case and top with fruit compote. Bake for another 5–8 minutes, until the pastry is golden.
6 Cool on a wire rack. If necessary, cut into small pieces before serving.

pinwheel sandwiches

3

makes: 2 toddler portions

½

storage: best eaten fresh

½

½

60g full-fat cream cheese

1tsp fresh parsley, chopped

1 slice cooked ham, very
  finely chopped

4 thin or medium slices of
  white bread, crusts
  removed

These are great sandwiches for children's parties. The pinwheel shape appeals to toddlers, and hopefully they will eat some savoury food rather than just overdosing on sweet things, which often seems to happen at parties!

1 In a bowl, beat the cream cheese until the mixture is soft, then stir in the parsley and ham.
2 Spread the cream cheese mixture evenly onto the four slices of bread.
3 Starting with a short end, tightly roll up one of the slices of bread. Chill for 15 minutes. Then, with a sharp knife, cut the "log" into 6 pinwheel sandwiches. Repeat with the remaining slices of bread.

cheese and sesame biscuits

1½

makes: 35 toddler portions
(35 biscuits)

½

storage: best eaten fresh or
keep for up to three days in an
airtight container or freeze for
up to three months

150g unsalted butter,
  softened

175g Parmesan cheese,
  finely grated

175g plain flour, sifted

pinch of salt

1tbsp olive oil

30–40g poppy seeds or
  sesame seeds, optional (do
  not give seeds or nuts to
  toddlers under the age of
  three if there is a family
  history of allergies)

The mixture for these biscuits can be made in advance and kept in the refrigerator or freezer until needed. The biscuits could also be frozen and just left to thaw before eating.

1 Put the butter in a large bowl and beat with a wooden spoon until it is soft and fluffy.
2 Add the cheese, flour, salt and olive oil and start to mix with a spoon. Use your hands to bring the dough into a ball and turn out onto a floured surface. Divide in half and roll each piece into a 25cm-long sausage shape.
3 Spread the seeds on a tray and roll the "sausages" in them. Wrap loosely in cling film and chill in the refrigerator for 40 minutes. When firm, cut into 5mm-thin rounds.
4 Preheat the oven to 180°C/350°F/gas mark 4. Put the rounds onto a lightly greased baking tray and bake for about 12 minutes, until pale golden. Cool on a wire rack.

You will be much more aware of your toddler's emerging personality during this year. She will be determined to let you know how she feels, particularly about food. This is just her way of testing you: stick to your guns about acceptable behaviour; she will feel more secure if she knows the limits. Often, toddlers' appetites slacken off as growth slows, so she may seem fussier about food. However, she needs lots of energy for development and exploration. Healthy snacks in-between meals will help give her energy. Toddlers learn by example, so eating together, even if you just eat a small portion at her suppertime, will help.

2-3
years

what's happening to
your toddler

Many parents think that this is going to be the worst year – the "terrible twos". This negative anticipation can exacerbate the problem, which is rarely as bad as we expect. You will become more aware of your toddler's personality and individuality at this stage and, in trying to express this, his behaviour can often seem unreasonable. But it is a learning process: he is finding out about himself and testing you to establish boundaries and where he fits in. Rules are an important part of this – knowing your limits will make him feel more secure.

At this stage his physical agility will increase and he may be able to walk up and down stairs, jump, hop and walk backwards. He is expending more energy and will need foods that are high in slow-release energy, such as bananas, dried fruits and chopped nuts (do not give nuts to toddlers under the age of three if there is a family history of food allergies). During this year your toddler's hand–eye co-ordination should improve, so self-feeding with a spoon will be much more successful. You can now introduce a fork, and chop food accordingly. He is likely to be able to eat most of his meal without any assistance.

By the age of two, he will probably put at least two words together and have a larger vocabulary. Pointing will also enable him to communicate more. Teach your toddler by talking to him and showing him things. One of the best ways for him to learn is by example, particularly about food. A difficulty he may have at mealtimes is sitting still, but it will encourage him if you eat together.

Talking about the food you are eating and how it was made or grown will make meals more interesting and help to keep him focused. Try to get your toddler involved in the kitchen, too, even if it is just carrying things or watching you cook. Many toddlers love playing "cooking" with kitchen utensils and having pretend meals with their toys.

This kind of involvement will help to avoid frustration when he doesn't have his own way or is unable to carry out certain tasks. Let him try things, even if you think the results may be unsuccessful, as this is how he will learn and in turn feel more confident and independent. By the end of this year you will find the frustrated outbursts few and far between.

Eating similar food as the rest of the family at shared mealtimes will not only make your life easier; it will also help to make him feel part of the family. But remember that while as a family you may be trying to reduce your fat intake, this kind of diet is not suitable for your toddler. He needs fat for energy and for the fat-soluble vitamins it contains. Good fat sources include full-fat dairy products, such as milk, cheese and yogurt, meat, chopped nuts and oils. If you are confident that your toddler is getting enough good fat in his diet, you can introduce semi-skimmed milk as a drink when your toddler is two.

Similarly, it is a mistake to give your toddler a high-fibre diet, particularly one containing large quantities of wholegrains or bran. These are very bulky foods that can hinder the absorption of important minerals, such as iron and calcium. However, high-fibre foods, such as brown rice or wholemeal bread, can be introduced gradually now, so that by the age of five your toddler will be used to a healthy adult diet. Just remember that high-fibre foods can be filling and toddlers have small tummies – give in moderation so that there is room for other foods.

A toddler's needs and abilities can be completely contradictory at this stage. While he needs lots of food for energy to fuel his increased physical activity and confidence, his attention span at meals and determination to test boundaries often means that very little gets eaten. The best way to keep him happy and energized throughout the day can be to take the view that a little food often is good: giving healthy, energy-boosting snacks when your toddler needs them. It is quite likely that your toddler will still need a nap during the day; giving a small snack or drink on waking can often increase his energy and improve his mood.

Your toddler needs a good calcium intake for the proper development of bones and teeth. The most obvious source of calcium is milk – he should be getting the recommended amount of 565ml per day, which includes milk used in cooking (see page 22). A toddler who is eating a broad and balanced diet should also be getting a plentiful supply of vitamins. If your toddler is having a fussy phase, or is a vegetarian or vegan, you may need to give him daily vitamin drops – but always consult your health care expert before doing so.

which nutrients
are key

your toddler's
routine

your toddler's feeds

There is no reason to deviate from the previous year's routine. However, at around this age your toddler may begin going to nursery or to a childminder and you may need to make some adjustments. A big part of my daughter Ella's routine at nursery is a mid-morning snack, which is a sociable and fun event. This tends to make her less interested in lunch, so I make up for it by giving her a more substantial mid-afternoon snack slightly earlier.

breakfast – around 7.30–8am
mid-morning snack – around 10am
lunch – around 12.30–1pm
mid-afternoon snack – around 3pm
supper – 5–5.30pm
bed – 7–7.30pm

your toddler's sleeps

During this year it becomes less necessary for your toddler to have a day-time sleep. You could start to reduce the amount of time that your toddler sleeps, for example, by cutting sleep time from one and a half hours to 45 minutes. However, with my second daughter Jasmine I cut out routine day-time sleeps altogether, but occasionally, if I feel she is particularly tired or has had a bad night's sleep – if she has been ill, for example – I will let her have a short nap during the day. When you cut out sleeps it is important to allow for a "quiet time" of at least 30 minutes during the day, where you may just sit quietly and read books or watch a short video. With my girls I found this pause was enough to keep them going for the rest of the afternoon.

why do children become fussy eaters?

Toddlers who ate really well as babies may still become faddy eaters as they grow older. A toddler who has never vehemently expressed a preference or dislike for a particular food is rare, but one who frequently refuses food can be a real challenge. However, as long as your toddler does not show any signs of illness – such as weight loss, fatigue, weakness, fever, irritability (in which case you should seek advice from your family doctor) – try not to be too concerned. Around the time of the "terrible twos", choosing what to eat and what not to eat, is just another way of asserting his budding independence and is normal. This problem can be exacerbated if toddlers are given too much choice or bribed or put under pressure to eat.

how to counteract fussy eating

There are a few ways to counter fussy eating habits, but the most important is not to make too much of an issue of it. Just calmly remove the food without comment and don't offer an alternative. While it may be tempting to rely on favourite foods, try to offer a wide variety of foods, or even some new ones, as this will encourage your toddler out of the rut. If he won't eat green vegetables, such as peas, offer a spoonful with other acceptable foods for a few meals on the trot. If they are left, don't comment. A new food may have been rejected, but the more often you offer it, the more likely he will be to try it – some toddlers just take a while to get used to new tastes and textures. Try to offer him food when you know he is going to be hungry, and don't offer snacks if he has eaten little at the previous meal. Try to eat together and eat some of the same things – one of the most important ways he will learn is by watching you. Above all, remember you are in charge.

playing with food

Some toddlers need to play with food by touching and smelling it, especially when they are learning to feed themselves. They enjoy the experience of mashing it up or pulling it into pieces before eating it. Try to remain relaxed about this and don't rush your toddler; he may be a naturally slow eater. When the play no longer involves eating, end the meal. Just keep showing him how you eat with a knife and a fork, and be encouraging.

trouble
shooting

2-3 year meal planners

key to meal planners

portions: all servings are 1 portion
drink: preferably water, tap or bottled.
Alternatively very diluted fruit juice.
breakfast: 7.30-8am; **mid-am:** 10am;
lunch: 12.30-1pm; **mid-pm:** 3pm;
supper: 5-5.30pm; **bed:** 7-7.30pm

There is no reason to deviate from the eating routine given for the previous year. However, if your toddler begins going to nursery or a childminder's at this age, you may need to make some adjustments. For instance, a mid-morning snack at nursery can be a sociable event, but this will tend to make him less interested in lunch, so give him a smaller lunch and then a larger mid-afternoon snack.

	breakfast	mid-am	lunch	mid-pm	supper	bed
menu 1	150ml milk, ham and cheese croissant, drink	pieces of peeled apple, drink	sticky chicken with mango, drink	drink	couscous with grated vegetables, drink	200ml milk
menu 2	150ml milk, muesli, drink	banana, drink	sweetcorn and coconut chowder, drink	drink	sausage stew, rhubarb and berries, drink	200ml milk
menu 3	150ml milk, fruit salad with yogurt sauce, drink	piece of toast with a little unsalted butter, drink	herby potato cakes with bacon, drink	drink	mushroom and garlic stuffed bread, drink	200ml milk
menu 4	150ml milk, poached egg and English muffin, drink	pot of raw vegetables, drink	tomato sauce with gnocchi, drink	drink	fried parsley potatoes with poached egg, drink	200ml milk
menu 5	150ml milk, pineapple and passion-fruit smoothie, piece of toast with a little unsalted butter, drink	muesli with blueberries, drink	chicken, apple and nut salad, drink	drink	Thai-spiced vegetables with rice, drink	200ml milk
menu 6	150ml milk, apricot scone, drink	peach and banana smoothie, drink	onion and potato tortilla, drink	pieces of peeled apple, drink	toad in the hole, drink	200ml milk

	breakfast	mid-am	lunch	mid-pm	supper	bed
menu7	150ml milk, yogurt and cereal sundae, drink	grapes, drink	lamb stew with olives, drink	drink	penne with chicken and broccoli, drink	200ml milk
menu 8	150ml milk, grated apple with raisin toast, drink	drink	rice with tuna and sweetcorn, drink	pieces of peeled apple, drink	potato salad with olives, tomato and egg, orange and passion-fruit sorbet, drink	200ml milk
menu 9	150ml milk, yogurt with banana, drink	drink	apple and hazelnut bread, drink	kiwi fruit in egg cup, drink	green vegetable crumble, drink	200ml milk
menu 10	150ml milk, toasted fruit bun, drink	grapes, drink	pea and bacon soup, drink	drink	chicken with parsley and garlic butter, drink	200ml milk
menu 11	150ml milk, doorstep with mushrooms, drink	drink	couscous with French beans and bacon, drink	grapes, drink	grilled salmon with steamed vegetables, drink	200ml milk
menu 12	150ml milk, warm fruit salad, drink	malt loaf with butter and pear, drink	grated carrot with pasta, drink	drink	hamburgers with cheese, apple bread and butter pudding, drink	200ml milk
menu 13	150ml milk, poached egg with toast soldiers, drink	scone with apple, drink	hummus and avocado dip, drink	drink	pork chop with parsnip and carrrot mash, rice pudding with prunes, drink	200ml milk
menu 14	150ml milk, pear, kiwi fruit and melon salad, drink	piece of toast with a little unsalted butter, drink	egg mayonnaise fingers, drink	drink	crispy baked chicken, plums and custard, drink	200ml milk

fresh breakfasts

fruit salad with yogurt sauce

 makes: 3 toddler portions

2

 storage: best eaten fresh or
½ keep in the refrigerator for up
to 24 hours

 200g fresh berries, eg
½ **blueberries, raspberries,**
1 **hulled and sliced strawberries**
200g fresh ripe watermelon
10½ **100ml orange juice**
2 drops vanilla extract
100ml full-fat natural yogurt

vitamin B₆

Any kind of fruit salad is popular with toddlers, as long as there is a good mix
of crunchy and soft fruit. Watermelon seems to be universally loved for its
colour and texture.

1 Place the berries in a bowl.
2 Peel the watermelon and cut into bite-size pieces, then add to the bowl with
the orange juice. Using a large spoon, gently mix the fruit together and leave
to marinate for at least 30 minutes. Meanwhile, mix the vanilla extract and
yogurt together, cover and leave in the refrigerator.
3 Serve the fruit at room temperature with the yogurt sauce over the top. If
necessary, cut the fruit into smaller pieces or mash lightly before serving.

ham and cheese croissant

10½ **makes:** 1 toddler portion

 storage: best eaten fresh
1

 1 croissant
2 **1 slice cooked ham, fat**
 removed
2 **25g Cheddar cheese, thinly**
 sliced

vitamins B₁, B₂, B₆, B₁₂ –
phosphorous

Filled croissants are great for weekend breakfasts, brunches or quick lunches.
I keep a big pack of them in the freezer as they only take about half an hour
to defrost.

1 Preheat the oven to 180°C/350°F/gas mark 4. Cut the croissant in half
lengthways. Place the ham on top of one half and cover with the cheese.
2 Put the other half back on top and place on a baking sheet. Cook in the oven
for 5–10 minutes, until the cheese is melted and the croissant is warm
through. If necessary, cut into smaller pieces before serving.

apricot scones

225g self-raising flour

pinch salt

1 level tsp baking powder

50g unsalted butter, plus
    extra for greasing

50g dried unsulphured
    apricots, finely chopped

150ml full-fat milk, plus
    extra for glazing

These are really quick and easy to make. You can use any kind of dried fruit. They make great breakfast food, especially served with fruit or full-fat natural yogurt.

1 Preheat the oven to 180°C/350°F/gas mark 4.

2 Sift the flour into a bowl with the salt and baking powder. Rub in the butter with your fingertips until the mixture looks like breadcrumbs, and then stir in the apricots. Make a well in the centre and gradually add the milk, stirring with a knife until the mixture comes together.

3 Turn out on to a floured surface and knead lightly for a minute, then roll out to 2cm thick. Cut out approximately 9 x 5cm rounds and put them onto a lightly greased baking sheet. Brush the tops with milk and bake in the oven for 12–14 minutes, until risen and golden.

4 Cool on a wire rack. If necessary, cut into smaller pieces before serving.

muesli

40g sunflower seeds, finely
    chopped

50g unsweetened shredded
    coconut

50g almonds, finely chopped

75g cashew nuts, finely
    chopped

300g rolled oats

4tbsp wheatgerm

125g dried unsulphured
    apricots, finely chopped

75g dried blueberries or
    raisins

pinch of ground cinnamon

full-fat milk or natural
    yogurt or apple juice, to
    serve

Making muesli is not an exact science, you can use pretty much any nuts, or dried fruits that you like (do not give nuts or seeds to toddlers under the age of three if there is a family history of food allergies). Most nuts and seeds have a nicer flavour if lightly toasted. Do this in the oven or, as I prefer, in a frying pan – just watch them carefully as they can over-brown very quickly.

1 Dry fry the sunflower seeds until pale golden and tip into a large bowl.

2 Dry fry the coconut. Add to the bowl with all the other ingredients and mix together well.

3 Serve with milk, apple juice or yogurt.

poached egg and English muffin

makes: 1 toddler portion

storage: best eaten fresh

1 medium egg
1 English muffin
small knob unsalted butter

vitamins A, B₂, B₁₂ –
phosphorous

Muffins have a lovely dense texture and make a change from ordinary toast.
You could make this for lunch and serve it with some baked beans for a really
nutritious meal.

1 Fill a small frying pan with water and bring to the boil. Turn the heat down to
barely simmering. Crack the egg into the pan. Cook for 5 minutes, until the
white is set and the yolk is firm, basting the top with the water as it cooks.

2 Meanwhile, split the muffin, then toast it under the grill and spread with a
little butter.

3 Gently remove the egg from the pan with a slotted spoon, then rest the
spoon on some kitchen paper to absorb the water. Place the egg on one half
of the toasted muffin and then season with freshly ground black pepper.

4 Serve with the other half of muffin. If necessary, cut into smaller pieces
before serving.

yogurt and cereal sundae

makes: 2 toddler portions

storage: best eaten fresh

100g raspberries, fresh or
frozen (defrosted)
100ml full-fat natural yogurt
100g granola (see page 153)
full-fat milk, to serve (optional)

vitamins B₁, B₂, B₆
– phosphorous

If you have them, use two clear plastic cups to serve these sundaes as they
would look really pretty. This is just as good made with ripe banana,
strawberries or fresh apricots. Try adding a pinch of ground cinnamon to
spice it up a little.

1 Mash the raspberries in a small bowl with a fork and swirl them through
the yogurt.

2 Place a couple of spoonfuls of the yogurt into a small bowl or cup. Spoon an
equal amount of the granola on top, then continue in layers. Repeat with a
second cup. If necessary, cut the granola into smaller pieces before serving.

3 You may need to add a little milk to make it less dry.

quick bites breakfasts

All of the recipes make one toddler portion unless stated otherwise.

vitamin B₆   7 **C** ½ ½

pineapple and passion-fruit smoothie

makes: 2 toddler portions
½ ripe large pineapple, peeled
2 passion-fruit
200ml apple juice

Cut the pineapple flesh into small chunks (making sure you remove any "eyes") and put the flesh into a bowl. Halve the passion-fruit and scoop the pulp into the bowl. Add the apple juice and whiz with a hand-held blender (or in a food processor or blender) until smooth. Where smoothies are concerned, it is a good idea to make enough for you as well as your toddler, as both of you can then benefit from a drink packed with nutrients. This smoothie is particularly high in vitamin C.

½  1 1 6½

vitamins B₂, B₆, B₁₂

poached egg with toast soldiers

1 medium egg
1 slice white toast

There are many ways to poach an egg, but this is one of my daughter Ella's favourites. Fill a shallow frying pan with water and bring up to simmering point. Crack the egg into the water and simmer for 5 minutes, or until the white is set and the yolk is firm, basting the top with the water as it cooks. Lift the egg out with a slotted sppoon and rest on kitchen paper for a few seconds. Cut the toast into fingers and serve with the egg, chopped into small pieces.

1½ **C** 2 1  4

vitamins B₂, B₆, B₁₂ – phosphorous

yogurt with banana

½ ripe large banana
100ml full-fat natural yogurt
1tsp runny honey

On the whole, breakfast recipes need to be quick to help busy mums and dads in the morning. This is really easy and universally popular. Mash the banana to a purée. Add the yogurt and honey and mix together.

2 **C** 2½ 1½ 10½

phosphorous

grilled bacon with a wholemeal bun

2 rashers unsmoked back bacon
1 wholemeal bun, halved
1 ripe small tomato, sliced
freshly ground black pepper

Grill the bacon until crisp, removing the rind if you prefer. Top one half of the wholemeal bun with the sliced tomato and season with a little freshly ground black pepper. Snip the bacon into pieces and put on top of the tomato. Cover with the other half of the bun. If necessary, cut into smaller pieces before serving. In season, try adding some sliced grilled mushrooms instead of, or as well as, the tomato.

doorstep with mushrooms

vitamin B₆

2tsp olive oil
2 large field mushrooms, thickly sliced
freshly ground black pepper
1 thick slice white bread

Make this when the lovely field mushrooms are in season. A thick slice of bread is a great energy booster. Heat the oil in a frying pan, add the sliced mushrooms and gently fry until they are soft and just beginning to give up their juices – approximately 5 minutes. Season lightly with freshly ground black pepper, then tip out over the slice of bread, so that it soaks up all the juices. If necessary, cut into smaller pieces before serving.

coconut milkshake

vitamin B₆

100ml tinned coconut milk
100g frozen exotic fruits
1 ripe large banana, chopped
juice of ½ lime

Check out the freezer section in your local supermarket for bags of exotic fruits. You will probably also find bags of frozen berries and summer fruits. (Do not serve nuts or nut products to toddlers under the age of three if there is a family history of allergies.) Put all the ingredients into a jug and purée with a hand-held blender (or in a food processor or blender) until smooth.

warm fruit salad

Vit B6 –

1tbsp runny honey
2tbsp apple juice
1 eating apple, peeled, cored, thinly sliced
1 slice pineapple, peeled, cored, cut in chunks
8 big seedless black grapes, halved

Toddlers enjoy the comfort of warm foods. Melt the honey with the apple juice in a small saucepan, add the sliced apples and cook them for 1–2 minutes. Stir in the pineapple chunks and grapes. Heat gently and stir until warmed through – approximately 2–3 minutes.

grated apples with raisin toast

15g unsalted butter
½ eating apple, peeled, cored and grated
½ ripe pear, peeled, cored and grated
pinch ground cinnamon (optional)
1 slice raisin bread

Heat the butter in a small saucepan, add the apple, pear and cinnamon and cook gently, stirring, for approximately 2–3 minutes. Toast the raisin bread and top with the warm fruit mixture. Cut into pieces and serve.

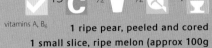

pear, kiwi fruit and melon salad

vitamins A, B₆

1 ripe pear, peeled and cored
1 small slice, ripe melon (approx 100g flesh), peeled
1 ripe kiwi fruit, peeled and chopped
50ml apple juice

These fruits have a cool texture, so are delicious for summer breakfasts. Chop the pear and melon into small pieces. Put into a bowl with the kiwi fruit. Pour over the apple juice. If necessary, lightly mash before serving.

toasted fruit bun

1 fruit bun
small knob unsalted butter
1 eating apple, eg Cox's, peeled and finely chopped

Look in your supermarket for yeast buns that have lots of dried fruit and very little sugar. Cut the bun in half and put into your toaster to toast. Spread the toasted halves with a little butter. If necessary, cut into smaller pieces before serving with the peeled, chopped apple.

fresh lunches

sticky chicken with mango

10

½

1

3

vitamin B$_6$
– phosphorous

makes: 3 toddler portions

storage: best eaten fresh or keep in the refrigerator for up to 24 hours

2 chicken breasts
2 garlic cloves, peeled and crushed
2tbsp runny honey
1tbsp sweet soy sauce or light soy sauce
juice of 1 lime
1 ripe mango, peeled, stoned and finely sliced
3–4 fingers of white or brown bread, to serve

This dish is always a hit with my children and their friends. They love to hold the sticky chicken and alternately munch on chicken, mango and fingers of bread.

1 Slice the chicken into thin strips (approximately 8 slices per breast).
2 In a bowl, mix together the garlic, honey, sweet soy sauce and lime juice. Add the chicken and marinate for at least 30 minutes, or preferably 1–2 hours.
3 Heat a griddle pan until really hot and cook the chicken over a medium heat, turning the pieces after about 1–2 minutes, then cook for another 2–3 minutes until cooked through. The honey and sweet soy should caramelize, making the chicken nice and sticky.
4 Serve the chicken pieces with pieces of mango and fingers of bread. If necessary, cut into smaller pieces before serving.

onion and potato tortilla

9½

1½

1½

1½

1

vitamins A, B$_2$,
B$_6$, B$_{12}$
– phosphorous

makes: 6 toddler portions

storage: best eaten fresh or keep in the refrigerator for up to 2 days

8 medium eggs, beaten
75g full-fat Cheddar cheese, grated (or half of each Parmesan and Cheddar)
freshly ground black pepper
2tbsp olive oil
1 large onion, sliced
150g potatoes, finely diced
50g baby spinach leaves

Once you have tried this recipe, have a go at experimenting with other vegetables. You may find that toddlers prefer this cut into small pieces and served with a dipping sauce.

1 In a bowl, mix the eggs with half the cheese and season with freshly ground black pepper.
2 Heat the oil in a heavy-based frying pan. Add the onion, cover and sauté until it is very soft and beginning to caramelize – approximately 10 minutes.
3 Add the potatoes and gently fry until soft – approximately 10 minutes.
4 Add the spinach, wilt and pour in the egg mixture, then sprinkle the remaining cheese over the top.
5 Cook over a low heat until the tortilla begins to set, then place under a medium grill and cook until pale golden. Wait a few minutes before turning out. If necessary, cut into smaller pieces before serving.

herby potato cakes with bacon

makes: 4 toddler portions

storage: keep in the refrigerator for up to 2 days

450g potatoes, peeled and chopped

50g unsalted butter, plus extra for greasing

75g plain flour

2tbsp fresh parsley, chopped

½tsp baking powder

freshly ground black pepper

8 rashers unsmoked back bacon, grilled and chopped

8 tomatoes, grilled and chopped

vitamins A, B₁, B₆ – phosphorous

Typical Scottish fare, these potato cakes make a good breakfast served simply with a little butter. For lunch, try serving them with grilled bacon or sausages and grilled tomatoes.

1 Boil the potatoes until they are tender – this should take approximately 15 minutes. Drain, then return them to the heat for a minute in order to dry them.

2 Add the butter and mash well. Add the flour, parsley and baking powder. Season with freshly ground black pepper and mix thoroughly.

3 Flour the work surface. Pat the dough out to 1cm thick and cut out 8 x 6cm circles.

4 Lightly butter a heavy-based frying pan, heat and fry the potato cakes for 2–3 minutes on each side, until golden. If necessary, cut into smaller pieces before serving immediately with bacon and tomatoes.

quick muffin pizzas

makes: 1 toddler portion

storage: best eaten fresh

1 English muffin

1tsp tomato purée

1 ripe tomato, thinly sliced

¼ courgette, thinly sliced

25g full-fat cheese, eg buffalo mozzarella or Cheddar, grated

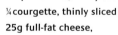

vitamins A, B₁, B₆, B₁₂ – phosphorous

These pizzas are perfect for those occasions when you do not have the time to make your own pizza base. You could also try using speciality breads such as olive bread or pitta.

1 Preheat the grill. Cut the muffin in half and spread with the tomato purée.

2 Top with the tomato and courgette slices, then sprinkle over the cheese.

3 Grill for 3–4 minutes, until the cheese is golden and bubbling and the pizza is hot through. If necessary, cut into smaller pieces before serving.

Jane's fish finger pie

makes: 4 toddler portions

storage: best eaten fresh

550g floury potatoes, peeled
 and chopped
knob unsalted butter
50ml full-fat milk
8 x 100% cod fish fingers
415g tinned low-sugar baked
 beans or spaghetti hoops
75g Cheddar cheese, grated

vitamins B₁,
 B₆, B₁₂
– phosphorous

This fish finger pie is a ridiculously easy to make and is always popular with children of all ages. It is very nutritious, being packed with protein and carbohydrate.

1 Preheat the oven to 180°C/350°F/gas mark 4.
2 Bring a pan of water to the boil and cook the potatoes until they are tender – approximately 15 minutes. Drain and mash with the butter and the milk.
3 Cook the fish fingers following the packet's instructions and put them into an ovenproof dish.
4 Pour over the baked beans or spaghetti and top with the mashed potato.
5 Sprinkle over the grated cheese and bake in the oven for 15 minutes, or until it is golden on top and hot through. If necessary, cut into smaller pieces before serving.

sausage and fennel pasta

makes: 6 toddler portions

storage: best eaten fresh or keep in the refrigerator for up to 2 days

2tsp olive oil
3 shallots, finely chopped
2 garlic cloves, peeled and
 finely chopped
6 good-quality pork
 sausages (approx 400g),
 skinned
1 level tsp fennel seeds
150ml no- or low-salt
 vegetable stock (see page 44)
400g tinned chopped
 tomatoes
freshly ground black pepper
400g pasta shells, cooked
fresh Parmesan cheese,
 grated, to serve

vitamins B₆, B₁₂
– phosphorous

The fennel seeds add a subtle aromatic flavour to this dish. It is a good idea to get your toddler used to different flavours from spices and herbs at an early age, so that he accepts them more readily as he grows older.

1 Heat 1tsp of the oil in a frying pan, and gently cook the shallots and garlic until soft, then reserve on a plate.
2 Heat the remaining oil and brown the sausage meat, breaking up any large pieces with a wooden spoon.
3 Add the fennel seeds and cook for 1 minute. Stir in the stock, then bring to the boil, stirring occasionally.
4 Add the tomatoes and cooked shallots and season with freshly ground black pepper. Simmer gently, uncovered, for 30 minutes.
5 Serve the sauce with the freshly cooked pasta and Parmesan. If necessary, cut into smaller pieces before serving.

quick bites lunches

All of the recipes make one toddler portion unless stated otherwise.

1 C **1** ▯ **½** ◀ **½** ✕ **4** ●

½ small ripe banana, peeled and mashed
1tsp runny honey
25g full-fat cream cheese
2 slices raisin or wholemeal bread

banana and honey sandwich

Mix the banana and honey together in a small bowl. Spread a slice of bread with cream cheese and top with the banana mix, then top with the other slice of bread. Cut into 4 triangles and serve.

2 C **1** ▯ **1½** ◀ **1½** ✕ **6½** ●

½ ripe avocado, peeled and stoned
4tbsp hummus
2 breadsticks
1 small carrot, peeled and cut into sticks

hummus and avocado dip

It's best not to make this dip too far in advance or it will go brown. Put the avocado and hummus into a bowl and mash with a fork until you have a rough purée. Serve as a dip with the breadsticks and carrot. To give the hummus a lovely sweet flavour, try adding a quarter of a roasted red pepper, skinned and finely chopped.

1 C **½** ▯ **1** ◀ **1½** ✕ **4½** ●

50g pasta
15g unsalted butter
2tbsp raisins
1 small carrot, peeled and grated

grated carrot with pasta

Bring a medium pan of water to the boil. Add the pasta and cook following the packet's instructions. Drain. Heat the butter in a saucepan, add the raisins and grated carrot and cook gently for 4–5 minutes. Tip the cooked pasta into the pan, stir through and serve. By barely cooking the carrots you are keeping most of their nutrients, and the crunchy texture of grated carrot tends to be popular with children. If necessary, cut into smaller pieces before serving.

▽ **1½** C **½** ✕ **1½** ●
vitamin B$_6$

50g gnocchi
1tbsp olive oil
1 spring onion, finely sliced
75ml passata (sieved tomato purée available
from supermarkets)
1tbsp full-fat cream cheese

tomato sauce with gnocchi

Bring a medium pan of water to the boil. Add the gnocchi and cook following the packet's instructions. Drain. Heat the olive oil in a saucepan, add the sliced spring onion and cook gently until soft – approximately 3–4 minutes. Add the passata and heat through for a few minutes, then stir in the cream cheese. Also, try adding one of the following variations, finely chopped: 1 slice cooked bacon or ham, half a cooked organic chicken breast, 2 fried mushrooms, 1 cooked broccoli floret, or a small handful of green beans (trimmed) and heat through until the meat is hot. Serve with the gnocchi, all chopped into smaller pieces if necessary.

6½ **C** ½ 2 1 14½

chicken, apple and nut salad

½ cooked organic chicken breast
1 Granny Smith apple, peeled and cored
½ stick celery
3 leaves baby gem lettuce
2–3 walnuts, shelled
1tbsp natural full-fat yogurt
1tsp runny honey
slice of focaccia bread, to serve (optional)

Finely chop the cooked chicken, apple, celery, lettuce and walnuts. Put them in a bowl (do not give nuts to toddlers under the age of three if there is a family history of allergies). Mix together the yogurt and honey and drizzle over the salad. Toss everything together and serve with a slice of focaccia.

 ½ **C** 1 1½ 14½

vitamins B₁, B₆, B₁₂, D, – phosphorous

rice with tuna and sweetcorn

50g white Basmati rice
25g frozen sweetcorn
25g peas, fresh or frozen
70g tinned tuna in oil or water, drained and flaked

Put the rice into a saucepan, add 100ml cold water, cover and bring to the boil. Reduce to a simmer and cook for 11 minutes, still covered. Remove from the heat and leave, still covered, for another 10 minutes. Bring a small pan of water to the boil and cook the sweetcorn and peas, then drain. Next, drain the rice before stirring in the peas, sweetcorn and tuna.

1 **C** 1 1 4

vitamins B₁, B₂, B₆ – phosphorous

Marmite toast with chunky salad

1 slice wholemeal bread
a little Marmite
5cm piece cucumber, peeled and chopped into bite-size pieces
3 cherry tomatoes, halved
2 button mushrooms, quartered

Marmite is a good source of B vitamins, but it is quite salty so spread it thinly. Toast the bread on both sides and spread with the Marmite. Cut into fingers and serve with the vegetables.

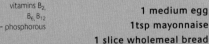 ½ 1½ 1½ 7½

vitamins B₂, B₆, B₁₂ – phosphorous

egg mayonnaise fingers

1 medium egg
1tsp mayonnaise
1 slice wholemeal bread

Bring a small pan of water to the boil, add the egg and cook it for 8 minutes once it has returned to the boil. Remove the egg, cool, peel and place in a bowl – making sure the egg is totally cooked. Using a fork, mash the egg with the mayonnaise. Toast the bread and spread with the egg, then cut into fingers.

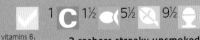 1 **C** 1½ 5½ 9½

vitamins B₁, B₆ – phosphorous

couscous with French beans and bacon

2 rashers streaky unsmoked bacon, rind removed
50g couscous
6 French beans, topped and tailed
3 ripe cherry tomatoes, quartered

Grill the bacon until cooked, then snip into bite-size pieces. Cook the couscous following the packet's instructions – try using no- or low-salt vegetable stock (see page 44), instead of water, to add more flavour. Bring a small pan of water to the boil and cook the beans until just done – approximately 2 minutes. Drain and cut into bite-size pieces. Tip the couscous into a bowl and mix through the tomatoes, bacon and beans.

lunches to freeze

lamb stew with olives

Make sure you buy good quality olives, otherwise they can add a slightly sour taste to the stew. Serve with rice or mashed or new potatoes.

makes: 9 toddler portions

storage: freeze for up to 4 months

11

1

3

1½ C

vitamins B₁, B₂, B₆, B₁₂ – phosphorous

4tbsp olive oil
900g lean lamb shoulder, diced
2 medium onions, finely chopped
2 garlic cloves, peeled and chopped
100ml no- or low-salt vegetable stock (page 44)
400g tinned chopped tomatoes
400g tinned cherry tomatoes
large pinch dark brown sugar
handful of fresh thyme sprigs
100g Kalamata olives, drained and pitted

1 Preheat the oven to 150°C/300°F/gas mark 2. Heat a large heavy-based casserole until really hot. Add 2tbsp oil and brown the lamb in batches. Transfer to a plate.
2 Heat the remaining oil and gently fry the onions and garlic until soft – approximately 5 minutes.
3 Add the stock and leave to bubble for a few minutes, stirring occasionally.
4 Add the lamb, chopped tomatoes, cherry tomatoes, sugar and most of the thyme. Season with freshly ground black pepper.
5 Bring to the boil, cover and cook in the oven for 1½ hours. Stir in the olives and cook for another 20 minutes. Scatter over the remaining thyme leaves. Cool completely. Transfer to freezerproof containers or freezer bags. Freeze.
6 Thaw thoroughly. Gently heat until piping hot. If necessary, cut into smaller pieces before serving.

pea and bacon soup

If you make this soup in the summer, be sure to use sweet fresh peas. I tend to sprinkle fresh Parmesan shavings on the top for extra flavour and a slight hint of saltiness.

makes: 8 toddler portions

storage: freeze for up to 3 months

6

3½

1

2 C

vitamin B₆

1tbsp olive oil
6 rashers unsmoked streaky bacon, rind removed and finely chopped
1 onion, peeled and chopped
1 litre no- or low-salt vegetable stock (page 44)
800g peas, fresh or frozen
2tbsp fresh mint, chopped
fresh Parmesan shavings

1 Heat the oil in a heavy-based pan and fry the bacon over a gentle heat until cooked and just golden.
2 Add the onion and cook until soft – approximately 3–4 minutes.
3 Add the stock and peas and simmer gently for 25 minutes. Add 1tbsp mint and cook for 2–3 minutes. Remove from the heat and cool slightly before whizzing in a blender (or food processor).
4 Cool completely. Pour into freezerproof containers or freezer bags. Freeze.
5 Thaw thoroughly. Gently reheat until just boiling, add the remaining mint, scatter with the Parmesan shavings and serve.

baked fish in tomato sauce

22½

½

1

2½ C

vitamins B₆, B₁₂
– phosphorous

makes: 4 toddler portions

storage: freeze for up to 4 months

2tbsp olive oil
1 medium onion, finely chopped
2 garlic cloves, peeled and crushed
100g chestnut (or other) mushrooms, finely chopped
400g tinned chopped tomatoes
small handful of fresh basil leaves, torn
4 small pieces white fish , fillet eg cod, haddock
juice of ½ lemon

You could always make a larger quantity of the sauce and keep to use with chicken pieces or pork chops. Serve with mash or rice and green vegetables.

1 Preheat the oven to 180°C/350°F/gas mark 4. Heat the olive oil in a heavy-based pan and gently fry the onion until soft and golden. Add the garlic and mushrooms and cook for another 5 minutes, stirring occasionally.

2 Stir in the tomatoes, season with freshly ground black pepper and simmer gently for 20 minutes. Stir in the torn basil.

3 Check the fish for bones before placing it in a buttered ovenproof and freezerproof dish, season with pepper and sprinkle with lemon juice. Pour over the tomato sauce. Cook in the oven for 20–25 minutes. Cool completely. Wrap the dish in foil or clingfilm and freeze.

4 Thaw thoroughly. Cook at 180°C/350°F/gas mark 4 for 20 minutes, or until piping hot. If necessary, cut into smaller pieces, cool and check the fish again for bones before serving.

apple and hazelnut bread

6½

1½

1½

1

phosphorous

makes: approx 8 toddler portions (900g loaf)

storage: freeze for up to 3 months

1tsp golden caster sugar
6g (2 level tsp) dried yeast
400g plain white flour
400g wholemeal flour
100g hazelnuts, toasted and finely chopped (do not give nuts to toddlers under the age of three if there is a family history of allergies)
50g dried apple, finely chopped
approx 360ml warm water

This easy-to-make loaf is deliciously nutty and moist.

1 Grease a 1kg loaf tin. Put 100ml warm water into a jug, stir in the sugar and yeast and leave for 10–15 minutes for a froth to form.

2 Sift the plain and wholemeal flour into a large bowl and mix in the nuts and apple. Make a well and pour in the yeast. Stir with a wooden spoon, gradually adding the rest of the warm water. Use your hands to mix it, adding a little more water if necessary, until you have a smooth dough.

3 Knead the dough briefly on a floured surface, shape it into an oblong and drop into the prepared tin. Sprinkle with flour, cover with a warm damp cloth and leave in a warm place for 30–40 minutes until doubled in size.

4 Preheat the oven to 200°C/400°F/gas mark 6.

5 Bake the bread for 40 minutes. Remove from the tin and bake upside down on the shelf for 10–15 minutes to crisp up. It is cooked if it sounds hollow when the bottom is tapped. Cool completely.

6 Slice, then wrap well in clingfilm or foil and freeze.

7 Thaw thoroughly. If necessary, cut into smaller pieces before serving.

macaroni bacon and cheese

19½

1½

1

4½

3 C

vitamins A, B₁, B₂,
B₆, B₁₂
– phosphorous

makes: 4 toddler portions

storage: freeze for up to 4 months

8 rashers unsmoked streaky bacon, rind removed

25g unsalted butter

1 medium onion, peeled and finely chopped

1tbsp plain flour

600ml full-fat milk

150g Cheddar cheese, grated

freshly ground black pepper

200g macaroni, cooked

4 ripe tomatoes, halved

olive oil

This is a really satisfying variation on an old favourite, and is absolutely packed with protein.

1 Preheat the grill to hot. Grill the bacon until cooked and crisp.
2 Heat the butter in a pan and gently fry the onion until soft – approximately 5 minutes.
3 Stir in the flour and cook for a minute. Whisk in the milk and stir over a gentle heat until you have a smooth sauce.
4 Add the grated cheese, freshly ground black pepper and macaroni, then crumble in the bacon. Stir together and spoon into an ovenproof and freezerproof dish. Cool completely, wrap the dish in foil and freeze.
5 Thaw thoroughly. Preheat the oven to 180°C/350°F/gas mark 4.
6 Put the tomatoes on a baking sheet, drizzle with a little oil and roast alongside the macaroni cheese for 20 minutes, or until piping hot and golden. If necessary, cut into smaller pieces before serving.

sweetcorn and coconut chowder

4½

½

½

1 C

vitamin B₆

makes: 5 toddler portions

storage: freeze for up to 3 months

7 ears fresh corn or 550g frozen sweetcorn, thawed

1 large onion, finely chopped

3 garlic cloves, finely chopped

2.5cm piece of root ginger, peeled and finely chopped

1 stick lemon grass, outer leaves removed

1 large potato, peeled and cut into small chunks

1 knob unsalted butter

400ml tinned full-fat coconut milk

300ml no- or low-salt veg stock (see page 44)

2tbsp fresh coriander, chopped

juice of ½ lime

This soup is thick and creamy and has a little texture from the corn and potatoes. For a vegan diet, just replace the butter with olive oil. Do not serve nut products to toddlers under the age of three if there is any family history of food allergies.

1 Preheat the oven to 200°C/400°F/gas mark 6. Peel the husks away from the fresh corn cobs and cut the kernels away.
2 Put the fresh or frozen corn into a heavy roasting dish with the onion, garlic, ginger, lemon grass and potato. Mix together, dot with butter and roast for 40 minutes, turning occasionally, until the vegetables are cooked and slightly soft. Remove the lemon grass.
3 Transfer half the vegetables to a bowl, add the coconut milk and stock, then purée with a hand-held blender (or in a food processor or blender). Transfer to a bowl with the remaining vegetables. Cool completely. Pour into freezerproof containers or freezer bags and freeze.
4 Thaw thoroughly. Gently reheat until boiling, add the coriander and lime juice. If necessary, lightly mash before serving.

quick bites snacks

Snacks play an important part in a toddler's diet. However, it is important not to rely on too many highly processed snacks, such as crisps and biscuits, that are often high in saturated fat, salt and sugar. Getting into this habit often results in a toddler becoming less interested in food at mealtimes, partly because he is not hungry and partly because the food is perceived to be less interesting than the attractively packaged snacks he has been munching during the day.

All of the recipes make one toddler portion unless stated otherwise.

vitamins B₆, B₁₂ – phosphorous

**1 small ripe banana, peeled and roughly chopped
100ml full-fat milk
small pinch ground cinnamon**

banana milk

Sometimes a thick milk drink is enough to keep your toddler satisfied until the next meal, particularly when made with bananas, which provide energy. You could also make this drink with other fruits, such as peaches or nectarines – just add a little natural yogurt to help thicken it slightly. Put the banana, milk and cinnamon into a blender (or food processor) and whiz until smooth.

**50g unsweetened muesli (do not give nuts to toddlers under the age of three if there is a family history of allergies)
50g fresh blueberries
100ml full-fat milk**

muesli with blueberries

Unsweetened muesli is great for toddlers, especially if you add some fresh fruit. If the muesli you choose has large whole nuts, give it a quick whiz with a hand-held blender (or in a food processor or blender) before serving. Put the cereal into a bowl, add the blueberries and pour over the milk. Leave for a few minutes and then serve.

**1 slice malt loaf
small scraping unsalted butter
1 ripe pear**

malt loaf with butter and pear

Look for a good-quality malt loaf without too many additives. Spread a slice with butter and cut into strips. Core the pear, peel and cut into chunks. Serve with the malt loaf.

1 ripe kiwi fruit

kiwi fruit in an egg cup

Kiwi fruits are particularly rich in vitamins C and E. To help make them more fun to eat, cut the top off the fruit and stick the fruit into an egg cup. Serve with a spoon and let your toddler scoop out the flesh. The fruit must be ripe so that it is easy for the toddler to eat.

1 **C** ½ ½ ½ 2½

vitamins B₁, B₆

1 fruit scone, preferably home-made (see page 104)
1 eating apple, eg Cox's

scone with apple

If you have the time, make a batch of home-made scones to keep in the freezer; they often taste better and will have far fewer additives than shop-bought ones. They make a great snack on a weekend afternoon, when your toddler may be eating supper slightly later in the day. Cut the fruit scone in half. Peel and core the apple and cut into chunks and serve with the scone.

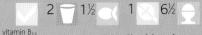

2 1½ 1 6½

vitamin B₁₂
– phosphorous

30g Cheddar cheese
2 oatcakes

oatcakes with cheese

Suitable for vegetarians and vegans, oatcakes make a quick and easy snack for toddlers. Organic oatcakes are also now available. Cut the cheese into chunks and serve with the oatcakes. A couple of oatcakes and a few fresh grapes also make a great snack.

3 **C** ½ ½

vitamins A, B₆

1 small carrot
5cm piece of cucumber
4 small ripe cherry tomatoes

pot of raw vegetables

Snacks do not need to be complicated, they just need to be made using fresh ingredients, such as raw fresh vegetables or fruit. Peel the carrot, trim the ends and cut into small sticks. Cut the cucumber into similar sized sticks. Cut the tomatoes in half and mix with the other vegetables and serve in a small pot. It's especially important to stay with your toddler while he eats raw vegetables.

1 ½ 4½

vitamins B₆, B₁₂

1 slice wholemeal bread
2tbsp meat or fish paté

toast with paté

Paté is the one food that I always spend a bit more on. Always read the label and look for one with a high meat percentage (around 70 per cent). Toast the slice of bread and spread with the paté. Cut into fingers and serve.

11 **C** ½ 1½

vitamin B₆

1 ripe fresh peach
1 small ripe banana, peeled and roughly chopped
100ml apple juice

peach and banana smoothie

Cut the peach in half, remove the stone, roughly chop the flesh and put into a blender (or food processor). Add the banana and apple juice and whiz until smooth. Pour into a plastic cup.

1½ **C** ½ ½ 4

vitamins B₆, B₁₂
– phosphorous

5cm piece of cucumber, peeled
2tbsp natural full-fat cottage cheese
1tbsp natural full-fat yogurt
1tsp extra-virgin olive oil
few leaves of fresh coriander or parsley, or a chive leaf, chopped
3 baby corn, halved

cottage cheese dip

Cut the cucumber in half and then into thins sticks. Mix the cottage cheese, yogurt, olive oil and herbs together and serve with the cucumber sticks and baby corn.

fresh **suppers**

Thai-spiced vegetables with rice

makes: 4 toddler portions

storage: best eaten fresh or keep Thai vegetables (not rice) in the refrigerator for up to 2 days

6
1
1½
½
3 **C**

vitamins A, B₁, B₆ – phosphorous

400ml tinned coconut milk
2–3tsp Thai 7 spice powder
2 medium sweet potatoes, peeled and cut into chunks
2 carrots, peeled and sliced
½ aubergine, cut in chunks
125g fine green beans
zest of 1 unwaxed lime
200g white Basmati rice

This is real energy food for vegetarians. Add some fresh coriander if your toddler likes the flavour. Do not serve coconut milk to toddlers under the age of three if there is a family history of allergies.

1 Put the coconut milk and Thai 7 spice into a heavy-based saucepan and gently heat for a few minutes. Add the potatoes, carrots and aubergine and simmer for 15–20 minutes.

2 Add the green beans and cook for a few more minutes, until all the vegetables are cooked. Meanwhile, put the rice into a pan, add 400ml water and simmer for 14 minutes (covered). Remove from the heat and leave covered for 11 minutes.

3 Serve the rice in bowls with the coconut vegetables on top. If necessary, cut into smaller pieces before serving.

stir-fried marinated chicken

makes: 6 toddler portions

storage: best eaten fresh or keep in the refrigerator for up to 2 days (do not reheat rice)

12½
½
1

4 **C**

vitamins A, B₆ – phosphorous

4 chicken breasts (500g)
2tsp dark soy sauce
2tbsp hoi sin sauce
2tsp sesame seeds
2.5cm freshly grated ginger
1tbsp runny honey
1tbsp vegetable oil
2 spring onions, finely sliced
1 red pepper, seeded and cut into thin strips
2 medium carrots, peeled and cut into thin strips
50g mange-tout, thinly sliced
white Basmati rice

Don't be surprised if forks get abandoned, there seems to be something quite appealing about picking up crunchy pieces of vegetables and sticky chicken strips with little hands. Do not serve seeds to toddlers under the age of three if there is any family history of allergies.

1 Cut the chicken into thin 5mm wide strips. Mix together the soy sauce, hoi sin sauce, sesame seeds, ginger and honey, then pour over the chicken, cover and chill for 30 minutes.

2 Meanwhile, put the rice into a saucepan, add twice the volume of water and simmer for 14 minutes (covered). Remove from the heat and leave covered for 11 minutes.

3 Heat the oil in a wok. Add the chicken and stir-fry until golden and almost cooked. Pour over the remaining marinade and cook over a high heat for 2 minutes, until the chicken is cooked.

4 Add the spring onions, pepper, carrots and mange-tout and stir-fry for a few more minutes. Serve with the cooked rice. If necessary, cut into smaller pieces before serving.

haddock with bacon and spinach

14½

1½

1½

1

1

makes: 6 toddler portions

storage: best eaten fresh

1½tbsp olive oil
550g unsmoked haddock
6 rashers unsmoked back
    bacon, rind removed and
    chopped into small pieces
2 shallots, finely chopped
2 garlic cloves, finely chopped
knob unsalted butter
225g baby spinach leaves
freshly ground black pepper
celeriac and potato mash,
    to serve

This requires nothing more complicated than shaking the frying pan for a few minutes. Make a mash of any vegetables that you fancy to go with the fish.

1 Check the haddock for bones. Heat the oil in a pan and fry the fish, skin side down, for 2 minutes. Turn over and fry for a few minutes more, until cooked.

2 Meanwhile, heat a little oil in another frying pan and fry the bacon until it starts to brown. Add the shallots and garlic and cook until golden and the bacon is cooked through.

3 Add the butter and spinach, then stir for a minute until the spinach has wilted. Season with freshly ground black pepper.

4 Serve the haddock on top of the bacon and spinach with some mash or rice. If necessary, cut into smaller pieces before serving.

chicken with herby mushrooms

19½

1½

2

½

½

makes: 4 toddler portions

storage: best eaten fresh or keep for up to 24 hours in the refrigerator

2tbsp olive oil
4 small chicken pieces
2 medium red onions, finely
    sliced
2 garlic cloves, peeled and
    finely chopped
250g chestnut mushrooms,
    finely chopped
1tbsp plain flour
600ml good low-salt chicken
    stock or no- or low-salt
    vegetable stock (page 44)
140ml double cream
2tbsp fresh herbs, eg
    tarragon, parsley, chopped
mashed potato or rice,
    to serve

You can make this dish with any sort of chicken pieces and any type of mushrooms. However, I do prefer the wonderful nutty flavour of chestnut mushrooms, and my children seem to agree.

1 Preheat the oven to 180°C/350°F/gas mark 4. Heat 1tbsp olive oil in a heavy-based casserole and brown the chicken pieces all over. Transfer to a plate.

2 Heat the remaining oil in a heavy-based frying pan and sauté the onions until soft – approximately 5 minutes. Add to the chicken.

3 Gently fry the garlic and mushrooms for 5 minutes in the casserole. Stir in the flour and cook for a minute.

4 Gradually add the stock, stirring constantly, and bring up to a gentle simmer. Return the chicken and onions to the pan, cover and transfer to the oven for 30–40 minutes, until the chicken is cooked through.

5 Remove from the oven and place on a low hob, add the cream, herbs and freshly ground black pepper and heat through. Serve immediately if cool enough or keep warm for 10 minutes in a low oven. If necessary, cut into smaller pieces.

crispy baked chicken

18

1

1½

½ C

vitamins B₆, B₁₂ – phosphorous

makes: 4 toddler portions

storage: best eaten fresh

1–2tbsp olive oil, for
  greasing
4 chicken breasts
2tbsp tomato ketchup
1 large egg, beaten
120g crisps (preferably with
  no added salt or low salt),
  crushed

If you feel tempted to give your toddler chicken nuggets, why not resist and make these instead?

1 Preheat the oven to 180°C/350°F/gas mark 4. Lightly oil a baking tray.
2 Lay the chicken breasts between 2 pieces of clingfilm and then bash them with a rolling pin in order to flatten them. Cut each breast into approximately 6 thin strips.
3 Brush the chicken strips with ketchup, then dip into beaten egg and finally roll in the crisps to coat thoroughly.
4 Put the chicken strips on the baking sheet and cook in the oven for 20 minutes, until crisp and golden. If necessary, cut into smaller pieces before serving.

toad in the hole

9½

1½

1½

1½

½ C

vitamins B₆, B₁₂ – phosphorous

makes: 4 toddler portions

storage: best eaten fresh

170g plain flour, sifted
3 large eggs
285ml full-fat milk
2tbsp cold water
2tbsp sunflower oil
6 good quality pork
  sausages
2tbsp olive oil (optional)

for the gravy
1tbsp olive oil (optional)
2 medium onions, skinned
  and finely sliced
1–2 garlic cloves, peeled and
  finely chopped
1tbsp plain flour
600ml low-salt chicken, beef,
  or no- or low-salt vegetable
  stock (see page 44)
freshly ground black pepper

This recipe needs to be served with a good rich gravy. Cook a little broccoli or some stir-fried greens to make the meal complete.

1 Preheat the oven to 220°C/425°F/gas mark 7. Put the first 5 ingredients into a food processor (or blender) and whiz until smooth. Leave the batter for 30 minutes.
2 Preheat the grill to hot and cook the sausages until golden brown.
3 Transfer the sausages to a roasting tin with 2tbsp sausage fat or olive oil. Heat the tin over a medium heat. When it is really hot, quickly pour in the batter and transfer to the highest shelf in the oven. Cook for 30–35 minutes, or until the batter is puffed up and golden brown.
4 To make the gravy, heat 1tbsp sausage fat or olive oil in a heavy-based saucepan. Add the onions and garlic and sauté, stirring occasionally, until soft and light brown – approximately 5–10 minutes. Stir in the flour and cook for a couple of minutes before gradually adding the stock. Simmer for 5 minutes, and then season with freshly ground black pepper.
5 If necessary, cut into smaller pieces before serving.

pork chops with cheesy mash

19½

makes: 6 toddler portions

storage: best eaten fresh

1

3½

1½

2 C

vitamins B₁, B₂, B₆, B₁₂ – phosphorous

900g floury potatoes, peeled
and chopped
50g unsalted butter
150ml full-fat milk
100g Cheddar cheese, grated
or finely chopped
freshly ground black pepper
4 pork chops (approx 400g)
3–4tbsp apple purée

This is a simple but satisfying supper. Children often enjoy the combination of fresh fruits with meat.

1 Boil a large pan of water, add the potatoes and simmer until tender. Drain.
2 Put 25g butter and all the milk into a small pan and heat until just melted, then remove from heat.
3 Return the potatoes to the pan and mash with the hot butter and milk until creamy, then add the cheese and stir. Season with freshly ground black pepper.
4 Meanwhile, grill the pork chops for 5–8 minutes on each side until cooked through. Put on a plate and keep warm.
5 Cut the pork chops into small pieces, top with the apple purée and serve with the mash.

pasta with carrots and chicken

11½

makes: 2 toddler portions

storage: best eaten fresh or keep for up to 24 hours in the refrigerator

2

3

3

2 C

vitamin B₆

150g pasta
75g sweetcorn, fresh or
frozen
1 chicken breast
1tbsp olive oil
2 medium carrots, peeled
and grated
2 handfuls of raisins
1 handful of Cheddar
cheese, grated (approx 75g)

Many of the ideas in this book are a result of having to find something quickly to feed 2 hungry toddlers. This is one of them.

1 Boil a large pan of water and cook the pasta following the packet's instructions. A couple of minutes before the end of the cooking time, add the sweetcorn. Drain.
2 Cut the chicken into small pieces. Heat the olive oil in a frying pan and sauté the chicken until just golden all over and cooked through.
3 Stir the carrots, chicken and raisins into the cooked pasta. Sprinkle the cheese over. If necessary, cut into smaller pieces before serving.

new potatoes with avocado

9½
½
1½
2
3 C

vitamins B₁, B₆, B₁₂
– phosphorous

makes: 2 toddler portions

storage: best eaten fresh

200g baby new potatoes, scrubbed

2 rashers unsmoked streaky bacon, rind removed

1 ripe avocado

90g feta cheese, crumbled

for the dressing

2tbsp sour cream or full-fat natural yogurt

handful of fresh mint, chopped

You could always omit the bacon and serve this with grilled fish or cooked chicken or on its own if you prefer.

1 Heat a grill to high. Boil a large pan of water, add the potatoes and simmer gently until just tender – approximately 10 minutes. Drain and chop into small pieces, then transfer to a bowl.

2 Grill the bacon until cooked through and crisp and cut into small pieces. Add to the potatoes.

3 Halve the avocado, remove the stone, peel and cut the flesh into small cubes. Add to the potatoes and bacon with the feta cheese.

4 Mix together the dressing ingredients, then mix well with the potato salad. If necessary, cut into smaller pieces before serving.

rice with honey and soy

6
½
½
½
4 C

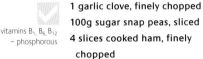

vitamins B₁, B₆, B₁₂
– phosphorous

makes: 2 toddler portions

storage: best eaten fresh or keep in the refrigerator for up to 24 hours and serve at room temperature (do not reheat rice)

100g white Basmati rice

1tbsp olive oil

1 medium red onion, finely chopped

1 garlic clove, finely chopped

100g sugar snap peas, sliced

4 slices cooked ham, finely chopped

for the dressing

1tbsp white wine vinegar

2tsp clear runny honey

2tsp soy sauce

freshly ground black pepper

As with so many of these fresh suppers, anything goes. If you do not have cooked ham, just add some more vegetables.

1 Put the rice with double its volume of water into a pan and cover. Bring up to the boil, then reduce the heat and simmer gently for 14 minutes. Remove from the heat and leave to stand, still covered, for another 11 minutes.

2 Heat the olive oil in a frying pan, and sauté the onion and garlic until just soft – approximately 5 minutes. Add the sugar snap peas and ham and sauté for a few more minutes. Stir this mixture into the rice.

3 In a small bowl, whisk together the dressing ingredients and pour over the rice, then mix together.

quick bites **suppers**

All of the recipes make one toddler portion unless stated otherwise.

1 **C** ½ 2 ½ 11½

pork chop with parsnip and carrot mash

1 small carrot, peeled and chopped
1 small parsnip, peeled and chopped
15g knob unsalted butter
1 medium pork chop (approx 100g)

Bring a small pan of water to the boil and cook the carrot and parsnip until soft – approximately 10 minutes. Drain, add the butter and roughly mash. Meanwhile, cook the pork chop under a hot grill for approximately 4–5 minutes on each side, or until cooked through. Cut into smaller pieces before serving with the mash.

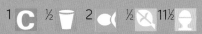 2 **C** 1½ ½ 12

vitamins B₁, B₆
– phosphorous

chicken with parsley and garlic butter

15g unsalted butter, softened
1 garlic clove, peeled, crushed
1tbsp fresh parsley, chopped
1 chicken thigh, with skin
2–3 new potatoes, washed and quartered
freshly ground black pepper
1tsp olive oil

Preheat the oven to 180°C/350°F/gas mark 4. Mix the butter, garlic and parsley together and push under the skin of the chicken thigh. Put into a small roasting tin with the potatoes and olive oil and season with freshly ground black pepper. Roast in the medium oven until the chicken and potatoes are cooked through – approximately 30–40 minutes. Cut into smaller pieces before serving.

1½ **C** 1½ ½ 10½

vitamin B₁₂
– phosphorous

fried parsley potatoes with poached egg

1 medium potato, peeled and halved
1tbsp unsalted butter
1tbsp fresh parsley, chopped
1 medium egg, poached (see page 106)

Bring a small pan of water to the boil and cook the potato for approximately 10 minutes, until still slightly firm in the centre. Drain, cool and cut into small cubes. Melt the butter in a heavy-based frying pan, add the potatoes and parsley and cook for 10–15 minutes, until the potato is cooked and golden. Serve with the poached egg, all chopped into small pieces if necessary.

3 **C** ½ 1 1½ 7½

potato salad with olives, tomato and egg

3 medium new potatoes, scrubbed
3 black Greek olives, stoned and chopped
1 small ripe tomato, finely chopped
1 medium egg, hardboiled and quartered

Bring a small pan of water to the boil and cook the potatoes until tender – approximately 10–12 minutes. Drain and cut into bite-size pieces. Put into a bowl with the chopped stoned olives and chopped tomato and top with the boiled egg quarters.

½   ½   ½   3½

mushroom and garlic-stuffed bread

1 small, part-baked white or wholemeal bread roll (available in the freezer section of most supermarkets)
15g unsalted butter
1 garlic clove, peeled and crushed
2 field mushrooms, halved

Preheat the oven to the temperature recommended for the bread. Make 4 slits into the top of the bread roll. Spread half of the butter in the slits. Melt the remaining butter in a small pan and gently fry the garlic and mushrooms briefly until the mushrooms are soft – approximately 5 minutes. Stuff the mushrooms into each slit, pouring over any pan juices. Bake in the preheated oven for the time recommended on the bread packet. Cut into small pieces, cool a little and serve.

½ C   ½   1   1½   7½
vitamins B₁, B₆

sausage stew

makes: 2 toddler portions
1 tsp olive oil
2 good pork sausages, skins removed
250ml storecupboard tomato sauce (see page 44) or 250ml passata
100g tinned cooked chickpeas, rinsed

Heat the oil in a heavy-based pan and fry the sausage meat, breaking it up with a wooden spoon as you go. When it is golden, add the tomato sauce. Bring to the boil, scraping the bottom to dislodge any bits that are sticking. Add the chickpeas and simmer for 10 minutes. Serve.

1½ C   1   1   14
vitamins B₁, B₆, B₁₂ – phosphorous

grilled salmon with steamed vegetables

1 small piece of salmon fillet (approx 75g), skinned
6 mangetout
4 baby corn
1tsp light soy sauce

Preheat the grill to high and cook the salmon for about 2–3 minutes on each side, until pale golden and cooked through. Meanwhile, cook the vegetables in a steamer over a pan of boiling water and cut into small pieces. Put the vegetables onto a small plate and flake over the salmon, checking carefully for bones. Sprinkle over the soy sauce and serve.

4 C 2½   2½   1   16½

penne with chicken and broccoli

75g penne
100g mixed broccoli and cauliflower florets
½ quantity (300ml) storecupboard white sauce (see page 45)
100g cooked chicken, shredded

Cook the penne following the packet's instructions. Steam the vegetables over a pan of boiling water until tender. Drain the pasta. Put the white sauce into a small, heavy-based pan and bring to simmering point. Stir in the pasta, vegetables and cooked chicken and bring back to simmering point, stirring often, until the chicken is heated through. If necessary, cut into small pieces before serving.

3 C 1   ½   2½   3½

couscous with grated vegetables

50g couscous
1 small carrot, peeled and grated
5cm piece of cucumber, peeled and grated
50g baby spinach, finely shredded
1tbsp extra-virgin olive oil
juice of ½ small lemon
1tsp runny honey

Cook the couscous following the packet's instructions, then mix in the vegetables. In a small bowl, whisk together the olive oil, lemon and honey and pour over the couscous. Mix well and serve.

suppers to freeze

meatballs in tomato sauce

You can make meatballs in many ways, but I always come back to this recipe.

makes: 10 toddler portions (30 small meatballs)

storage: freeze for up to 4 months

4tbsp olive oil

4 large onions, finely chopped

2 garlic cloves, peeled and finely chopped

1tbsp balsamic vinegar

2 x 400g tin chopped tomatoes

300ml no- or low-salt vegetable stock (page 44)

freshly ground black pepper

large pinch soft brown sugar

2tbsp fresh parsley, chopped

2tbsp basil leaves, torn

800g lean beef mince

2tbsp fresh parsley, chopped

flour, for coating

vitamins B₆, B₁₂ – phosphorous

1. To make the tomato sauce, heat 2tbsp oil in a heavy-based saucepan and sauté half the onions until soft. Add the garlic and sauté for a few minutes before adding the balsamic vinegar. Cook for a minute.
2. Stir in the tomatoes and stock. Season with a pinch of salt, black pepper and sugar, then simmer, uncovered, for 20 minutes. Add the herbs.
3. For the meatballs, heat the remaining oil in a frying pan and sauté the remaining onions until soft. Transfer to a bowl and cool. Mix in the mince, parsley and seasoning. Lightly flour your hands and make small meatballs. Roll each in flour.
4. Heat 2tbsp oil in a heavy-based frying pan and brown the meatballs in batches. Drain on kitchen paper. Add the meatballs to the sauce, cover and simmer for 15 minutes. Turn the meatballs, then cook, uncovered for 10–15 minutes. Cool completely. Spoon into freezerproof containers or freezer bags. Freeze.
5. Thaw thoroughly. Gently heat in a saucepan until boiling. If necessary, cut into smaller pieces before serving.

smoked haddock soup

Many toddlers will love this soup and its smoky flavour.

makes: 6 toddler portions

storage: freeze for up to 3 months

450g smoked haddock fillets

450ml full-fat milk

450ml water

2 small onions, peeled

40g unsalted butter

2 medium potatoes, peeled and cubed

2 ripe tomatoes, skinned, seeded and chopped

1tbsp fresh parsley, chopped

vitamins B₁, B₆, B₁₂ – phosphorous

1. Put the fish into a saucepan with the milk, water and 1 onion. Simmer very gently for 5 minutes, until the fish is cooked, then leave to stand for 10 minutes. Strain and reserve the liquid and fish separately.
2. Finely chop the remaining onion. Melt the butter in a large pan and cook the onion until soft, then add the potatoes and cook for a few minutes, stirring.
3. Pour over the poaching liquid and cook until the potato is soft. Purée with a hand-held blender (or in a food processor or blender). Return to the pan.
4. Flake the cooked fish, removing any bones. Stir into the soup with the tomatoes, freshly ground black pepper and parsley. Leave to cool completely, then pour into freezerproof containers and freeze.
5. Defrost thoroughly, then heat through until boiling. Cool a little to serve.

beef burgers with cheese

 15½

 1

 4

 1

makes: approx 6 toddler portions (12 small burgers)

storage: freeze for up to 4 months

1tbsp olive oil

1 medium red onion, finely chopped

500g good-quality lean beef mince

1 medium egg, beaten

freshly ground black pepper

75g Cheddar cheese, finely chopped (optional)

bread rolls, shredded lettuce, cheese slices, tomatoes slices, to serve

vitamins B₁, B₆, B₁₂ – phosphorous

It does not take long to mix together some minced beef with a few seasonings to make hamburgers – giving you peace of mind as you know exactly what went into them. Never refreeze raw meat that has already been frozen.

1 Heat the oil in a frying pan and sauté the onion until soft – approximately 5 minutes. Transfer to a large bowl and cool.

2 Add the mince and egg and season lightly with freshly ground black pepper. Mix well with the cheese, if using.

3 Wet your hands slightly and make small beef burgers. Layer in a freezerproof container with greaseproof paper and freeze.

4 Thaw thoroughly. Keep the burgers at room temperature for 30 minutes before cooking.

5 Grill the burgers for 3–4 minutes on each side, until cooked through.

6 Serve with bread rolls, lettuce and tomato and cheese slices. If necessary, cut into smaller pieces before serving.

lamb stew

 16½

 1½

 1

 2½

makes: 8 toddler portions

storage: freeze for up to 4 months

4tbsp olive oil

150g unsmoked back bacon, rind removed, chopped

900g lean lamb shoulder, diced

2 medium onions, finely chopped

2 garlic cloves, peeled and finely chopped

100ml no- or low-salt vegetable stock (page 44)

400g tin chopped tomatoes

400g tin cherry tomatoes

large pinch dark brown sugar

handful of fresh thyme sprigs

freshly ground black pepper

 vitamins B₁, B₆, B₁₂ – phosphorous

You may like to add some mushrooms or olives to this stew. I often serve it with a creamy plain or pesto mash, but it is also great with rice.

1 Preheat the oven to 150°C/300°F/gas mark 2. Heat a large heavy-based casserole until hot. Add 2tbsp olive oil and brown the bacon and lamb. Transfer to a plate.

2 Heat the remaining oil and gently sweat the onions and garlic until soft – approximately 5 minutes.

3 Add the stock and leave to bubble for a few minutes, stirring occasionally.

4 Add the lamb, bacon, chopped tomatoes, cherry tomatoes, sugar and most of the thyme. Season with freshly ground black pepper.

5 Bring to the boil, cover and cook in the oven for 1 hour 50 minutes, stirring occasionally. Scatter over the remaining fresh thyme leaves and season. Cool completely. Transfer to freezerproof containers, cover and freeze.

6 Thaw thoroughly. Gently heat until boiling. If necessary, cut into smaller pieces before serving.

green vegetable crumble

makes: 5 toddler portions

storage: freeze for up to four months

10
2
2
3
6

2 heads broccoli, cut into florets

2 leeks, washed and sliced

200g green beans, topped and tailed

250g fresh spinach, washed and destalked

30g unsalted butter

30g plain flour

400ml full-fat milk

75g Cheddar cheese, grated

2tbsp fresh herbs, chopped

50g fresh breadcrumbs

50g nuts, finely chopped

25g Parmesan cheese, grated

vitamins A, B$_1$, B$_2$, B$_6$, B$_{12}$
folic acid – phosphorous

A variety of textures make this crumble popular with toddlers. Do not give nuts to children under the age of three if there is a family history of food allergies.

1   Steam or boil broccoli, leeks and beans separately until just tender. Drain.

2   Wilt the spinach in a pan with a tiny amount of water. Drain thoroughly in a sieve, pressing with a wooden spoon. Roughly chop and mix with other vegetables in an ovenproof and freezerproof dish.

3   Melt the butter in a pan, stir in the flour and cook for 1 minute. Gradually add the milk, stirring constantly, and simmer until the sauce is smooth and thickened. Stir in the cheese and add pepper. Pour over the vegetables.

4   Mix together the herbs, breadcrumbs, nuts and Parmesan and scatter over the top. Cool completely. Wrap the dish in foil and freeze.

5   Thaw thoroughly. Cook in a preheated oven at 180°C/350°F/gas mark 4 for 20–25 minutes, until golden and piping hot. If necessary, cut into smaller pieces before serving.

creamy chicken and leek pie

makes: 8 toddler portions

storage: freeze for up to 4 months

24
1½
2½
½
2

1.25kg whole chicken

2 medium onions, peeled and quartered

1 large carrot, peeled and cut into chunks

bunch of fresh herbs, eg rosemary, thyme and parsley

salt and 4 peppercorns

3tbsp olive oil

130g pancetta, cubed

250g chestnut mushrooms, chopped

25g unsalted butter

3 medium leeks, finely sliced

25g plain flour

4tbsp double cream (optional)

1 x 375g pack puff pastry

vitamins A, B$_1$, B$_2$, B$_6$ – phosphorous

This is a richly satisfying supper that is packed with protein.

1   Put the chicken in a casserole with the onions, carrot, half the herbs, a pinch of salt and the peppercorns. Cover with water and a lid. Bring to the boil. Simmer for 1 hour. Pierce a thigh with a knife to see if the juices run clear, then leave to cool in stock. Remove the meat from the bones and cut into small chunks, then put into a freezerproof pie dish. Skim any fat off stock, strain and reserve 565ml.

2   Heat the olive oil in heavy-based saucepan. Add the pancetta and mushrooms and cook until golden – about 5 minutes. Transfer to a bowl and cool.

3   Heat the butter in the pan and sauté the leeks until soft. Stir in the flour and cook for 2 minutes, then gradually add the stock and stir, until sauce thickens.

4   Chop the remaining herbs, then add them with some seasoning. Cool completely. Add the cream (if using) and the mushroom and pancetta mixture, mix well.

5   Pour the cool sauce over the cool chicken.

6   Cut thin strips of the pastry and place on the dampened pie dish lip. Rest the remaining pastry sheet over the pie. Crimp the edges together and trim. Make a small slit in the lid and wrap in clingfilm or foil and freeze.

7   Thaw thoroughly. Cook in a preheated oven at 190°C/375°F/gas mark 5 for about 30 minutes, until piping hot and the pastry is puffed and golden. If necessary, cut into smaller pieces before serving.

fresh & frozen puddings

banana and toffee ice-cream

makes: 8 toddler portions

storage: freeze for up to 3 months

150ml full-fat milk
juice of ½ lemon
125g golden caster sugar
300g full-fat cream cheese
3 very ripe bananas, peeled and roughly chopped
2 x 45g Crunchie bars

vitamin B₆

Use the ripest bananas you can find to give the best flavour. This has to be one of the easiest ways to make ice-cream – and one of the tastiest.

1   Put all of the ingredients, except the Crunchie bars, into a food processor and whiz until really smooth.
2   Roughly crush the Crunchy bars into very small pieces.
3   Tip into a freezerproof bowl, add the Crunchies, stir once, cover and freeze for at least 6 hours.
4   Leave at room temperature for 5 minutes before serving.

apple and blackberry crumble

makes: 6 toddler portions

storage: best eaten fresh or freeze for up to 4 months

100g plain flour, plus 1tbsp
25g hazelnuts, toasted and finely chopped
50g unsalted butter, chilled and diced
1 medium egg yolk
3 apples, eg Bramley, peeled, cored and sliced
100g blackberries
3tbsp light soft brown sugar

for the crumble topping
50g unsalted butter, chilled and diced
75g white flour
50g soft brown sugar
25g hazelnuts, toasted and finely chopped

This makes a change from the traditional crumble. It is a tart with a crumble topping. You could use any fruit that is in season. Do not give nuts to toddlers under the age of three if there is any family history of food allergies.

1   Put the flour and nuts into a food processor, add the butter and process until the mixture resembles fine breadcrumbs. (Alternatively, rub in the butter with your fingertips.)
2   Add the egg yolk and a little water, if necessary, and process until the pastry just draws together. Knead briefly on a lightly floured surface to form a flat 22cm round.
3   Line a chilled 20cm loose-bottomed tin with the pastry, trim the edges with a generous hand and chill for 30 minutes. Line with baking paper and baking beans and bake blind in a preheated oven at 180°C/350°F/gas mark 4 for 10 minutes, then remove the paper and beans and bake for a further 5 minutes.
4   In a bowl, mix together the apples, blackberries, soft brown sugar and 1tbsp flour. Spoon into the pastry case.
5   For the topping, rub the butter into the flour (or in a food processor) until the mixture resembles fine breadcrumbs. Stir in the remaining ingredients. Sprinkle over the fruit and bake for 20–25 minutes.

little fruit puddings

4½

makes: 6 toddler portions

1

storage: best eaten fresh or keep in the refrigerator for up to 3 days

½

½

½ C

3 apricots, stoned and sliced

3 nectarines, stoned and sliced

150g unsalted butter, plus extra for greasing

140g golden caster sugar

2 medium eggs

vitamins A, B₆, B₁₂

125g self-raising flour, sifted

60ml full-fat milk

custard or full-fat natural yogurt, to serve

You could use any fruit for these – just make sure it is ripe for the best flavour and texture possible.

1 Preheat the oven to 180°C/350°F/gas mark 4. Butter 6 muffin tins.

2 Put the fruit into a roasting tin, then dot with 25g butter and sprinkle with 15g sugar. Roast for 5–10 minutes, until slightly soft.

3 Beat the remaining butter and sugar in a bowl until light and fluffy. Add the eggs, one at a time, and beat until thoroughly incorporated.

4 Fold in the flour, then add the milk, mixing quickly.

5 Spoon the mixture into the muffin tins, layering with the fruit – the muffin tins should be about three-quarters full. Bake in the oven for 15–20 minutes, until golden.

6 Serve with home-made custard or yogurt. If necessary, cut the muffins into smaller pieces before serving.

fruit tea loaf

3½

makes: approx 20 toddler portions (2 x 450g loaves)

1

storage: best eaten fresh or keep in an airtight container for 4–5 days or freeze for up to 4 months

1

1

phosphorous

300g ready-to-eat dried pineapple

300g ready-to-eat dried pawpaw

225g ready-to-eat dried unsulphured apricots

250ml pineapple juice

100g Brazil nuts, very finely chopped

225g light muscavado sugar

2 medium eggs, beaten

225g wholemeal self-raising flour

225g white self-raising flour

If my girls still seem hungry after lunch, I tend to give them some fresh fruit with yogurt or a piece of a fruit loaf. This loaf also works well at a party. Do not give nuts to toddlers under the age of three if there is any family history of food allergies.

1 Chop the dried fruit into very small pieces. Put into a large bowl. Put the pineapple juice and 225ml water into a pan, bring to the boil, then pour it over the dried fruit. Leave to soak for a minimum of 1 hour, or overnight if possible.

2 Preheat the oven to 170°C/325°F/gas mark 3. Grease and line the bottom of 2 x 450g loaf tins.

3 Mix the soaked fruit and liquid with the Brazil nuts, sugar, eggs and sifted flour. Divide the mixture equally between 2 tins.

4 Bake for 55–60 minutes, until well risen and firm to touch. Cool in the tin for 10 minutes. Turn out onto a wire rack and cool completely.

5 Slice. If necessary, cut into smaller pieces before serving.

apple bread and butter pudding

7½

1

1

1

½

vitamin B₂ –
phosphorous

makes: 4 toddler portions

storage: best eaten fresh or keep in the refrigerator for up to 2 days

3 Cox's apples, peeled, cored and chopped

50g golden caster sugar, plus 1tbsp

4–5 slices white bread (approx 120g), lightly buttered and crusts removed

35g raisins

3 medium eggs

275ml full-fat milk

pinch of ground cinnamon

This bread and butter pudding has a lovely squishy apple layer. It's a real hit with children of all ages and is particularly good with a dollop of custard.

1 Preheat the oven to 180°C/350°F/gas mark 4. Butter an ovenproof dish.
2 In a small pan, cook the apple with 1tbsp water and 1tbsp sugar for 5–6 minutes, until just softened.
3 Cut each slice of bread into 4 triangles and lay half of the triangles into the buttered dish. Sprinkle over half the raisins and then the apple mixture. Add the remaining bread triangles and the rest of the raisins.
4 Whisk the eggs in a large bowl, then add the milk, sugar and cinnamon. Pour over the bread, gently pressing down the triangles so that they are covered in the egg mix.
5 Bake in the oven for 30–40 minutes, until risen and golden. If necessary, cut into smaller pieces before serving.

saucy chocolate pudding

3½

½

½

1

vitamins B₂, B₆, B₁₂ – folic acid – phosphorous

makes: 6 toddler portions

storage: best eaten fresh or keep in the refrigerator for up to 2 days

40g unsalted butter, melted, plus extra for greasing

100g self-raising flour

65g golden caster sugar

2tbsp cocoa

90g milk chocolate, chopped

120ml full-fat milk

1 medium egg, beaten

few drops vanilla extract

for the sauce

165g light soft brown sugar

2tbsp cocoa

250ml boiling water

To enjoy the sauce at the bottom of the pudding you need to serve this straight away, otherwise it may be absorbed by the sponge. Try other types of chocolate instead of milk chocolate, such as orange or white chocolate.

1 Preheat the oven to 180°C/350°F/gas mark 4 and then butter a 750ml ovenproof dish.
2 Sift the flour, caster sugar and cocoa into a bowl. Stir in the chocolate.
3 Whisk together the milk, melted butter, egg and vanilla, then mix with the dry ingredients. Pour into the buttered dish.
4 To make the sauce, mix together the brown sugar and cocoa, then sprinkle over the pudding mixture. Carefully pour the boiling water over the top and bake in the oven for 30 minutes, until the pudding feels firm and has puffed up.
5 If necessary, cut into smaller pieces before serving.

quick bites puddings

Try not to make a habit of always offering something sweet after a savoury course, as most toddlers will very quickly learn that if they don't eat their main course they can still fill up on pudding.

All of the recipes make one toddler portion unless stated otherwise.

1½ 2 1 ½ 5½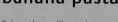

banana pasta

makes: 3 toddler portions
600ml full-fat milk
25g golden caster sugar
100g macaroni
2 ripe small bananas, peeled and sliced

Bring the milk and sugar to the boil in a heavy-based pan. Add the macaroni and bring back to the boil, then simmer, stirring often, until tender – approximately 10–15 minutes. Spoon into a bowl, add the sliced bananas and serve.

1 ½ ½ ½ 3½

quick passion-fruit trifle

1 ripe passion-fruit
2 sponge fingers, broken
into pieces
2tbsp natural full-fat yogurt

Passion-fruit are a good source of both beta-carotene and vitamin C. Cut the passion-fruit in half and scoop out the pulp. Put the sponge fingers into the bottom of a small plastic bowl. Top with the yogurt and then the passion-fruit. Cover and leave for at least 10–15 minutes for the sponge fingers to go slightly soft.

 1 ½ ½ 2½

phosphorous

1 portion of home-made rice
pudding (see page 86) or
100g tinned rice pudding
3 "ready to eat" prunes

rice pudding with prunes

Chop the prunes into very small pieces and simply stir into the rice pudding before serving. Do not reheat home-made rice pudding.

 1½ ½ ½ 4

vitamin B₆ –
phosphorous

1tbsp nuts, eg cashews,
hazelnuts, almonds (do not give
nuts to toddlers under the age of
three if there is a family history
of allergies)
3tbsp natural full-fat yogurt
1tsp runny honey
1tbsp raisins

yogurt with honey and raisins

Finely chop the nuts and put into a bowl. Add the yogurt, honey and raisins and mix together.

orange and passion-fruit sorbet

5

makes: 10 toddler portions
juice of 1kg fresh oranges
125g golden caster sugar
5 passion-fruit

This is how sorbets should taste – full of flavour. The reason for this is because it is made of pure, fresh fruit juice without any added water. It does contain sugar, as this is a vital ingredient for determining the soft and creamy texture. Put the juice in a pan, scoop out any pips, then add the sugar and heat gently until all the sugar is dissolved, stirring occasionally. Leave to cool. Put a sieve over the pan. Halve the passion-fruit and scrape the flesh into the sieve. Press it through with a wooden spoon. Stir well, then freeze in an ice-cream machine or pour the mixture into a freezer-proof container, cover and freeze for 2 hours. Remove the sorbet from the freezer and whiz in a food processor (or blender), then return it to the freezer for another 2 hours. Repeat the process. Freeze for at least 6 hours. Leave at room temperature for 5 minutes before serving.

vitamins B₂, B₆,
B₁₂ – phosphorous

plums and custard

makes: 2 toddler portions
1tbsp custard powder
2tsp golden caster sugar
300ml full-fat milk
2 ripe plums, halved and stoned

Make the custard following the packet's instructions. Chop the plums into very small pieces and divide the fruit between 2 bowls. Cover each with custard. When it is in season, try using stewed rhubarb instead of the plums; it goes really well with custard.

6 C **1**  **1**

peach with dried pawpaw

1 ripe peach
2 pieces dried pawpaw, finely chopped
full-fat natural yogurt, to serve

Peel the peach if necessary. Cut in half and remove the stone. Cut the flesh into small pieces and put into a bowl. Scatter over the dried pawpaw. If you are serving this to a vegan toddler, keep as it is. Alternatively, you may like to add a dollop of natural yogurt.

4 C **1** **6½**

rhubarb and berries

makes: 2 toddler portions
200g fresh rhubarb
handful of blueberries (approx 50g)
4 ripe strawberries, hulled, chopped
75ml apple juice
1–2tbsp golden caster sugar – enough to taste

Trim the rhubarb and chop into small pieces. Put it into a saucepan. Add the berries, 50ml water and the apple juice and simmer for 5 minutes, until the rhubarb is just tender. Stir in the caster sugar to taste. Transfer the fruit into small bowls.

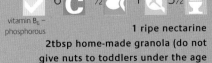

vitamin B₆ –
phosphorous

nectarine crumble

1 ripe nectarine
2tbsp home-made granola (do not give nuts to toddlers under the age of three if there is a family history of allergies)
small knob unsalted butter

If you don't have home-made granola to hand, use a bought cereal. Preheat the oven to 180°C/350°F/ gas mark 4. Cut the nectarine in half and remove the stone. Put each half in a small ovenproof dish. Spoon the granola on top of the fruit. Dot with butter and bake for 15 minutes, until the nectarine is soft and the topping is crunchy. If necessary, cut into smaller pieces before serving.

celebration food

pink meringues

makes: 20 toddler portions
(approx 40 meringues)

storage: keep in an airtight
container for up to 2 weeks or
freeze for up to 3 months

175g golden caster sugar
a couple of drops pink food
colouring
3 medium egg whites

When I served these for Jasmin's birthday tea her eyes nearly popped out of
her head. You do need to use a good quality food colouring otherwise the
colour can vanish on cooking.

1   Preheat the oven to 110°C/225°F/gas mark ¼. Line 2 baking trays with
    Bakewell paper.
2   Put the sugar into a bowl, add the food colouring and mix together.
3   Put the egg whites into a clean, grease-free bowl and whisk until stiff peaks
    form. Add a little of the coloured sugar and whisk, then continue to add the
    sugar, whisking after each addition – whisk quickly to prevent the egg whites
    from collapsing.
4   Put little spoonfuls of the mixture onto the trays, leaving a small space
    between each. Put the trays into the oven and bake for 1 hour, then turn off
    the oven and leave to cool.
5   When cool, peel away the paper.

bicycle pump

2½
½
1

makes: 10 toddler portions

storage: keep in the
refrigerator for up to 2 days

135g packet flavoured jelly
410g tinned evaporated milk

vitamin B₆

This works best with a red or black-coloured jelly, such as strawberry,
raspberry or blackcurrant. If you don't have an electric whisk, you could try
whisking it by hand, but it may take quite a while! Do not serve nuts to
toddlers under the age of three if there is any family history of food allergies.

1   Put the jelly into a small saucepan with 2tbsp water and melt over a very
    gentle heat. Do not allow it to boil or simmer. Keep warm.
2   Meanwhile, put the evaporated milk into a large bowl and whisk with an
    electric whisk for about 10 minutes, until thick and mousse-like and almost
    tripled in volume. Continue to whisk and slowly pour in the melted jelly so
    that the mousse is evenly coloured. Quickly pour into a clear bowl and leave
    in the refrigerator for at least 2 hours, until set.

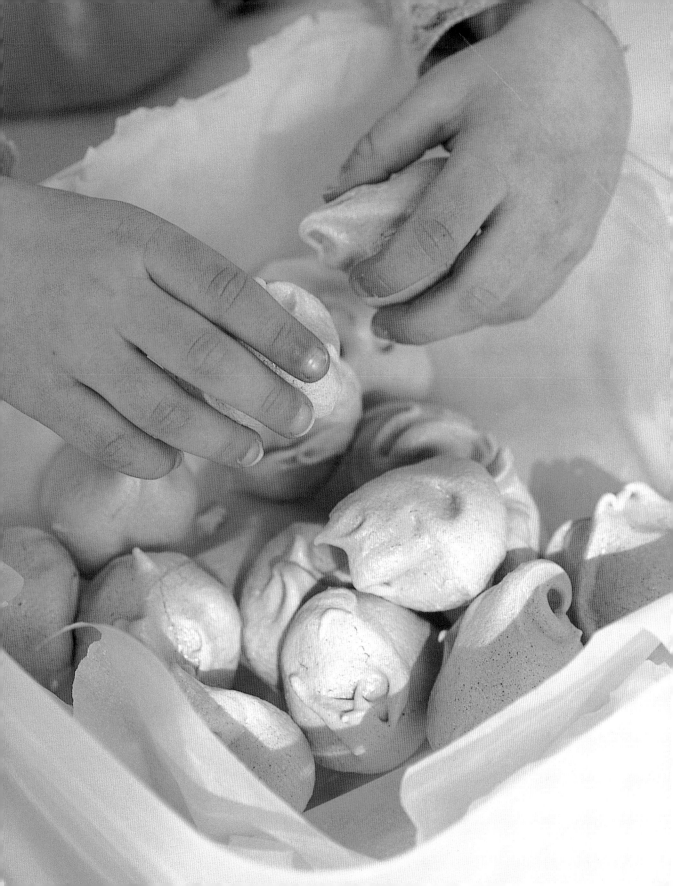

banana and apricot tea bread

makes: approx 10 toddler portions (approx 1kg loaf)

storage: best eaten fresh or keep in airtight container for up to 3 days or freeze for up to 3 months

C

100g unsalted butter, melted, plus extra for greasing

vitamins B₆, B₁₂

3 large bananas (450g unpeeled weight)

juice of ½ lemon

2 large eggs

150g golden caster sugar

½tsp salt

200g self-raising flour, sifted

50g dried unsulphured apricots, finely chopped

50g dried cranberries, finely chopped

75g sifted icing sugar, to glaze

juice of ½ lemon, to glaze

Really ripe bananas, even ones with blackened skin, give the best banana flavour. If you do not have any dried cranberries, just use 50g more dried unsulphured apricots.

1   Preheat the oven to 180°C/350°F/gas mark 4. Grease and line a 1kg loaf tin or butter 10 mini loaf tins.

2   Whiz the bananas in a food processor (or blender) with the lemon juice until really smooth.

3   Whisk the eggs until foamy, then add the sugar, a little at a time, and the melted butter and salt. Fold in the flour alternately with the banana mixture. Stir in the apricots and cranberries.

4   Spoon into the loaf tin and bake in the oven for 50–55 minutes (or 25 minutes for the mini loaf tins). Turn out and cool on a wire rack.

5   Mix together the icing sugar and lemon juice, if using and drizzle over the top.

fruit cookies

makes: 20 toddler portions (approx 20 cookies)

storage: keep in an airtight container for up to 3 days or freeze for up to 3 months

100g unsalted butter, softened, plus 2tbsp for the topping and extra for greasing

100g golden caster sugar, plus 2tbsp for the topping

1 large egg

175g plain flour, sifted

50g ground almonds

1tsp ground mixed spice

75g currants

Ella calls these squashed-fly cookies. They are sweet but not too messy to eat – something I am sure many parents consider when planning a celebration that involves toddlers! Once cooked, these can be frozen and just thawed when needed.

1   In a bowl, beat the butter and sugar together until pale and fluffy. Add the egg and beat well.

2   Add the flour, ground almonds, mixed spice and currants and mix to a firm dough. Cover and chill for 15–20 minutes.

3   Preheat the oven to 180°C/350°F/gas mark 4. Grease a baking tray. On a lightly floured surface, roll out the dough to 3–4mm thick. Use a 5cm biscuit cutter to cut out rounds and place on the tray.

4   Brush the biscuits with a little melted butter and sprinkle with sugar. Bake in the oven for 8–10 minutes, until lightly golden. Cool on a wire rack.

lemon drizzle cake

makes: 10 toddler portions

storage: keep in an airtight container for up to 4 days or freeze for up to 3 months

vitamin B₆

175g unsalted butter, softened

175g golden caster sugar

grated zest and juice of 1 unwaxed lemon

2 medium eggs, beaten

3–4tbsp full-fat milk

175g self-raising flour, sifted

2tbsp golden icing sugar, sifted

You could make an orange drizzle cake instead of this lemon cake – just use the zest of 2 unwaxed oranges in the cake mix and the juice of 1 orange for the topping.

1 Preheat the oven to 180°C/350°F/gas mark 4. Grease and line the bottom of a 900g loaf tin.

2 Beat the butter, sugar and lemon zest together in a bowl until light and fluffy. Gradually beat in the eggs and milk.

3 Fold the flour into the mixture. Spoon into the prepared tin. Bake in the oven for 45–55 minutes, until the cake is golden and firm to touch.

4 Mix together the lemon juice and icing sugar.

5 Poke a cocktail stick all over the hot cake and then pour over the lemon icing immediately.

6 Cool in the tin for 5 minutes, then turn out onto a wire rack.

piggies in blankets

makes: 25 toddler portions

storage: keep in the refrigerator for up to 2 days or freeze for up to 3 months

40g unsalted butter, plus extra for greasing

225g self-raising flour

pinch of salt

½tsp baking powder

50g sundried tomatoes, finely chopped

25g fresh parsley, chopped

75g Cheddar cheese, grated

150ml full-fat milk, plus extra for glazing

25 chipolata sausages, cooked and cooled

These little sausages wrapped in a herby scone mixture make a great alternative to sausage rolls.

1 Preheat the oven to 200°C/400°F/gas mark 6. Grease a baking sheet. Sift the flour, salt and baking powder into a bowl.

2 Rub in the butter with your fingertips (or in a food processor) until the mixture resembles breadcrumbs. Stir in the tomatoes, parsley and cheese. Make a well in the centre, then mix in enough milk to give a soft dough.

3 On a lightly floured surface, roll into a square, 6mm thick. Cut into 25 squares.

4 Wrap each chipolata in a square of dough, then use a little milk to stick down the edges. Put on the baking sheet and brush the tops with milk. Bake in the oven for 8–10 minutes, until risen and golden. Serve warm. If necessary, cut into smaller pieces before serving.

Now is the time to get your toddler involved in all aspects of food, not just mealtimes. Encourage his interest by taking him to stimulating places, such as farmers' markets, where he will be able to taste seasonal produce. Or involve him in the preparation of meals. Toddlers at this stage get bored quickly, particularly at mealtimes, so don't insist he eats everything; just serve smaller portions so that he has the satisfaction of finishing a meal and asking for more. And he will really pick up on your attitude to food: try to be relaxed and encourage him to eat well by giving him the wide variety of foods that you eat yourself. What you do now will set him up for the rest of his life.

3-4 years

what's happening to
your toddler

During this year you will notice that your toddler is becoming more self aware. If she is anything like my three-year-old she will be chatting for Britain, with a favourite word being "why" – in Ella's case, partly because she is naturally inquisitive, but also because she likes to keep me talking!

Your toddler will be more independent and sure of herself. She will like to play with siblings and other children, but she will also be content to play by herself. She will love to do "grown-up" things, such as choosing and paying for goods in a shop. Encourage this when you are out shopping for food and, if you get the chance, go to farmers' markets, where she may be able to taste as well as look at food.

Of course, her physical skills will have improved. She will enjoy hopping, skipping and running. She will also be more capable of carrying out everyday tasks – for example, she will probably be able to dress herself (albeit haphazardly), and feed herself quite easily, perhaps even using a big knife and fork. Mealtimes should become less challenging, especially as she becomes more reasonable and willing to accept substitutes – for example, if she asks for a banana but you only have an apple.

At this age, toddlers will have a fairly clear idea of what they do and don't enjoy and will be able to let you know this. They think more deeply than they have before but will get bored quickly, often at mealtimes: when they have lost interest, don't drag things out by insisting plates are cleared. If you offer varied and interesting meals, most inquisitive toddlers will take up the challenge. Try offering fun foods such as cherry tomatoes, little cheeses or small bread rolls rather than processed foods aimed at children.

Your toddler will also become far more aware of others, learning from them, but also acknowledging how they feel about things. At this stage, your attitude to food will really have an effect on her. Having a relaxed but healthy approach to eating is vital. You can also encourage her to eat well by simply giving her the same wide variety of foods that you eat yourself. What she eats in her formative years may have some impact on her health later in life.

By the age of three, you will notice your toddler becoming more interested in the food that she eats. The main concern at this stage can be what your toddler is eating while she is out of your care, for example at friends, grandparents or a nursery. You will also begin to notice some of the effects of peer pressure – my daughter Ella has become aware of the kinds of convenience foods available and looks for them when we go shopping, even though I don't keep them in the house.

If your toddler is eating less than usual, this may be because she has been eating foods such as crisps, that are too energy-dense, without enough other nutrients. You may also see other behavioural changes, particularly those induced by the over-consumption of sugar or additives. I am aware that Ella becomes "hyper" after children's parties, where she has eaten lots of high-sugar foods such as cakes, sweets and biscuits.

Of course, regular sugar consumption can also cause tooth decay. It can be more problematic and unrealistic to completely ban all sugary foods. Giving a few sugary foods every now and then is fine. If, like Ella, your toddler has a sweet tooth, give other sweet foods, such as fruit-based smoothies or milkshakes, chunks of fresh fruit, handfuls of dried fruits or low-sugar muesli bars (do not give nuts to toddlers under the age of three if there is a family history of food allergies).

At this stage, your toddler is likely to be active and full of energy. Playing outside is something that should be encouraged, not only because it is good for your child's well-being but also because it has important nutritional benefits. The main source of vitamin D for most toddlers is from the action of sunlight on their skin. Vitamin D, along with calcium, is needed to help make bones stronger. However, if you live in a more northerly country, or your toddler is kept covered for religious or medical reasons, or if she is on a restricted diet, such as vegan, you should speak to your family doctor or registered dietician about vitamin D supplements.

which nutrients
are key

your toddler's
routine

your toddler's feeds

Snacks will be more of a contentious issue, as your toddler becomes aware of the types of foods available – and junk food in particular. It is really important to give healthy snacks. Make sure that they are given at least two hours before the next meal, so that they do not spoil your toddler's appetite.

Continue with the previous two years' routine:
breakfast – around 7.30–8am
mid-morning snack – around 10am
lunch – around 12.30–1pm
mid-afternoon snack – around 3pm
supper – 5–5.30 pm
bed – 7–7.30 pm

your toddler's sleeps

It is unlikely, between three and four years old, that your toddler will need a sleep during the day. However, she will be a lot more active and inquisitive, and she can become overtired. Ella, my oldest, who is three and half years old, still has a quiet time during the day, usually after lunch, when she is happy to sit and look at books or watch a video by herself for at least half an hour. It is important for toddlers to feel relaxed about spending some quiet time on their own.

how important is variety?

From the age of one, your goal should be to gradually increase the variety of foods included in your toddler's diet, so that by the age of four she is eating as wide a variety of foods as possible. Although variety is best, inevitably there will be times when it seems she has eaten the same thing for two or three days in a row. Some parents worry that it will affect their toddler's nutritional intake, but many studies have shown that even if a toddler eats the same healthy meals for a few consecutive days, they will usually manage to consume the right kind of food for normal growth and development.

constipation

Almost all toddlers will suffer from constipation at some point. It is likely that your toddler is suffering if she finds it difficult to go the toilet, passing only hard and dry faeces infrequently. Stools should always be quite soft and not cause pain or discomfort. However, constipation is normally a short-term problem. Try to give her more fresh fruit, vegetables, wholemeal bread and other fibre-rich foods that toddlers like, such as low-sugar baked beans and high-fibre white bread. It is also very important to get her to drink lots of water, as this will help with bowel movement: sometimes constipation is just the result of insufficient fluid. If the problem persists for more than a week, seek advice from your family doctor or registered dietician.

toddler diarrhoea

Toddler diarrhoea is also relatively common. There are several possible causes, but the most likely is a change in diet. If your toddler has eaten more fruit, fruit juice, sugary drinks or dried fruit than usual, she is likely to suffer from diarrhoea. The most important thing to do is to make sure she drinks enough fluids to compensate for those lost, or she may become dehydrated surprisingly quickly. Diarrhoea may sometimes be accompanied by a fever, lack of appetite, vomiting and abdominal pain. If your child shows any of these any of these symptoms, consult your family doctor.

trouble
shooting

3-4 year meal planners

key to meal planners

portions: all servings are 1 portion
drink: preferably water, tap or bottled.
Alternatively very diluted fruit juice.
breakfast: 7.30-8am; **mid-am:** 10am;
lunch: 12.30-1pm; **mid-pm:** 3pm;
supper: 5-5.30pm; **bed:** 7-7.30pm

By the age of four, your child should be eating more or less the same variety of foods as the rest of the family, so try to vary her diet as much as possible in this year. This will have the added bonus of encouraging her interest in mealtimes – by the time they are three, toddlers can get bored easily, so meals with challenging textures and "naturally" toddler size foods, such as cherry tomatoes, individual homemade tarts or vegetable sticks, can appeal.

	breakfast	mid-am	lunch	mid-pm	supper	bed
menu 1	150ml milk, banana and chocolate pastry, drink	orange segments, drink	smoked mackerel paté, drink	drink	courgette cream cheese pasta, raspberry yogurt ice, drink	200ml milk
menu 2	150ml milk, dried fruit compote, drink	apple, drink	quick tomato chicken, drink	drink	home-made pizza, very quick apple crumble, drink	200ml milk
menu 3	150ml milk, fried bread and eggs, drink	drink	chickpea and bacon soup, drink	pear, drink	lamb burgers with lemony beans, grilled fruits, drink	200ml milk
menu 4	150ml milk, granola, drink	grapes, drink	warm bacon with beans, drink	drink	couscous with roasted ratatouille, drink	200ml milk
menu 5	150ml milk, James' boiled egg with soldiers, drink	banana, drink	tomato, mozzarella and basil on ciabatta, drink	drink	baked beans and cheese on toast, drink	200ml milk
menu 6	150ml milk, bacon eggy bread, drink	drink	roasted vegetables with pasta bake, drink	drink	lamb koftas, drink	200ml milk

	breakfast	mid-am	lunch	mid-pm	supper	bed
menu7	150ml milk, blueberry buttermilk pancake, drink	banana, drink	noodles with peanuts, drink	drink	lamb chop with French beans, choc chip steamed pudding, drink	200ml milk
menu 8	150ml milk, kedgeree, drink	drink	cottage cheese and olive bagel, drink	grapes, drink	tortellini with cauliflower and cheese, fruit with raspberry dipping sauce, drink	200ml milk
menu 9	150ml milk, grilled kipper, drink	cereal bar with melon, drink	courgettes with rosemary and pasta, drink	satsuma, drink	roast chicken with tomatoes and beans, drink	200ml milk
menu 10	150ml milk, croissant with apple, drink	pitta bread with cottage cheese, drink	vegetable korma, drink	satsuma, drink	broccoli, chickpeas bacon and red pepper, drink	200ml milk
menu 11	150ml milk, mango smoothie, toast, drink	drink	sardine and tomato toast, drink	piece of fresh fruit, drink	beef stew with mushrooms, drink	200ml milk
menu 12	150ml milk, muesli with fresh raspberries, drink	drink	Mediterranean bean stew, drink	satsuma, drink	potato wedges with fish fingers, Malteser and caramel ice-cream, drink	200ml milk
menu 13	150ml milk, crunchy yogurt, drink	drink	noodles with peanut sauce, drink	piece of fresh fruit, drink	lentil and root vegetable stew, drink	200ml milk
menu 14	150ml milk, James' boiled egg with soldiers, mango smoothie, drink	drink	roasted vegetable and pasta bake, drink	piece of fresh fruit, drink	garlic prawns in white sauce with pasta, drink	200ml milk

fresh breakfasts

blueberry buttermilk pancakes

3½ **makes:** 7 toddler portions (14 pancakes)

½ **storage:** best eaten fresh or keep in the refrigerator for up to 2 days

1 15g unsalted butter
1 medium egg
1 284ml buttermilk
2 drops vanilla extract
125g plain flour
1tsp bicarbonate of soda
100g dried pears, finely chopped
150g fresh blueberries
2tsp vegetable oil

vitamin B₁₂ – phosphorous

These are really popular with toddlers. If you can't get hold of blueberries, just add a little more pear. To really gild the lily, try serving them with a little golden or maple syrup.

1 Melt the butter in a small pan over a gentle heat.
2 In a mixing bowl, whisk together the egg, buttermilk, vanilla extract and melted butter.
3 Sift the flour and bicarbonate of soda into a separate bowl mix, then add the egg mixture and mix together. Don't worry if the batter is lumpy.
4 Stir in the dried pears and blueberries.
5 Heat 1tsp oil in a heavy-based frying pan. Spoon 1–2tbsp of batter for each pancake into the pan and cook for 2–3 minutes, then flip over and cook for a further 1–2 minutes until the pancakes are lightly browned. Keep warm in a low oven in-between sheets of greaseproof paper while you cook the rest, adding the second teaspoon of oil when you have cooked half the pancakes.

banana and chocolate pastries

2½ **makes:** 6 toddler portions (6 pastries)

½ **storage:** best eaten fresh or keep in an airtight container for up to 2 days

1 x 280g tube *pain au chocolat* dough (available from supermarkets)
2 large ripe bananas, sliced
handful of raspberries, fresh or frozen (defrosted)
apricot jam, to glaze

vitamin B₆ – folic acid

These are definitely designed to be a treat rather than the norm. Instead of bananas and raspberries, you could try finely chopped breakfast apricots – dried apricots soaked in juice, which have a wonderful texture and flavour.

1 Preheat the oven to 190°C/375°F/gas mark 5. Remove the dough and little bag of chocolate sticks from the tube, then cut along the dough's perforated lines.
2 Put 3 banana slices into the middle of each rectangle of pastry, top with 2–3 chocolate sticks and a few raspberries, and put onto a baking sheet.
3 Bake the pastries for 8–12 minutes, until risen and golden.
4 Warm some apricot jam in a small pan and brush it over the top of the cooked pastries. If necessary, cut into smaller pieces before serving

kedgeree

18

½

2

1½

vitamins A, B₁, B₂,
B₆, B₁₂ – folic acid
– phosphorous

makes: 4 toddler portions

storage: best eaten fresh

300ml full-fat milk

350g unsmoked haddock

3 medium eggs, soft to
hardboiled (see page 155),
roughly chopped

50g unsalted butter

150g long grain white or
brown rice, freshly cooked

2tbsp fresh parsley, chopped

freshly ground black pepper

You could make this with salmon instead of haddock. Originally an Indian dish, it would have been served slightly spiced. Try adding a little mild curry powder to the butter and cooking for a minute before adding the rest of the ingredients. The rice should be freshly cooked – it is important not to reheat rice.

1 Put the milk and 300ml water into a wide pan with the haddock and bring up to the boil. When it boils, turn the heat off and leave to stand for 15 minutes.
2 Lift the fish from the pan and flake onto a plate, carefully removing any bones and skin.
3 Roughly chop up the boiled eggs.
4 Heat the butter in a pan and add the cooked rice, flaked haddock, chopped boiled eggs and parsley. Stir gently until hot through, then season with freshly ground black pepper.

fried bread and eggs

6½

1

1

½

vitamins A, B₂, B₆,
B₁₂ – folic acid –
phosphorous

makes: 2 toddler portions

storage: best eaten fresh

2 slices sliced bread

25g unsalted butter

1tbsp olive oil

2 medium eggs

This is a neat way to serve fried eggs. You can experiment with different types of bread, but pre-sliced does seem to work best. This makes a great breakfast, with plenty of protein and carbohydrate.

1 Using a 7.5cm cutter, cut out a circle from the centre of each piece of bread. Reserve the circles.
2 Melt the butter and oil in a large frying pan. When it foams, add the bread and cut-out rounds and fry on one side until golden brown – approximately 2–3 minutes.
3 Turn the pieces over and carefully break an egg into the circular hole in each slice of bread. Spoon some of the hot fat over the yolk in order to help to cook it. Cook over a gentle heat until the eggs are completely cooked through – approximately 4 minutes.
4 Transfer to plates and put the fried bread lids onto the eggs. If necessary, cut into smaller pieces before serving.

granola

This is just a crunchier version of muesli – excellent served with fruit, full-fat natural yogurt or full-fat milk for breakfast. You can adapt the recipe according to the kind of nuts or dried fruits you have in the house. But remember, do no not give nuts or seeds to toddlers under the age of three if there is any family history of allergies.

makes: 11 toddler portions

storage: keep in an airtight container for up to 4 weeks

5½

2

2½

½

vitamins B₁, B₆, B₁₂ – phosphorous

unsalted butter, for greasing
350g porridge oats
50g wheatgerm
50g unsweetened shredded coconut
50g sesame seeds
75g sunflower seeds
75g hazelnuts, finely chopped
125ml sunflower oil
75ml runny honey
½tsp vanilla extract
175g dried fruit, chopped into small pieces

1 Preheat the oven to 150°C/300°F/gas mark 2. Grease a large baking tin.
2 In a large bowl, mix the oats, wheatgerm, coconut, sesame seeds, sunflower seeds and hazelnuts.
3 In a large saucepan, combine the oil, honey and vanilla. Heat gently until the honey has melted. Pour the honey mixture into the bowl containing the dry ingredients and mix thoroughly. Spread the mixture out in the tin. Bake in the oven for 35–45 minutes, stirring the mixture every 10 minutes.
4 Cool, then add the dried fruit.

dried fruit compote

You can use pretty much any kind of dried fruit. Serve this compote cold for breakfast with muesli (see page 104) or full-fat natural yogurt. Alternatively, serve it warm with custard on cold days.

makes: 11 toddler portions

storage: keep in the refrigerator for up to 3 days

copper

100g ready-to-eat prunes
100g dried apples
100g dried apricots
100g dried mango
50g dried pineapple
200ml apple juice
pinch of ground cinnamon (optional)
2 ripe pears, peeled, cored and chopped

1 Cut all the dried fruit into small pieces and put into a large saucepan.
2 Add the juice, 300ml water and cinnamon, if using, and bring to the boil. Simmer over a gentle heat for 15 minutes.
3 Add the fresh pear and simmer for another 5 minutes. Cool completely, then marinate for at least an hour before serving.

quick bites breakfasts

All of the recipes make one toddler portion unless otherwise stated.

vitamin B₆
~ folic acid

makes: 2 toddler portions
½ ripe large mango, peeled
and stone removed
1 ripe small banana, peeled and cut into
chunks
200ml orange juice
approx 50g berries, eg blueberries

mango smoothie

Look for tree-ripened mangoes, as they should be ripe and ready to eat with the best flavour. Often Asian supermarkets have really good fruit to choose from, so it's worth looking around for your fruit if you have the time. Cut the mango into small pieces and put into a bowl. Add the banana chunks, orange juice and berries and whiz with a hand-held blender (or in a food processor or blender) until smooth.

vitamins A, B₂, B₆,
B₁₂ ~ phosphorous

approx 200ml full-fat milk
2–3tsp drinking chocolate powder

hot chocolate

Use a good-quality hot chocolate powder that relies on chocolate for flavour rather than sugar. This is a great drink for cold wintry mornings. Make it following the packet's instructions.

3½

makes: 2 toddler portions
100g muesli (do not give nuts to
toddlers under the age of three if there
is a family history of allergies)
approx 50g raspberries, fresh or frozen
(defrosted)
100ml full-fat milk

muesli with fresh raspberries

If necessary, whiz the muesli, then put it into a bowl. Lightly mash the raspberries and scatter over the muesli. Pour over the milk. The mashed raspberries will make the milk go a lovely pink colour.

vitamins B₂, B₆, B₁₂
~ phosphorous

1 children's muesli bar (do not
give nuts to toddlers under the
age of three if there is a family
history of allergies)
½ ripe small pear, cored, peeled
and chopped
100g natural full-fat yogurt
approx 50ml full-fat milk

crunchy yogurt

Lots of unsweetened or low-sugar museli bars are available that make great breakfast stand-bys. This is an easy way of using them to make a more substantial breakfast. Crumble the museli bar into a bowl. Add the chopped pear and yogurt and mix together. If it's a little too thick, thin with some milk.

½ 1 1 6½

vitamins A, B₂, B₆,
B₁₂ – folic acid –
phosphorous

1 medium egg
small knob unsalted butter
1 slice wholemeal bread, toasted

boiled egg with soldiers

Children love boiled eggs, especially if you serve them in some fun egg cups. Bring a small pan of water to the boil. Add the egg and simmer for 6 minutes, or until completely cooked, then transfer to an egg cup. Immediately chop the top off. Butter the toast – you could also spread it with Marmite if you prefer – cut into fingers and serve with the egg.

10 C 1 ½ 2½

vitamins B₂, B₆, B₁₂
– phosphorous

makes: 2 toddler portions
approx 125g berries, fresh or
frozen (defrosted)
200ml full-fat milk
½ ripe medium banana (optional)

berry milkshake

Any combination of soft fruits will work well for this milkshake. You can add a little banana or a few crushed ice cubes if you would like a drink that is a bit thicker. Simply put the fruits and milk together into a jug and purée them with a hand-held blender (or in a food processor or blender) until you have a smooth milkshake.

1 1 6½

vitamins B₆, B₁₂, D
– folic acid –
phosphorous

1 kipper fillet
25g unsalted butter, melted
1 slice granary toast

grilled kipper

When choosing kippers, look for ones that are plump and oily and have a nice smokey smell. Covering the grill-pan with foil prevents the smell from recurring when you grill other foods. Preheat the grill. Line the pan with foil and brush it with half the melted butter. Put the kipper, skin side up, onto the foil and grill for 1 minute. Turn over the kipper, brush the flesh with the remaining melted butter and grill for a further 4–5 minutes, until cooked through. Double-check for bones, then serve with toast. If necessary, flake into small pieces to serve.

1 C ½ ½ 2

vitamin B₆ –
folic acid

1 croissant
1 eating apple, eg Cox's

croissant with apple

Preheat the oven to 180°C/350°F/gas mark 4. Place the croissant on a baking tray and warm through for 4–5 minutes. Peel, core and chop the apple and serve with the croissant. Or you could do as they do in France and let your toddler dunk the croissant into some hot chocolate (see page 154).

       1 1 1 6

vitamins B₂, B₆, D –
folic acid –
phosphorous

1 medium egg, whisked
2tbsp full-fat milk
freshly ground black pepper
1 slice bacon and parsley bread (see
page 54) or other savoury bread of
your choice
small knob unsalted butter

bacon eggy bread

In a shallow bowl, whisk together the egg and milk with a little freshly ground black pepper. Dip the bread into the egg mixture, making sure it is completely coated. Heat the butter in a frying pan, then cook the bread for 2–3 minutes on each side, until just starting to go golden. Cut into fingers.

fresh lunches

noodles with peanut sauce

2½

1½

1½

3

vitamins B₁, B₆ –
folic acid –
phosphorous

makes: 4 toddler portions

storage: best eaten fresh or keep in fridge for up to 2 days

1tbsp olive oil
1 garlic clove, peeled, crushed
4 spring onions, finely sliced
½ orange pepper, deseeded
  and thinly sliced
100g mange-tout, thinly sliced
100g creamed coconut
300ml no- or low-salt veg
  stock (see page 44)
4 heaped tbsp crunchy
  peanut butter
juice of ½ lime
250–300g medium egg
  thread noodles
1tbsp sesame seeds, toasted

Nuts are a great source of protein, especially for vegetarians and vegans. Serve with some stir-fried green vegetables or steamed vegetables. You do not need to serve vegetables with this dish as it is already packed with them. Do not give nuts or seeds to toddlers under the age of three if there is any family history of allergies.

1 Heat the oil in a heavy-based saucepan and fry the garlic and spring onions for a minute. Add the orange pepper and mange-tout and fry for a minute.
2 Roughly chop the creamed coconut. Add the stock and coconut. Stir in the peanut butter, then simmer for 2–3 minutes, stirring often.
3 Stir in the lime juice and season with freshly ground black pepper.
4 Meanwhile, boil a large pan of water and cook the noodles following the packet's instructions.
5 Drain, and add the noodles to the pan with the peanut sauce, then stir well. Sprinkle over the toasted sesame seeds. If necessary, cut into smaller pieces before serving immediately.

smoked mackerel paté

6½

½

½

vitamins B₂, B₆,
B₁₂, D –
phosphorous

makes: 6 toddler portions

storage: keep in the refrigerator for up to 2 days

2 garlic cloves, peeled and
  crushed
400g smoked mackerel
  fillets (approx 3 fillets), flaked
4tbsp full-fat natural yogurt
juice of ½ lemon
wholemeal toast, to serve
carrot, cucumber and celery
  sticks, to serve
tomato chunks , to serve

Oily fish, such as mackerel, is great brain food and it is fine to offer your toddler smoked fish occasionally, as long as it is not a regular occurrence.

1 Put the first four ingredients into a bowl and purée with a hand-held blender (or in a food processor or blender) until smooth.
2 Cover and chill for 10 minutes, or serve immediately with toast, carrot, cucumber and celery sticks, and tomato chunks.

baked eggs

makes: 2 toddler portions

storage: best eaten fresh

9½

1

1½

2

knob unsalted butter

½ small leek, washed and
finely sliced

2 medium eggs

freshly ground black pepper

1

50g Cheddar cheese, grated

vitamins A,, B₂, B₆,
B₁₂, D – folic acid
– phosphorous

These are quick and easy and toddlers love the fact that they are served in individual dishes. You could try using some gently fried mushrooms, or cooked flaked haddock or smoked salmon trimmings, instead of the leeks.

1 Preheat the oven to 180°C/350°F/gas mark 4. Melt the butter in a small pan and fry the leek over a gentle heat until soft – approximately 4–5 minutes.

2 Butter 2 ramekins or small oven-proof dishes. Divide the leek mixture between the dishes, then crack an egg over each and season with freshly ground black pepper. Sprinkle over the grated cheese.

3 Put the ramekins into a roasting tin and pour boiling water into the tin to come about halfway up the sides of the dishes. Bake for 15–18 minutes, or until the egg is completely cooked through.

Mediterranean bean stew

makes: 6 toddler portions

storage: keep in the
refrigerator for up to 3 days

6½

1½

1

1½

3

vitamins A, B₁, B₆ –
folic acid –
phosphorous

50g unsalted butter

3 medium leeks, washed and
finely sliced

1 medium red onion, sliced

2tbsp olive oil

1 red pepper, chopped

2 garlic cloves, crushed

200g courgettes, cut in chunks

400g tinned tomatoes

1tbsp tomato purée

400g tinned cooked butter
beans, drained and rinsed

300g tinned cooked canellini
beans, drained and rinsed

200ml good-quality no- or
low-salt veg stock (page 44)

handful fresh basil leaves,
torn, or parsley, chopped

3tbsp Parmesan or Cheddar
cheese, grated, to serve

brown or white bread

This is a hearty vegetarian dish that can be made in advance and kept in the refrigerator until needed. Serve with bread for a complete meal.

1 Heat the butter in a large casserole and fry the leeks and onion until soft and pale golden – approximately 5 minutes. Remove from the pan and reserve.

2 Heat the oil in the casserole and gently fry the red pepper for 4–5 minutes, until soft and golden. Add the garlic and fry for 1 more minute.

3 Add the courgettes, tomatoes and purée and cook for a few minutes. Add the beans and stock and return the leeks and onions to the pan. Stir well and bring to the boil. Simmer for 20 minutes.

4 Stir in the basil and parsley and cook for another 5 minutes. Season with freshly ground black pepper and serve in bowls with grated cheese over the top and bread to mop up the juices.

souffléd baked potatoes

8

1

1½

1

1

vitamins B₄, B₆, B₁₂,
– folic acid –
phosphorous

makes: 8 toddler portions

storage: best eaten fresh

4 baking potatoes, scrubbed

olive oil

4tbsp full-fat milk

25g unsalted butter

30g Cheddar cheese, grated

2 medium eggs, separated

freshly ground black pepper

2 rashers unsmoked streaky
  bacon, rind removed,
  grilled and chopped

1tbsp fresh parsley, chopped

These are a little more special than a plain jacket potato, and are a good way of encouraging your toddler to enjoy eggs.

1   Preheat the oven to 200°C/400°F/gas mark 6. Rub a little olive oil into the potatoes, then cook in the oven for 1 hour until the skins are crisp and the insides are soft.

2   Slice the potatoes in half and carefully scoop out the flesh into a bowl, reserving the skins.

3   Add the milk and butter to the flesh and mash the potatoes well. Add the cheese, egg yolks and some pepper, then mash again. Stir in the bacon and fresh parsley.

4   Whisk the egg whites in a grease-free bowl until stiff and then fold them into the potato mixture. Spoon this mixture back into the reserved potato skins and put onto a baking tray. Cook in the hot oven for 20 minutes, until risen and golden.

quick tomato chicken

18½

2

2½

2

vitamins B₁, B₆ –
folic acid –
phosphorous

makes: 3 toddler portions

storage: best eaten fresh or keep in the refrigerator for up to 2 days

2tbsp olive oil

10g unsalted butter

2 chicken breasts, skinned
  and cut into bite-size pieces

300ml passata (sieved
  tomato purée available
  from supermarkets)

large handful fresh basil
  leaves, torn

400g spaghetti or tagliatelli

4tbsp full-fat crème fraîche,
  cream cheese or Greek
  yogurt

freshly ground black pepper

Billy, who has been assisting me on this book, was served something similar to this for supper at a friend's house. She was so enthusiastic about it that I had a go – it is delicious.

1   Heat the oil and butter together in a frying pan, then fry the chicken pieces until golden. Add the passata and basil and simmer for 5–8 minutes, until the chicken is cooked through.

2   Meanwhile, boil a large pan of water and cook the spaghetti following the packet's instructions. Drain.

3   When the chicken is cooked, stir in the crème fraîche and season with pepper. Serve with the spaghetti. If necessary, cut into smaller pieces before serving.

quick bites lunches

All of the recipes make one toddler portion unless stated otherwise.

1½ **C** 2 1½ 1 6½

1 slice wholemeal bread
3 tinned sardines in oil, drained and
lightly mashed
1 juicy ripe tomato, finely chopped
lemon wedge (optional)

sardine and tomato toast

Tinned sardines are a great source of calcium and, like other oily fish, they are also high in essential fats and zinc. Preheat the grill, then grill the bread on one side. Turn over and top with the mashed sardines, then sprinkle over the tomato. Return to the grill and cook for 3–4 minutes until hot through. Your toddler may like to squeeze some lemon juice over the top. Cut into pieces.

½ **C** ½ ½ ½ 2½

2 small beetroots (approx 75g),
cooked
2tbsp full-fat cream cheese
3 fresh chives, finely snipped
1 slice granary toast

creamy beetroot dip

Chop the beetroots into tiny pieces and put into a bowl. Add the cream cheese and chives and mash really well with a fork. Serve the dip with toast fingers. If this goes down well with your toddler, try using it as a sauce for pasta – just add it when the pasta is still hot and stir thoroughly.

1½ **C** ½ ½ 3½

vitamins A, B₂, B₁₂ –
folic acid –
phosphorous

50g pasta
15g unsalted butter
1 sprig rosemary
1 courgette, grated
50g buffalo mozzarella or full-fat
cream cheese (optional)

courgettes and rosemary with pasta

Bring a medium pan of water to the boil. Add the pasta and cook following the packet's instructions, then drain. Heat the butter in the pan, add the rosemary sprig and grated courgette and cook gently for 4–5 minutes, stirring occasionally. Return the pasta to the pan and heat through briefly. Remove the rosemary before serving. You could add a little mozzarella or cream cheese to make the sauce creamier.

½ **C** 2 1 10

vitamins B₁, B₆ –
folic acid –
phosphorous

50g medium egg noodles
1tsp sesame oil
1 spring onion, finely chopped
1tbsp smooth peanut butter
25g peanuts, finely chopped
1tsp lime juice

noodles with peanuts

Bring a medium pan of water to the boil and cook the noodles following the packet's instructions, then drain. Heat the oil in a pan and gently fry the spring onion until soft. Add the peanut butter, peanuts and lime juice. Add the noodles and toss everything together to mix thoroughly. If necessary, chop into small pieces before serving. Do not serve nuts, seeds or their products to toddlers under the age of three if there is any family history of allergies.

vitamins B₁, B₆ – folic acid

6 medium new potatoes
2 rashers unsmoked streaky bacon, rind removed
1tbsp pesto (or less if this is too strong for your toddler)

new potatoes with bacon and pesto

Cut the potatoes into small pieces. Bring a small pan of water to the boil, add the potatoes and cook until just tender – approximately 10–12 minutes. Drain and return the potatoes to the pan. Preheat the grill. Grill the bacon until cooked and slightly golden around the edges. Chop the bacon into small pieces and add to the potatoes with the pesto, then mix everything together.

vitamins A, B₁, B₆, B₁₂ – folic acid – phosphorous

1 soft ciabatta roll
1tbsp olive oil
1 ripe tomato, thinly sliced
3 thin slices buffalo mozzarella (approx 50g)
2 fresh basil leaves

tomato, mozzarella and basil on ciabatta

Cut the ciabatta roll in half, and drizzle each half with the olive oil. Place the tomato slices onto one half, with the mozzarella and basil on top. Place the other half on top, squidge down and cut into small pieces.

50g full-fat cottage cheese
4 Kalamata olives, stoned and finely chopped
1 plain bagel, sliced in half
1 ripe small tomato, chopped into bite-size pieces

cottage cheese and olive bagel

Bagels are soft but chewy enough to make them interesting. If you are feeling adventurous, look for flavoured varieties, such as onion bagels. Mix the cream cheese and chopped olives together in a small bowl. Toast the bagel halves and top with the cheese mixture. Serve with the tomato pieces.

50g Camargue red rice
3 small broccoli florets
2 dried unsulphured apricots, finely chopped
30g feta cheese, crumbled

Camargue rice with apricots and feta

Cook the rice following the packet's instructions, then drain. Bring a pan of water to the boil and steam the broccoli for a few minutes until just tender, then cut into small pieces. While the rice is still warm, mix through the broccoli, apricots and feta. Serve immediately.

2 broccoli florets
2tsp olive oil
2 rashers unsmoked streaky bacon, rind removed and chopped
100g tinned cooked cannellini beans, drained and rinsed

warm bacon with beans

Steam the broccoli for a few minutes over a pan of boiling water until just tender. Cut into small pieces. Heat the olive oil in a saucepan, add the bacon and fry until lightly golden and cooked. Add the cannellini beans and broccoli, then heat through briefly.

lunches to freeze

easy mini quiches

makes: 12 toddler portions (12 mini quiches)

storage: freeze for up to 4 months

175g plain flour, sifted
pinch of salt
90g unsalted butter, chilled and diced, plus 15g for the filling
1 medium egg yolk plus 1tbsp cold water
1 medium leek, washed and finely chopped
1 large courgette, sliced
50g Gruyère cheese, grated
sprig of rosemary
2 large eggs, beaten
200ml full-fat milk

vitamins B₆, B₁₂

Toddlers love miniature foods, so these quiches are always popular.

1   Chill a muffin tin. Put the flour and a pinch of salt into a food processor and whiz to aerate. Add 90g butter and process until the mixture resembles fine breadcrumbs (or rub the butter in with your fingertips). Add the egg yolk and, if necessary, water, and process until the pastry just draws together.

2   Roll out the pastry to 2.5mm thick and cut out circles to line your muffin tin. Chill for 1 hour. Preheat the oven to 180°C/350°F/gas mark 4. Heat 15g butter in a frying pan and sweat the leek for 5 minutes. Add the courgette and brown a little, turning often. Spoon into the pastry cases and sprinkle with cheese.

3   Chop the rosemary leaves. Whisk the milk into the eggs with the herbs and season with black pepper. Pour over the filling. Cook for 18–20 minutes, or until the filling is golden and puffy. Cool, then freeze in a freezerproof container.

4   Thaw thoroughly. Warm in the oven at 180°C/350°F/gas mark 4 for 10 minutes. If necessary, cut into smaller pieces before serving.

carrot and coriander soup

makes: 6 toddler portions

storage: freeze for up to 3 months

800g large carrots, peeled
2 medium onions, peeled
25g unsalted butter
1tbsp olive oil
2 sticks celery, chopped
2 garlic cloves, chopped
2cm piece of fresh root ginger, finely chopped
1tbsp runny honey
2tbsp fresh coriander
2–3tbsp double cream

vitamins A, B₆

This is one of my girls' favourites, and I have not found a toddler yet who dislikes it. Making soups yourself has the advantage that you can leave the texture quite thick, making it easier for toddlers to spoon it up!

1   Thinly slice the carrots and finely chop the onions.

2   Melt the butter and oil together in a large heavy-based saucepan. Add the carrots, onions, celery, garlic and ginger. Cover and sweat over a gentle heat for 20 minutes. Add 750ml water, the honey and freshly ground black pepper, then simmer until the vegetables are soft – about 10 minutes.

3   Purée until smooth using a hand-held blender (or in a processor or blender).

4   Cool completely, then transfer to freezerproof containers or freezer bags and freeze.

5   Thaw thoroughly. Reheat gently until boiling with more water to make the desired consistency. Chop the coriander and add with the cream, if using.

chickpea and bacon soup

6

makes: approx 10 toddler portions

1

storage: freeze for up to 3 months

1

1tbsp olive oil

2

1 large onion, finely chopped

2 garlic cloves, finely chopped

2 sticks celery, finely chopped

2 medium carrots, finely chopped

vitamins A, B₁, B₆

130g pancetta or unsmoked streaky bacon

400g tin chopped tomatoes

2 x 400g tin cooked chickpeas, drained and rinsed

1 litre no- or low-salt veg stock (see page 44)

100g small pasta

You could always make a larger quantity of the sauce and keep to use with chicken pieces or pork chops. This is delicious served with mash, or rice and green vegetables.

1 Heat the oil in a heavy-based saucepan. Sauté the onion, garlic, celery and carrots until soft – approximately 5–10 minutes. Transfer to a plate.

2 Cut the pancetta or bacon into small cubes and add to the pan. Fry until golden and crisp – approximately 5 minutes.

3 Add the cooked vegetables, tomatoes, chickpeas and stock, season with freshly ground black pepper, and simmer for 10 minutes.

4 Put a third of the soup into a bowl and purée with a hand-held blender (or in a food processor or blender). Pour in the remaining soup, stir and cool completely. Pour into freezerproof containers or freezer bags and freeze.

5 Thaw thoroughly. Add the pasta and gently reheat in a saucepan until boiling and the pasta is cooked.

roasted veg and pasta bake

10½

makes: 4 toddler portions

storage: freeze for up to 3 months

1½

2

1 large red onion, peeled

1 large aubergine

2

1 large courgette

1 red and 1 orange pepper, seeded and sliced

6

2tbsp olive oil

2–3tbsp pesto

vitamins A, B₆, B₁₂ – folic acid – phosphorous

125ml double cream

50ml full-fat milk

freshly ground black pepper

250g pasta, cooked

75g Cheddar cheese, grated

handful of parsley, chopped

This protein-packed lunch is a great way to serve vegetables to toddlers.

1 Preheat the oven to 190°C /375°F/gas mark 5. Cut the onion into thin wedges and cut the aubergine and courgettes into 2cm chunks

2 Put all the vegetables into a roasting dish, drizzle with olive oil and roast in the oven for 40 minutes, until cooked and golden-edged.

3 Put the pesto, cream and milk into a saucepan, season with freshly ground black pepper, then heat gently for 2 minutes, stirring.

4 Mix the pasta and vegetables into the sauce. Spoon the mixture into 4 ovenproof and freezerproof dishes, sprinkle with cheese and parsley. Cool completely. Wrap in foil and freeze.

5 Thaw thoroughly. Preheat the oven to 190°C/375°F/gas mark 5. Cook for 15–20 minutes, until piping hot and golden. If necessary, cut into smaller pieces before serving.

shepherd's pie

Toddlers love this nutritious British classic.

16

2

4

½

3

vitamins A, B₁, B₂,
B₆, B₁₂ – folic acid –
phosphorous

makes: 6 toddler portions

storage: freeze for up to
4 months

2tbsp olive oil
550g lean lamb mince
1 medium leek
2 medium carrots
100g mushrooms
1 garlic clove, crushed
200g tinned cooked kidney
  beans, drained and rinsed
400g tinned tomatoes
2tbsp fresh herbs, chopped
300ml water
900g potatoes
3–4tbsp full-fat milk, plus a
  little extra
knob unsalted butter

1. Preheat the oven to 180°C/350°F/gas mark 4. Heat 1tbsp olive oil in a heavy-based casserole and brown the mince. Reserve on a plate.
2. Wash the leek and peel the carrots, then dice them. Wash and thinly slice the mushrooms. Heat the remaining oil and fry the leek and carrots until soft and pale golden. Add the mushrooms and garlic and fry for 5 minutes, stirring often.
3. Add the kidney beans, tomatoes and herbs, and stir well. Stir in the water and mince. Season with black pepper, then simmer gently for 35 minutes.
4. Meanwhile, peel and halve the potatoes and cook them in a pan of boiling water until tender. Drain and mash with the milk and butter.
5. Put the mince into a freezerproof pie dish, then top with the potato. Brush with a little milk. Cool completely. Wrap in foil and freeze.
6. Thaw thoroughly. Cook in a preheated oven at 180°C/350°F/gas mark 4 for 30–35 minutes, until the top is golden and crunchy.

vegetable korma

Do not give nuts or their products to toddlers under the age of three if there is a family history of food allergies.

4½

2

1½

1

3

vitamins B₁, B₆ –
folic acid –
phosphorous

makes: 6 toddler portions

storage: freeze for up to
4 months

2 medium onions
5 garlic cloves
8cm piece of ginger
2 medium parsnips
1 medium swede
2 small turnips
2 medium potatoes
50g unsalted butter
2tbsp sunflower oil
3tsp mild curry powder
200g creamed coconut
1.2 litres no- or low-salt veg
  stock (see page 44), boiling
4tbsp full-fat natural yogurt
fresh coriander leaves
50g roasted cashews
brown or white rice, to serve

1. Peel and finely chop the onion, garlic and ginger. Peel and dice the remaining vegetables. Heat the butter and oil in a heavy-based saucepan and sauté the onions for 5 minutes.
2. Add the garlic and ginger and cook for a few minutes, then add the curry powder and cook for a minute. Add the peeled and diced vegetables and cook for 10 minutes, stirring often.
3. Chop the coconut, put it into a bowl and dissolve in the boiling stock. Add to the vegetables, season with freshly ground black pepper, then simmer for 1 hour, stirring occasionally. Leave to cool, transfer to a freezer-proof container and freeze.
4. Thaw thoroughly, put into a saucepan and bring to the boil. Just before serving, stir in the yogurt and adjust the seasoning. Finely chop the coriander and cashew nuts, then sprinkle them over the korma. Serve with the cooked rice.

quick bites snacks

Some of the problems associated with children's eating habits are linked to snacking. Often parents give children snacks without realizing how high in sugar and fat they are. Such snacks spoil the childrens' appetites and provide empty calories, which give a short-lived burst of energy but have little nutritional value. Bite-size pieces of fruits and vegetables make the best snacks, with more substantial snacks given when a toddler needs a quick energy fix.

All of the recipes make one toddler portion unless otherwise stated.

vitamins A,
B₁, B₆, E
– folic acid –
phosphorus

dried mango with Brazil nuts

40g Brazil nuts
50g dried mango with
no added sugar

Just one Brazil nut can provide your toddler with all the mineral selenium she needs (selenium helps boost the immune system). There are many dried fruits to choose from – offer a variety to your toddler so that she benefits from the nutrients each one gives. Dried mango is a great source of beta-carotene and vitamin C. Chop the nuts and mango into bite-size pieces and mix. Do not give nuts to toddlers if there is any history of food allergies.

vitamins B₂, B₆,
B₁₂,
– folic acid –
phosphorous

home-made ice-cream with fresh fruits

1 scoop of home-made
ice-cream (see page 132)
handful fresh ripe berries,
eg raspberries, strawberries

Good-quality homemade ice-cream, made with cream, unrefined sugar, and fresh fruit, is delicious. In small quantities it's fine for your toddler – much better than many of the cheap children's ready-made ice-creams, which often contain hydrated fats, chemical additives, lots of sugar, and other baddies. Serve the ice-cream in a pretty plastic bowl or cup and scatter over the fruit. Often an attractive bowl and spoon are all that is needed to make this treat extra exciting.

vitamin B₁₂ –
folic acid

pitta bread with cottage cheese

½ pitta bread
1 tbsp full-fat cottage cheese
1 chive stalk, finely chopped
(optional)

Keep a packet of pittas in the freezer – you can slice and grill them almost as soon as you take them out. They are really handy for a quick snack or lunch. Grill the pitta bread half, with the cut side facing uppermost. When it is ready, mix the cottage cheese with the chopped chives and spread on to the pitta. Cut into small strips.

corn with butter

10g unsalted butter
½ fresh, or equivalent of frozen,
corn on the cob

As much as possible, make your toddler's snacks fresh fruits or vegetables. To make this corn on the cob, melt the butter in a small saucepan. Bring a large pan of salted water to the boil and boil or steam the corn on the cob until it is just tender. Drain and serve with melted butter drizzled over the top.

vitamin B₆ –
phosphorus

cereal bar with melon

1 large slice ripe Galia melon
1 cereal bar

Cut the skin away from the melon, then cut the fruit flesh into chunks. Chop the cereal bar into small pieces and mix with the melon in a small pot. (There are many good cereal bars on the market – try to look for ones that don't have too much added sugar and be aware that sugar can come in many guises including syrup, honey, and dextrose.)

vitamin B₆

popcorn

1 tbsp vegetable oil
100g dried corn kernels

Heat the oil in a saucepan until hot. Add the corn kernels in a single layer and put the lid on the pan. When the kernels begin to pop, reduce the heat and shake gently. When the popping stops, remove the pan from the heat. Allow to cool slightly. Serve 40g cooked popcorn per toddler and keep the rest in an airtight container. Only serve to toddlers who are very confident with chewing.

vitamin B₆ –
folic acid

frozen satsumas with raisins

1 seedless satsumas
2 tbsp raisins

We all know that oranges and satsumas are good sources of vitamin C, but many of us do not realize that they also provide a good supply of potassium and they even have a little folic acid. This may seem like an easy snack to suggest, but something as obvious as a handful of raisins and a satsuma can be forgotten. Peel the satsuma, scatter the segments in a freezerproof container, cover and freeze. Serve with a little pot of raisins. Frozen segments make a great thirst-quencher on a hot day.

ice lollies

makes: 3 toddler portions
100g natural full-fat yogurt
400ml fresh apple juice

During the summer, toddlers will inevitably ask for lollies. You can choose whether you keep these for a pudding or an occasional snack. They are a great way of cooling little ones down. Put the yogurt into a large jug and gradually whisk in the apple juice. Divide the mixture between ice cube trays, lolly pop containers, or small paper cups. Insert a lolly pop stick into the middle of each and freeze for 3-4 hours, or until firm.

fresh suppers

sticky salmon

makes: 4 toddler portions

storage: best eaten fresh or keep in the refrigerator for up to 2 days

9½

½

vitamins B$_6$, B$_{12}$ – phosphorous

4 salmon fillets (450g)
lemon or lime wedges

for the marinade:
5cm ginger, peeled, grated
2 garlic cloves, peeled, crushed
1tbsp light soy sauce
juice of ½ lemon
1tsp sesame oil
a little olive oil

A tasty marinade can help to entice the slightly less willing to get stuck into eating fish. Some rice or a few noodles and a steamed green vegetable would make the meal complete. Do not serve seeds or their oils to toddlers under the age of three if there is any family history of allergies.

1 Preheat the oven to 220°C/425°F/gas mark 7. Mix together the marinade ingredients and pour over the salmon in a non-metallic bowl. Cover and chill for 30–60 minutes.

2 Take the salmon out of the marinade and place on a roasting tray. Pour over the marinade and roast in the oven for approximately 10-12 minutes, or until the fish is cooked through. If necessary, cut into smaller pieces before serving with the citrus wedges.

lamb koftas

makes: 6 toddler portions (12 small koftas)

storage: keep uncooked in the refrigerator for up to 2 days or keep cooked in the refrigerator for up to 3 days

8

1

2

½

vitamins B$_6$, B$_{12}$ – phosphorous

250g lean lamb mince
2 onions, finely chopped
2 garlic cloves, peeled and
   roughly chopped
2tsp mixed spice
2 slices white bread, crumbed
2tbsp fresh parsley, chopped
1tbsp fresh mint, chopped
1 medium egg, beaten
2tbsp pine nuts, chopped
   and toasted
seasoned flour

I tend to serve these little lamb koftas with cherry tomatoes, strips of pitta bread and a dip of full-fat natural yogurt mixed with chopped fresh mint. Remember to soak the sticks in water before cooking, to prevent them from catching fire under the grill. Do not serve nuts to toddlers under the age of three if there is any famly history of allergies.

1 Put the first seven ingredients into a food processor and whiz together for a couple of minutes.

2 Transfer to a bowl, add the egg and chopped pine nuts, mix well and mould into 12 sausage shapes. Cover and refrigerate for 30 minutes.

3 Roll in seasoned flour. Stick a skewer into each (which is traditional) or leave as they are, then grill or shallow fry for 3–4 minutes on each side, until cooked through (8-10 minutes in total).

4 Mix together some yogurt and mint and serve with the lamb koftas, cherry tomatoes and pitta bread. If necessary, cut into smaller pieces before serving.

lamb chops in herb crust

4

½

1

½ C

vitamins B₆, B₁₂ –
phosphorous

makes: 4 toddler portions

storage: best eaten fresh or keep in the refrigerator for up to 24 hours and serve at room temperature

4 lamb chops, approx 1cm thick

50g white or brown fine breadcrumbs

small handful of fresh parsley, chopped

handful of cheese, eg fresh Parmesan, finely grated

2 medium eggs, beaten

olive oil, for frying

Many toddlers love the texture of a crunchy coating. Serve these chops with some freshly cooked green vegetables and potatoes or a few fingers of bread.

1 Put the chops in a plastic bag and flatten with a rolling pin. You may like to cut out the bone at this point (alternatively, cut the meat into small pieces once it is cooked).

2 Mix together the breadcrumbs and parsley in a bowl. Dip the chops into the grated cheese – pressing it into the meat, then into the beaten eggs and finally the breadcrumb mixture.

3 Heat the oil in a large heavy-based frying pan over a medium heat and brown the chops on one side – approximately 3–4 minutes. Do not move them earlier, as the coating will stick to the pan. Turn over and brown the other side for another 3-4 minutes, or until cooked through.

4 Rest on kitchen paper for 2 minutes. If necessary, cut into smaller pieces before serving.

courgette cream cheese pasta

8½

2

2

1

3 C

vitamins A, B₁, B₆ –
folic acid –
phosphorous

makes: 4 toddler portions

storage: best eaten fresh

300g tagliatelle

2tbsp olive oil

6 small courgettes, very thinly sliced lengthways

2 garlic cloves, peeled and finely chopped

2 sprigs of fresh rosemary, leaves only, chopped

200g full-fat cream cheese, roughly chopped

juice of ½ lemon

This also works really well with half cream cheese and half goat's cheese, which some toddlers will love and others will hate, it's just a case of experimenting to see what they like.

1 Bring a large pan of water to the boil, add the tagliatelle and cook until *al dente*.

2 Heat the oil in a large frying pan. Add the courgettes, garlic and rosemary and sauté until just soft, but not golden.

3 Add the cream cheese and cooked tagliatelle, and season well with freshly ground black pepper, then add lemon juice to taste. If necessary, cut into smaller pieces before serving.

Thai green chicken and peas

makes: 5 toddler portions

storage: keep in the refrigerator for up to 3 days

2tbsp groundnut or vegetable oil

500g chicken meat, cut into small pieces

1–2tbsp Thai green curry paste

400ml tinned coconut milk

200ml no- or low-salt veg stock (see page 44)

2 fresh lime leaves or juice of ½ lime

large handful of basil leaves, torn

15½

½

1

vitamin B₆ – phosphorous

You may like to add just 1tbsp of the Thai green curry paste the first time you make this for your toddler – although, if she's anything like my daughter Ella she will be quite happy with the heat from 2tbsp paste. Alternatively, if you want to make the curry quite hot for the rest of the family but not too spicy for your toddler, take a little of the juices out of the pan and dilute them with more coconut milk for her. You could bulk the dish out by adding chopped vegetables about 5 minutes before the end of the cooking. Do not serve nut products to toddlers under the age of three if there is a family history of allergies.

1 Heat 1tbsp oil in a heavy-based saucepan. Fry the chicken pieces, leave until it comes away from the pan easily – approximately 2–3 minutes. Turn over and cook until just golden – approximately 3–4 minutes more.

2 Stir in the Thai green curry paste and cook for a few more minutes. Add the coconut milk, vegetable stock and lime leaves or lime juice. Gently simmer for 10 minutes.

3 Add the basil and season. If necessary, cut into smaller pieces before serving.

herby roast chicken

makes: 8 toddler portions

storage: keep in the refrigerator for up to 2 days

2 seedless oranges, cut into wedges

6 sprigs fresh rosemary handful of fresh thyme sprigs

2 large knobs unsalted butter

1 chicken (approx 1.8kg) olive oil

700g new potatoes, scrubbed

peas or green beans, to serve

10

½

1

3

vitamins B₁, B₆ – folic acid – phosphorous

A roast chicken normally provides you with a few extra meals – when you can use up any leftover meat.

1 Preheat the oven to 180°C/350°F/gas mark 4. Push the orange wedges, half the herbs and a good knob of butter inside the chicken.

2 Stuff the remaining butter and herbs under the skin of the chicken breasts. Season the bird.

3 Heat the oil in a large roasting tin and add the chicken. Roast for 15 minutes per 450g plus an extra 15 minutes.

4 30 minutes before the end of cooking, add the potatoes to the roasting tin and continue to cook.

5 Remove the chicken and potatoes from oven when the chicken is thoroughly cooked. Place the chicken on a plate to rest for 5 minutes before carving, while keeping the potatoes warm. Serve slices of the chicken with the potatoes and green vegetables. If necessary, cut into smaller pieces before serving.

barbecue chicken

makes: 4 toddler portions (2 chicken pieces each)

storage: keep in the refrigerator for up to 2 days

11½

1

1

2

vitamins A, B₁, B₆ – phosphorous

8 chicken pieces, eg thighs, skinned

2 medium red onions, finely chopped

8tbsp tomato ketchup

2tbsp soft dark brown sugar

1tbsp grainy mustard

1tbsp Worcester sauce

1 garlic clove, peeled and crushed

3tbsp olive oil

600g sweet potatoes, peeled and chopped

This is a quick and easy dish, popular in both summer and winter – the chicken is just as good served cold – perfect for packed lunches or picnics.

1 Preheat the oven to 200°C/400°F/gas mark 6. Score each piece of chicken two or three times.

2 In a large bowl, mix all the other ingredients together, except the oil and sweet potatoes. Add the chicken and stir well to coat the chicken – you may prefer to use your hands to really work the marinade into it. Cover and leave for 30 minutes.

3 Heat 1tbsp olive oil in a roasting tin, carefully put the chicken in and roast it in the oven for 40–50 minutes, until the chicken is cooked through.

4 Meanwhile, put the sweet potatoes in a separate roasting dish, drizzle with the remaining oil and season with freshly ground black pepper. Cook alongside the chicken for 40–50 minutes. If necessary, cut into smaller pieces before serving.

butter beans with bacon

16½

2½

3

2½

½

vitamins B₁, B₂, B₆, B₁₂ – phosphorous

makes: 2 toddler portions

storage: best eaten fresh or keep in the refrigerator for up to 2 days

4 rashers unsmoked streaky bacon, rind removed

1tbsp olive oil

1 medium onion, finely chopped

400g tinned cooked butter beans, drained and rinsed

125ml no- or low-salt veg stock (see page 44)

75ml double cream

50g Cheddar cheese, grated

2 slices buttered brown toast, to serve

This is a comforting supper that we all enjoy eating. If you want to make enough for the whole family, just double the ingredients.

1 Chop the bacon into small pieces. Heat the oil in a frying pan and fry the bacon until it starts to go golden – approximately 3–4 minutes.

2 Add the onion and sweat until soft and translucent, then pour away most of the fat.

3 Add the beans and stock, then simmer gently until the liquid has reduced by half – approximately 5 minutes.

4 Stir in the cream, simmer for 2 minutes, then stir in the cheese. Serve with buttered toast.

lentils with sausages

makes: 2 toddler portions

storage: best eaten fresh or kept in refrigerator for 24 hours

4 pork sausages

50g pancetta, cubed

1 small onion, finely chopped

1 garlic clove, peeled and finely chopped

100g puy lentils, rinsed

handful of fresh parsley, chopped

17½

4

3½

½

½

vitamins B₁, B₂,B₆,B₁₂ – phosphorous

Lentils are relatively quick to cook and make a good change from potatoes or pasta. You may want to reduce this recipe to two sausages depending on your toddler's appetite.

1 Preheat the oven to 180°C/350°F/gas mark 4. Put the sausages in a roasting dish and bake for approximately 20 minutes, turning halfway through the cooking time, until golden and cooked through.

2 Meanwhile, fry the pancetta in a heavy-based saucepan until golden – for approximately 3-4 minutes – adding a little olive oil if the pancetta is very lean.

3 Add the chopped onion and garlic and cook for 3–4 minutes until soft.

4 Add the lentils and approximately 500ml boiling water – enough just to cover the lentils. Simmer for approximately 20 minutes, until the dish is cooked.

5 Slice the sausages and add to the lentils, season with freshly ground black pepper and parsley and mix everything together.

stir-fried pork with greens

13

1½

2½

1½

2

vitamins B₁, B₁₂,B₆ – phosphorous

makes: 3 toddler portions

storage: best eaten fresh or keep in the refrigerator for up to 2 days

250g boneless lean pork shoulder

1tsp sesame oil

1tbsp light soy sauce

1tsp cornflour

2tbsp olive oil

3 spring onions, finely sliced

200g spring greens, shredded

There are so many ways to make stir fries and so many combinations of meat, fish and vegetables that you can use. Most toddlers love the flavour of sesame oil and soy, so this could be a good way to encourage them to eat their greens. Do not serve seeds or their products to toddlers under the age of three if there is any family history of food allergies.

1 Cut the pork into 1cm cubes. Mix the sesame oil, soy sauce and cornflour in a bowl. Add the pork and roughly mix.

2 Heat a wok and add the oil, then the pork and stir-fry for a few minutes until the pork is brown around the edges.

3 Add the spring onions, spring greens and freshly ground black pepper. Stir-fry for 4–5 minutes, until the pork is cooked through and the greens have just started to wilt. If necessary, chop into smaller pieces before serving.

quick bites **suppers**

All of the recipes make one toddler portion unless stated otherwise.

vitamin A, B₁, B₆, B₁₂
– folic acid –
phosphorous

lamb chop with beans, carrots and potatoes

2 new potatoes, scrubbed
and quartered
8 thin French beans, topped
and tailed
1 small carrot, peeled and cut into chunks
1 medium lamb chop (approx 75g)
1tsp mint sauce (optional)

Bring a pan of water to the boil, add the potatoes and simmer gently for 10 minutes or until tender, then drain. Steam the other vegetables over boiling water for 5 minutes, or until tender. Meanwhile, grill the lamb chop under a hot grill for 3–4 minutes each side, until cooked through. Serve the lamb with the vegetables and, if you like, the mint sauce. If necessary, cut into smaller pieces before serving.

tortellini with cauliflower and cheese

75g tortellini
3 cauliflower florets, cut into
small pieces
50g Cheddar cheese, grated

Bring a pan of water to the boil and cook the tortellini following the packet's instructions, then drain. Steam the cauliflower over the boiling water until tender. Chop the cauliflower into small pieces and add to the drained tortellini. Stir in the grated cheese. If necessary, cut into smaller pieces before serving.

vitamin B₁, B₂, B₆ –
phosphorous

roasted chicken with beans and tomato

½ chicken breast, cut into
bite-size pieces
2tsp olive oil
freshly ground black pepper
100ml passata (sieved tomato
purée available in supermarkets)
75g tinned cooked cannellini
beans, rinsed and drained
pinch soft brown sugar
a few fresh coriander leaves,
chopped (optional)

Preheat the oven to 190°C/375°F/gas mark 5. Put the chicken pieces into an ovenproof dish with the olive oil, season with freshly ground black pepper and mix well. Roast in the moderately hot oven for 15 minutes until the pieces are pale golden. Stir in the passata, beans, sugar and coriander and return the chicken to the oven for 15 minutes, or until it is cooked and the sauce hot through. If necessary, cut into smaller pieces before serving.

vitamins B₁, B₆, B₁₂
– folic acid – phosphorous ½ 4

potato wedges with fish fingers

small baking potato,
scrubbed and cut into wedges
2tsp olive oil
freshly ground black pepper
2 x 100 per cent cod fish fingers

Preheat the oven to 180°C/350°F/gas mark 4. Put the potato wedges into a small roasting tray, pour over the oil and season with freshly ground black pepper. Mix well and roast for 30 minutes. Add the fish fingers to the roasting tray alongside the wedges and cook following packet's instructions. Serve the wedges with the fish fingers. If necessary, cut into smaller pieces before serving.

 6 C 1 ½ 4½

vitamins A, B₁, B₆
– folic acid –
phosphorous

broccoli, chickpeas, bacon and red pepper

2 rashers unsmoked
streaky bacon, rind removed
2 broccoli florets
80g tinned cooked chickpeas,
rinsed and drained
½ red pepper, seeded and finely chopped

Preheat the grill and cook the bacon until just golden and slightly crisp. Chop into small pieces and put into a bowl. Steam the broccoli over boiling water until just tender, then chop up and add to the bacon with the chickpeas and red pepper. Pour into a saucepan and heat through. If necessary, cut into smaller pieces before serving.

 2 1 ½ 6½

tamins A, B₁, B₆, B₁₂
– folic acid –
phosphorous

baked beans and cheese on toast

1 slice white or brown bread
small knob unsalted butter
40g full-fat Cheddar cheese, grated
100g low-sugar baked beans

Preheat the grill and toast the bread on one side. Spread the untoasted side with butter and cover with the cheese. Grill until bubbling and melted. Meanwhile, warm though the baked beans and serve with the cheese on toast. If necessary, cut into smaller pieces before serving.

 1 ½ 4

vitamins A, B₁, B₂, B₆, B₁₂
– folic acid –
phosphorous

garlic prawns in white sauce with pasta

75g penne
15g unsalted butter
1 small garlic clove, peeled
and crushed
6 raw medium prawns, shelled
½ quantity (300ml) storecupboard
white sauce (see page 45)

Bring a large pan of water to the boil and cook the pasta following the packet's instructions, then drain. Melt the butter in a small saucepan, add the garlic and prawns and cook until the prawns are just pink – this will only take a few minutes. Add the white sauce and heat through. Stir in the pasta and heat through for another couple of minutes. If necessary, cut into smaller pieces before serving.

 3 C ½ 1½ 2½

vitamins B₁, B₆
– folic acid

couscous with oven-roasted ratatouille

makes: 2 toddler portions
1 ripe small tomato,
chopped into small pieces
1 small courgette, thinly sliced
½ aubergine, chopped into small cubes
1tbsp olive oil
freshly ground black pepper
50ml passata (sieved tomato purée
available at supermarkets)
50g couscous

Preheat the oven to 190°C/375°F/gas mark 5. Put all the vegetables into a small roasting tray, pour over the oil and season with freshly ground black pepper. Mix well and roast for 25 minutes. Add the passata, stir well and roast for a further 5 minutes. Meanwhile, make the couscous following the packet's instructions. Serve with the roasted ratatouille. If necessary, cut into smaller pieces before serving.

suppers to freeze

beef stew with mushrooms

Kids love the sweetness of the prunes in this otherwise richly savoury dish.

14

2

4

½ C

vitamins A, B₆,
B₁₂
– phosphorous

makes: 8 toddler portions

storage: freeze for up to
4 months

4tbsp olive oil
2 medium onions, sliced
2 carrots, finely chopped
sprig of thyme
25g unsalted butter
250g field mushrooms, sliced
2tbsp fresh parsley, chopped
750g lean stewing steak
2tbsp flour, seasoned
500ml no- or low-salt veg
   stock (see page 44)
1tbsp tomato purée
2tsp English mustard
   (optional)
200g prunes, stoned

1   Preheat the oven to 150°C/300°F/gas mark 2. Heat 2tbsp oil in a frying pan and fry the onions and carrots until soft and pale golden, then tip them into a casserole with the thyme. Add the butter to the frying pan and sauté the mushrooms until they begin to give up their juices, then stir in the parsley and tip into the casserole.

2   Cut the stewing steak into chunks. Turn the chunks in the flour. Heat the remaining oil in the pan until hot and brown the meat. Add to the casserole.

3   Stir any remaining flour into the frying pan with 150ml water and leave to bubble for a few minutes. Add the stock, tomato purée and mustard (if using), then pour into the casserole. Chop the prunes and add, stir well, cover and cook in the oven for 1 hour 45 minutes – stir occasionally to prevent the meat overbrowning. You may also need to add more stock.

4   Cool completely, transfer to freezerproof containers and freeze. To serve, thaw thoroughly. Gently heat until boiling. If necessary, cut into smaller pieces.

home-made pizzas

These pizzas are so tasty that they might not make it to the freezer! Try adding herbs, cheese or tomato purée to the base.

6½

½

1

2

vitamin B₆
– phosphorous

makes: 4 toddler portions

storage: freeze for up to
3 months

200g self-raising flour
100ml full-fat milk or soya
   drink
50ml olive oil, plus extra
4tbsp tomato passata
2 chestnut mushrooms,
   finely sliced
1 slice cooked ham, finely
   chopped
50g Cheddar cheese, grated

1   Preheat the oven to 180°C/350°F/gas mark 4. Sift the flour into a bowl and make a well in the centre. Pour in the milk and olive oil and, using a fork, draw the mixture together into a dough. Tip the dough out onto a floured surface and divide into four. Roll each chunk into a ball and roll out to a flat circle (10cm diameter), then press it flatter still on a lightly greased baking sheet.

2   Spread 1tbsp tomato passata on each circle and top with the mushrooms and ham. Sprinkle over a little cheese and bake for 5–10 minutes. Cool completely. Wrap in foil and freeze.

3   Thaw thoroughly. Reheat in a preheated oven at 170°C/ 325°F/ gas mark 3 for 5 minutes or until hot through and bubbling on top.

chicken, olive and bean stew

18

1½

1½

½

1

vitamins B₁, B₆ –
phosphorous

makes: 8 toddler portions

storage: freeze for up to
4 months

850g chicken breast, skinned

large pinch of paprika

3tsp ground coriander

3tbsp olive oil

1 onion, peeled, finely chopped

300g tinned cooked black-
   eyed beans

400g tinned cooked
   cannellini beans

250ml low-salt veg stock

400g tinned cherry tomatoes

2tbsp tomato purée

125g Kalamata olives

handful of fresh coriander

1tbsp balsamic vinegar

This is a great way to get your toddler used to the more intense flavours of ingredients such as olives.

1 Cut the chicken into small chunks and put them in a bowl with the paprika and coriander. Season with freshly ground black pepper and mix well.

2 Heat 1½tbsp oil in a heavy-based casserole. Brown the chicken and reserve. Add the remaining oil to the pan and sweat the onion until soft.

3 Drain and rinse the beans. Add the chicken, beans, stock, tomatoes and tomato purée to the onion, then simmer for 20 minutes. Stone and chop the olives and chop the coriander.

4 Add the olives, vinegar and coriander and simmer for 5–10 minutes more, until the chicken is cooked. Cool completely, transfer to freezerproof containers and freeze.

5 Thaw thoroughly. Heat gently in a saucepan until boiling.

6 Serve with couscous, rice or mashed potato. If necessary, cut into smaller pieces before serving.

lentil and root vegetable stew

5½

1½

1

½

3

vitamin A, B₁, B₆, –
folic acid –
phosphorous

makes: 8 toddler portions

storage: freeze for up to
4 months

2tbsp olive oil

25g unsalted butter

1 red onion, finely chopped

2 medium leeks, finely sliced

2 garlic cloves, crushed

2 large parsnips, peeled

2 large carrots, peeled

2 sweet potatoes, peeled

100g split red lentils

1 bay leaf

1 sprig rosemary

850ml no- or low-salt veg
   stock (see page 44)

410g tinned cooked butter
   beans, drained and rinsed

2 courgettes, sliced

handful of fresh parsley

This is a great dish to serve to your toddler on a cold winter's night.

1 Heat the oil and butter together in a heavy-based saucepan. Gently fry the onion, leeks and garlic until soft, but not browned – approximately 5 minutes.

2 Cut the parsnips, carrots and sweet potatoes into bite-size chunks, then add to the pan to lightly brown.

3 Stir in the lentils, bay leaf, rosemary and stock. Cover and gently simmer for 45 minutes.

4 Add the butter beans and courgettes, then simmer for 15 minutes more, until just tender.

5 Chop the parsley and add to the stew. Season with freshly ground black pepper. Leave to cool completely. Transfer to a freezerproof container and freeze.

5 Thaw completely. Heat through thoroughly until boiling. If necessary, chop into smaller pieces before serving.

lamb burgers with lemony beans

9½
1½
2½

vitamins B₁, B₁₂
– folic acid –
phosphorous

makes: 7 toddler portions
(approx 14 burgers)

storage: freeze for up to
3 months

4tbsp olive oil plus 3tbsp for
   the beans
3 garlic cloves, finely chopped
800g lean lamb mince
1tbsp runny honey
1tbsp lemon juice
2tsp ground cumin
2tsp ground coriander
4tbsp fresh mint, chopped
4tbsp pine nuts, toasted
600g tinned cooked
   cannellini beans, drained
juice of ½–1 lemon
2tbsp fresh parsley, chopped
2tbsp fresh mint, chopped

I sometimes toss chopped baby spinach leaves and watercress in with the beans. Do not give nuts to toddlers under the age of three if there is a family history of allergies. Never refreeze raw meat that has already been frozen.

1 To make the burgers, heat 2tbsp olive oil in a frying pan and sauté the garlic for a few minutes until soft. Transfer to large bowl.
2 Add the mince, honey, lemon juice, spices and mint and mix together. Flour your hands and shape the mixture into 14 balls. Cover and chill for 15 minutes.
3 Layer in a freezerproof container between greaseproof paper and freeze.
4 Thaw thoroughly. Heat a griddle or frying pan until really hot, add 2tbsp olive oil and fry the burgers over a medium heat, until golden and cooked through – approximately 6–8 minutes on each side, turning occasionally. Alternatively, grill them. If necessary, cut into smaller pieces before serving.
5 Meanwhile, roughly chop the pine nuts. Blanch the cannellini beans in boiling water, drain. Mix with the olive oil, lemon juice, herbs and pine nuts.
6 Serve each toddler two burgers with a spoonful of the beans.

crispy vegetable bake

16½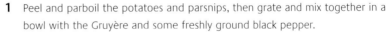
2½
3
6
4

vitamins B₁, B₂,
B₆, B₁₂
– folic acid –
phosphorous

makes: 4 toddler portions

storage: freeze for up to four
months

200g potatoes
200g parsnips
100g Gruyère cheese, grated
50g unsalted butter
2 leeks, washed and sliced
2 carrots, peeled and
   chopped
30g plain flour
565ml full-fat milk
100g Cheddar cheese, grated
2tbsp parsley, chopped
200g green beans, cooked
   and chopped
200g frozen peas or
   sweetcorn, or a mixture

This highly nutritious dish is always popular with my daughter Ella.

1 Peel and parboil the potatoes and parsnips, then grate and mix together in a bowl with the Gruyère and some freshly ground black pepper.
2 Melt 25g butter in a pan and fry the leeks and carrots until soft and pale gold. Reserve.
3 Melt the remaining butter in the pan, stir in the flour and cook for 1 minute. Gradually add the milk, whisking constantly. Return to the heat and bring to the boil, stirring constantly until thick and smooth.
4 Stir in the Cheddar until melted. Add the parsley, leeks, carrots, beans and peas or sweetcorn. Tip into an ovenproof and freezerproof dish. Sprinkle the potato mixture on top. Cool completely. Wrap in foil or clingfilm and freeze.
5 Thaw thoroughly. Bake in a preheated oven at 180°C/350°F/gas mark 4 for 20–30 minutes, until golden.

fresh & frozen puddings

choc chip steamed pudding

3½

2

½

½

vitamins B₆, B₁₂

makes: 8 toddler portions

storage: best eaten fresh or keep in the refrigerator for up to 3 days

100g unsalted butter
100g light soft brown sugar
2 large eggs, beaten
1tsp vanilla extract
170g plain flour
30g cocoa
2 heaped tsp baking powder
50g good-quality milk chocolate, finely chopped

for the sauce:
470g jar Morello cherries in juice
2tbsp soft brown sugar

If you do not fancy making the cherry sauce, serve with full-fat natural yogurt or vanilla ice-cream or custard instead. Do invest in a 900ml plastic pudding basin with lid: they are so easy to use. This pudding reheats well – just steam.

1 Butter a 900ml pudding basin. In a bowl, cream the butter and sugar together until pale and fluffy. Gradually beat in the eggs and vanilla extract until completely mixed in.

2 Sift the flour, cocoa and baking powder onto the egg mixture. Fold in. Stir in the chocolate and just enough cold water to make a loose dropping consistency.

3 Pour into the pudding basin. Cover with greaseproof paper or foil, with a fold in the centre to create space for the pudding to rise. Steam over boiling water for 1½ hours. Top up with boiling water as necessary. Turn out onto a warmed plate.

4 Meanwhile, to make the sauce, strain the cherry juice into a saucepan. Add the sugar and bring slowly to the boil. Simmer for 2 minutes.

5 Add three-quarters of the cherries and simmer for 2 minutes. Whiz with a hand-held blender or mash until smooth. Mix with the whole cherries and serve with pudding. If necessary, cut into smaller pieces before serving.

raspberry smush

2½

½

½

½

4½ C

makes: 8 toddler portions

storage: freeze for up to 3 months

550g frozen raspberries
100g golden caster sugar
250g Greek yogurt

If it is the season for raspberries, have a go at "pick your own" – they are much cheaper than their shop-bought counterparts and you could try to get your child to help. The first time my daughter Ella saw strawberries growing she thought someone had dropped them on the floor!

1 Put the frozen raspberries, sugar and yogurt together in a food processor. Quickly whiz to make a quick and slightly chunky dessert.

2 Serve straight away – it will be semi-frozen.

banana and vanilla risotto

makes: 4 toddler portions

4½

storage: best eaten fresh or keep in the refrigerator for up to 2 days (do not reheat rice)

½

½

750ml full-fat milk

1½

25g light soft brown sugar

3–4 drops vanilla extract

1

50g unsalted butter

125g Arborio rice

2 ripe large bananas, chopped

vitamins A, B₂, B₆, B₁₂ – phosphorous

freshly grated nutmeg

This is a great source of carbohydrate, perfect for feeding the little ones before they go to bed, helping to ensure a good night's sleep – for you as well as them!

1 Put the milk, soft brown sugar and vanilla extract into a small saucepan and heat to simmering point.

2 Melt the butter in a heavy-based saucepan, add the Arborio rice and stir to coat the grains.

3 Add one of the chopped bananas and a ladleful of the hot milk and stir continuously, until all the milk is absorbed. Add another ladleful, and continue until the rice is *al dente*, with a creamy sauce.

4 Stir in the other chopped banana and sprinkle with nutmeg.

Eve's pudding

5½

makes: 6 toddler portions

storage: best eaten fresh or keep in the refrigerator for up to 24 hours

1

½

450g cooking apples

1

75g light soft brown sugar

zest of 1 unwaxed lemon

1

150g unsalted butter, plus extra for greasing

150g golden caster sugar

2 medium eggs, beaten

vitamins A, B₆, B₁₂

300g self-raising flour, sifted

4tbsp full-fat milk

For a variation on this recipe, replace 25g of the flour with 25g ground almonds. Or add a pinch of ground cinnamon to the sponge mixture. You could also make this pudding with other soft fruits – fresh apricots or plums work particularly well – just make sure they are really ripe. Do not give nuts to toddlers under the age of three if there is any family history of allergies.

1 Preheat the oven to 180°C/350°F/gas mark 4, then butter a 900ml ovenproof dish.

2 Peel, core and finely slice the apples into the dish, sprinkle over the soft brown sugar and lemon zest. Mix well.

3 Cream the butter and caster sugar together in a bowl until pale and fluffy. Add the beaten eggs and beat well.

4 Fold in the flour and then stir in the milk.

5 Spoon this sponge mixture over the apples. Use a palette knife to smooth lightly over the top. Bake in the oven for 40–45 minutes, until the sponge is risen and golden.

pear and blueberry crisp

1½

1

makes: 4 toddler portions

storage: best eaten fresh or
store in fridge for 2-3 days

½

700g ripe pears
5tbsp light soft brown sugar
½ 100g blueberries
50g plain flour
1½ pinch of ground cinnamon
pinch of freshly grated
nutmeg
50g unsalted butter

vitamin B₆

I have also made this with blackberries and raspberries instead of the blueberries. This is delicious served warm with custard or cold with yogurt.

1 Preheat the oven to 200°C/400°F/gas mark 6. Peel the pears, core and cut them into chunks. Put into a saucepan with 1tbsp sugar, a little water and the blueberries.

2 Cook over a low heat for 3–4 minutes, until the berry juice just begins to run. Tip into a small ovenproof dish or 2–3 ramekins.

3 Sift the remaining sugar, plus the flour, cinnamon and nutmeg into a bowl. Rub in the butter with your fingertips (or in a food processor) until the mixture resembles fine breadcrumbs. Sprinkle over the fruit. Bake in the oven for 30 minutes, until golden.

grilled fruits

½
4C

makes: 4 toddler portions

storage: best eaten fresh or keep for up to 2 days in the refrigerator

½ vanilla pod
4tsp golden caster sugar
4 ripe peaches (or plums, nectarines, peeled pears, figs, etc), halved and stoned
4tbsp Greek yogurt, to serve

A delicious pudding for summer months, when fruit is plentiful. Use anything you like really – it also works well with bananas. If you don't have a grill you can just as easily bake them in a hot oven.

1 Split the vanilla pod lengthways and scrape out the seeds into a small bowl. Add the sugar and mix well.

2 Put the fruit, cut side up, into a ovenproof dish and sprinkle over the sugar. Grill for 5–8 minutes, until softened and the tops are golden and bubbling.

3 Cool slightly before serving, ideally with a dollop of Greek yogurt. If necessary, cut into smaller pieces before serving.

quick bites **puddings**

I tend not to put a lot of emphasis on puddings, so the quicker they are to make the better.

All of the recipes make one toddler portion unless stated otherwise.

quick jam tarts with fruit

makes: 12 toddler portions
375g ready-made sweet shortcrust pastry
12–16 raspberries, fresh or frozen (defrosted)
12–16tsp low-sugar good quality jam (avoid those containing surbitol)

Preheat the oven to 150°C/300°F/gas mark 2. Roll out the pastry to 2.5mm thick and cut out circles a little larger than the jam tart tins. Put in the tins, then place a raspberry in the middle of each pastry circle and top each with a teaspoon of jam or stewed compote. Cook for 18 minutes, until the pastry is golden. Leave to cool in the tins for a couple of minutes before lifting out. Cool on a wire rack.

fast strawberry ice-cream

makes: 3 toddler portions
200g frozen strawberries
60ml natural Greek yogurt
60ml crème fraîche
1–2tbsp golden icing sugar

Take the berries out of freezer 10 minutes before you want to eat the pudding. Put the berries into a food processor (or blender), add the natural Greek yogurt, crème fraîche and icing sugar, and whiz until smooth. Serve the ice-cream immediately.

lemon yogurt

3–4tbsp natural full-fat yogurt
1–2tsp lemon curd

I rarely buy little pots of yogurt. I tend to add fruits and jams to natural yogurt to avoid giving the girls unnecessary flavourings, colours or too much sugar. Put the yogurt into a bowl, add the lemon curd and mix together.

vitamin B$_K$ – folic acid

fruit with a raspberry dipping sauce

approx 100g raspberries, fresh or frozen (defrosted)
1 small slice ripe melon, eg Canteloupe or Galia
3 ripe large strawberries, hulled and halved

Put the raspberries into a bowl and mash with a fork until smooth. Spoon into a little serving dish. Peel the melon and cut the flesh into chunks. Put the melon and strawberries onto a little plate and serve with the crushed raspberries for dipping.

vitamins B₂, B₆ –
phosphorous

very quick apple crumble

2 eating apples, eg Cox's
pinch ground cinnamon
2tbsp apple juice
3tbsp crunchy granola (see page
153; do not give nuts to toddlers
under the age of three if there is
any family history of food allergies)

If you don't have any home-made granola, buy a small bag of granola, preferably without too much added sugar. Preheat the oven to 180°C/350°F/gas mark 4. Peel, core and cut the apples into small pieces. Put the fruit into a saucepan with the cinnamon and apple juice and cook for 10 minutes, or until soft, then spoon into 2 ramekins. Top with the granola and bake for 10–15 minutes, until golden. Leave to cool slightly before serving.

folic acid –
phosphorous

pineapple and pear dipped in chocolate

50g good-quality plain
or milk chocolate
1 thick slice ripe
pineapple
1 ripe small pear

This is a quick pudding, which I find especially handy when fussy toddlers come to tea – they tend to find room for a piece of fresh fruit dipped in chocolate. Break the chocolate into pieces and place in a bowl over a pan of gently simmering water until melted. Cut the slice of pineapple into small chunks. Core, peel and thickly slice the pear. Dip the fruit pieces into the melted chocolate and then rest on a cooling rack or piece of greaseproof paper, and leave in a cool place to dry for 20 minutes, or until the chocolate has set.

vitamins B₂, B₆,
B₁₂ – phosphorous

stewed fruits with custard

makes: 2 toddler portions
2 ripe pears
1 eating apple eg Cox's
50ml apple juice
1tbsp custard powder
1tbsp golden caster sugar
300ml full-fat milk

Peel the pears and apple, core and cut into chunks. Put the fruit into a saucepan with the apple juice. Simmer, covered, for 10–15 minutes, until the fruit is soft. Put the custard powder and sugar into a bowl and mix to a paste with 2tbsp of the milk. Bring the remaining milk to the boil, gradually pour into the custard mix, whisking constantly, then return the custard to the pan and cook for a few minutes, until it is smooth and thick. Serve the fruit with the custard.

Vit B6 –

fruit kebabs

makes: 3 toddler portions
1 ripe kiwi fruit
1 seedless orange
1 ripe small banana
2tsp runny honey
6 wooden sticks, soaked in water

Line a grill-pan with foil. Preheat the grill to medium. Peel the kiwi fruit and cut the flesh into 1cm chunks. Peel and segment the orange. Cut the ripe banana into chunks. Skewer the fruit onto each wet, wooden stick, alternating the type of fruit as you go. Drizzle the honey onto the fruit and grill, turning occasionally, for 3–5 minutes, until the fruit is just starting to caramelize. Leave to cool slightly before serving before removing the fruit from the sticks, then serve.

celebration **food**

vanilla strawberry cakes

 6½

 1

 1

 1½

 2C

vitamins A, B₁₂

makes: 10 toddler portions
(10 cakes)

storage: keep for up to 3 days
in an airtight container

125g unsalted butter, softened

125g golden caster sugar

2 drops vanilla extract

2 large eggs

125g self-raising flour, sifted

1–2tbsp full-fat milk

150g white chocolate, chopped

5 ripe strawberries, hulled
and halved, or 10 whole
raspberries

These fairy cakes are for the nostalgically–minded. You are doing better than me if you can wait until they have cooled down before you tuck in.

1 Preheat the oven to 180°C/350°F/gas mark 4. Line a muffin tin with some paper cases.

2 In a bowl, beat the butter, sugar and vanilla extract together until pale and fluffy. Beat in 1 egg and then 1tbsp flour. Beat in the other egg, then gradually fold in the remaining flour.

3 Fill the paper cases with spoonfuls of the mixture and bake in the oven for 15 minutes. Cool on a wire rack.

4 Melt the chocolate in a bowl over a pan of gently simmering water and put a blob on top of each cake. Top each with half a strawberry and leave to set.

Malteser and caramel ice-cream

 4½

 ½

 ½

1

vitamins A, B₂, B₁₂

makes: 6 toddler portions

storage: freeze for up to
3 months

75g golden caster sugar

4 egg yolks, separated

600ml full-fat milk

2 drops vanilla extract

450ml whipping cream

2 x 37g bags of Maltesers,
crushed

2 x 50g Caramel bars,
roughly chopped

This special occasion ice-cream is quite soft and can be eaten 5 minutes after taking it out of the freezer.

1 Put the sugar and egg yolks in a bowl and beat until light and fluffy.

2 Put the milk and vanilla extract into a saucepan and bring to simmering point.

3 Pour the hot milk over the eggs and mix well. Pour back into the pan and gently heat, stirring constantly, until the custard is thick. Leave to cool.

4 Whisk the cream to soft peaks, then fold into the cooled custard. Pour into a freezerproof container and freeze for 1 hour, or until the ice-cream has just started to freeze and is slightly thick. Mix in the maltesers and caramel bars and freeze for another 5 minutes.

lemon sandwich cookies

½

makes: 10 toddler portions

storage: keep in an airtight container for up to a week

1 **C**

125g self-raising flour

zest of 1 unwaxed lemon

60g golden caster sugar

75g unsalted butter, chilled and diced, plus extra

1tbsp full-fat milk

golden icing sugar, for dusting

for the icing

1tbsp lemon juice

125g golden caster sugar

75g unsalted butter, softened

Sandwich the cookies together with the cream just before serving to prevent the crisp cookies from going soft.

1 Preheat the oven to 350°F/180°C /gas mark 4. Sift the flour into a bowl. Add the lemon zest and sugar.

2 Rub in the butter with your fingertips (or in a food processor) until the mixture looks like breadcrumbs. Add the milk and mix until the dough comes together in a ball. Knead briefly on a floured surface until smooth, then refrigerate for 5 minutes.

3 Roll out on a floured surface to 3mm thick and cut into 5cm rounds and place on a greased baking sheet.

4 Bake for 6–8 minutes, until pale golden. Cool on the baking sheet, then lift gently onto a wire rack.

5 In a small bowl, mix the icing ingredients together well and chill for 5 minutes. Sandwich the biscuits together and dust with icing sugar. If necessary, cut into smaller pieces before serving.

triple chocolate cookies

1½

makes 15 toddler portions

storage keep in an airtight container for up to 4 days or freeze for 4 months

100g unsalted butter, softened

100g light muscovado sugar

few drops vanilla extract

1 medium egg, beaten

2tbsp golden syrup

150g self-raising flour

2tbsp cocoa

100g mixture of milk, orange and white chocolate

You could use any chocolate chunks for these cookies, but the combination of white and orange chocolate is sublime.

1 Preheat the oven to 180°C/350°F/gas mark 5. In a bowl, cream the butter until very soft. Add the sugar and vanilla extract and beat well for a minute or 2, until pale and fluffy.

2 Gradually beat in the egg and stir in the golden syrup. Sift in the flour and cocoa and gently mix until incorporated.

3 Cut the chocolate into big chunks and gently but thoroughly stir it in.

4 Shape the mixture into 15 walnut-size balls, flatten the tops slightly, then place on a non-stick baking tray or tray lined with baking paper. Bake for 7 minutes – the mixture will continue to set as it cools.

5 Remove from the tray when the cookies are firm and cool on a wire rack.

chocolate-dipped flapjacks

makes: 16 toddler portions

storage: keep in an airtight container for up to 4 days or freeze for up to 4 months

75g unsalted butter, plus extra for greasing
75g golden caster sugar
2tbsp golden syrup
175g rolled oats
75g good-quality milk chocolate

Dipped in a little chocolate, these flapjacks are extra special.

1 Preheat the oven to 180°C/350°F/gas mark 4. Butter a 20cm tin. Melt the butter, sugar and syrup in a large pan over a gentle heat. Stir well, then thoroughly mix in the oats.
2 Tip into the tin and level off. Bake for 15 minutes, until pale golden.
3 Cool slightly in the tin and mark into 8 fingers, then mark each finger diagonally so that you have 16 triangular flapjacks. Cool completely.
4 Melt the chocolate in a bowl over a pan of simmering water. Dip one end of each flapjack finger into the melted chocolate and leave to cool on a wire rack. If necessary, cut into smaller pieces before serving.

pancetta-wrapped fruit

makes: approx 10 toddler portions

storage: best eaten fresh or keep in the refrigerator for up to 2 days

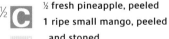
vitamin B6

½ fresh pineapple, peeled
1 ripe small mango, peeled and stoned
10–15 thin slices pancetta or unsmoked streaky bacon, rind removed
handful of ready-to-eat dried unsulphured apricots

for the sauce
4tbsp crunchy peanut butter
½ small onion, finely chopped
1 garlic clove, peeled, crushed
1tsp fresh ginger, peeled and finely chopped
2tsp soft brown sugar
½tsp mild chilli powder
40g creamed coconut, roughly chopped
150ml boiling water

These are a little different for a toddlers' party, but a good way of encouraging them to eat something savoury. Do not give nuts to toddlers under the age of three if there is any family history of allergies.

1 Preheat the oven to 190°C/375°F/gas mark 5. Cut the pineapple and mango into small chunks.
2 Cut the pancetta or bacon in half and wrap each piece around a chunk of fresh or dried fruit. Secure with a cocktail stick.
3 Put the pancetta-wrapped fruits on a baking tray and bake in the oven until the pancetta is just crisp and the fruit is starting to caramelize – approximately 15–20 minutes.
4 To make the peanut sauce, combine all the ingredients in a small pan and bring to the boil. It will spit violently but stir frequently for 10 minutes to prevent it from catching.
5 If necessary, remove the cocktail sticks and cut up the fruit before serving with the sauce as a dip.

Index

additives, artificial 28, 30-1, 33, 145
allergies 11-12, 23, 26, 33
almonds (ground) 89
anaemia 13, 26, 49
antioxidants 28
apple
  and blackberry crumble 132
  bread and butter pudding 135
  and hazelnut bread 116
  , pea and banana smoothie 58
  pie 87
  purée with raisin toast 71
  chicken, apple and nut
    salad 113
  with croissant 155
  Eve's pudding 182
  in fruit salad 107
  grated, with honey and
    bread 71
  grated, with raisin toast 107
  sausage and apple pastry 72
  scone and 119
  stewed apple and
    blackberries 59
  very quick apple crumble 185
apricot
  bagel with cream cheese and
    apricot 59
  banana and apricot tea
    bread 140
  with rice and feta 161
  lamb with spice and apricot 83
  scones 104

asthma 11, 28
aubergine
  with chicken and tomato
    sauce 79
  moussaka-stuffed 80
avocado 16, 19-20
  and cream cheese dip 64
  hummus and avocado dip 112
  mashed, with corn thins 70
  with new potatoes 125
  with pasta and tuna 64

babies, bottle-fed 24
bacon 19
  with broccoli, chickpeas and
    red pepper 175
  with butter beans 172
  and cheese on toast 58
  with chicken and rice 65
  chickpea and bacon soup 164
  couscous with French beans
    and bacon 113
  and egg scramble 57
  eggy bread 155
  grilled bacon with wholemeal
    bun 106
  with haddock and spinach 122
  with herby potato cakes 110
  macaroni bacon and
    cheese 117
  with new potatoes and
    pesto 161

new potatoes wrapped in
  bacon 79
and parsley bread 54
pea and bacon soup 114
warm bacon with beans 161
bagel
  with cottage cheese and
    olive 161
  with cream cheese and
    apricot 59
baked beans 13, 25, 29, 30, 32
  and cheese on toast 175
banana 17, 19, 96
  apple, pear and banana
    smoothie 58
  and apricot tea bread 140
  and chocolate pastries 150
  and date cake 90
  and honey sandwich 112
  ice 89
  and mango smoothie 54
  milk 118
  pasta 136
  and peach smoothie 119
  scones 87
  and toffee ice-cream 132
  and vanilla risotto 182
  with yogurt 89, 106
barbecue chicken 172
bean sprouts 25
beans 12-4, 25, 29, 30, 32, 41-2
  chicken, olive and bean
    stew 178
  couscous with French beans
    and bacon 113
  with lamb chop, carrots and
    potatoes 174
  lemony, with lamb burgers 179
  Mediterranean bean stew 158
  quick sausage and beans 82
  with roasted chicken and
    tomato 174
  with warm bacon 161
beef, hamburgers with cheese 130
beetroot, creamy dip 160
behavioural problems 28, 30, 145
berry
  compote with yogurt 88
  fast berry ice-cream 184
  milkshake 155
betacarotene, see vitamins, A
biscuits 32-3, 49, 118
  cheese and sesame 93
  fruit cookies 140
  lemon sandwich cookies 188
  triple chocolate cookies 188
blackberries
  and apple crumble 132
  and stewed apple 59
blood 14, 19
blueberries
  and buttermilk pancakes 150
  in muesli 118
  pear and blueberry crisp 183
bones, nutrients for 14, 20, 97
bran 13, 25, 97
bread 17, 19, 21, 25, 43
  apple and hazelnut bread 116
  with apple and honey 71
  bacon eggy bread 155

breadsticks and dips 70
and butter pudding 135
ciabatta 161
doorstep with mushrooms 107
egg mayonnaise fingers 113
fried bread and eggs 152
fried bread with mushrooms 59
garlic-stuffed 127
wholemeal 13, 14,25, 97
wholemeal bun, bacon 106
breakfasts 10
  1-2 years 54-9
  2-3 years 102-7
  3-4 years 150-5
  cereals 13, 17, 19, 20, 25, 31-2
breast milk 18, 21, 22, 24
breastfeeding, weaning 24
broccoli
  with chicken and penne 127
  with chickpeas, bacon and
    red pepper 175
  with lemon fish 76
  with bacon and beans 161
burgers 87
  hamburgers with cheese 130
  lamb burgers with beans 179
butter beans 12, 32
  with bacon 172
  with tuna, tomato and
    lettuce 79
butter, unsalted 16, 18, 20
buttermilk, and blueberry
  pancake 150

Caffeine 13, 25, 31
cakes 32-3
  banana and date cake 90
  chocolate-dipped flapjacks 189
  lemon drizzle cake 141
  malt loaf with pear 118
  oatcakes with cheese 119
  pink meringues 138
  raspberry muffins 56
  vanilla strawberry cakes 186
  white chocolate krispies 92
calcium 14, 20, 22, 97, 145
  vegan/vegetarian 14, 25, 145
carbohydrates 10, 17
carrot
  and coriander soup 162
  grated, with pasta 112
  with lamb chop, beans and
    potatoes 174
  and parsnip mash with pork
    chop 126
  with pasta and chicken 124
  , squash and orange soup 66
cauliflower, with tortellini and
  cheese 174
celebration food
  1-2 years 90-3
  2-3 years 138-41
  3-4 years 186-9
cereal bars, with melon 167
cereals 12-4, 17, 19, 20-1, 25
  breakfast (fortified) 13, 17, 19,
    20, 25, 31-2
  Ready Brek with prunes 58
  to avoid 31-2
  yogurt and cereal sundae 105

charts, how to use 6-7
cheese
  and bacon on toast 58
  in bacon and parsley bread 54
  and baked beans on toast 175
  Cheddar, with scrambled
    egg 59
  sauce 60
  and sesame biscuits 93
  mash with pork shops 124
  pasta bake 83
  cottage cheese 78, 119, 161
  cream cheese 42, 59, 64, 71,
    74, 93, 170
  crumbly 14
  dips 64
  feta 161
  frittata 77
  full-fat 18, 19, 20, 42, 97
  and ham croissant 102
  with hamburgers 130
  and macaroni bacon 117
  and marmite straws 90
  oatcakes with cheese 119
  with pasta and sweetcorn 64
  tomato, mozzarella and basil
    on ciabatta 161
  with tortelloni and
    cauliflower 174
chicken 10
  , apple and nut salad 113
  with aubergine and tomato
    sauce 79
  with bacon and rice 65
  baked, with rice 76
  barbecued 172
  stuffed with mushrooms 78
  crispy baked 123
  with herbs and cheese 74
  with herby mushrooms 122
  herby roast 171
  and leek pie 131
  low-salt chicken stock 43
  minty with vegetables 65
  nuggets 31
  and olive and bean stew 178
  with parsley and garlic
    butter 126
  with pasta and carrots 124
  with penne and broccoli 127
  pesto chicken 60
  quick tomato chicken 159
  roasted, with beans and
    tomato 174
  sticky chicken with mango 108
  stir-fried marinated 120
  Thai green and peas 171
  tomato and chicken pasta 77
chickpeas 12, 17, 21
  with broccoli, bacon and red
    pepper 175
  and bacon soup 164
chocolate 13, 31, 32
  and banana pastries 150
  chip steamed pudding 180
  -dipped flapjacks 189
  hot chocolate 154
  Malteser and caramel
    ice-cream 186
  pineapple and pear in 185

saucy chocolate pudding 135
triple chocolate cookies 188
white chocolate krispies 92
ciabatta, with tomato,
  mozzarella and basil 161
coconut
  creamed 42
  milkshake 107
  sweetcorn and coconut
    chowder 117
  oil 16
coeliac disease 26
coffee 31
coleslaw, with jacket potato 78
compotes
  berry compote with yogurt 88
  dried fruit (3-4 years) 153
  dried fruit with yogurt (1-2
    years) 71
  stewed fruit compote 45
  warm fruit compote 89
constipation 147
cooking, help from toddlers 96
corn thins, with avocado 70
courgette
  and cream cheese pasta 170
  with pasta and rosemary 160
couscous 42
  with beans and bacon 113
  with grated vegetables 127
  with roasted ratatouille 175
  salad with tuna 62
cream 22
crisps 33, 49, 118, 145
croissants
  with apple 155
  ham and cheese 102
crumble
  apple and blackberry 132
  green vegetable 131
  nectarine 137
  very quick apple 185
custard 86
  baked (egg) 84
  plums and 137
  with stewed fruits 185

dates, banana and date cake 90
dental problems 17, 30
desserts see puddings
diabetes 26, 30
diarrhoea 26, 147
diets
  bowel movements and 147
  high-fibre 10, 25, 97
  low-fat 10, 16
  special 26-7
dips
  cottage cheese 119
  cream cheese 64
  creamy beetroot 160
  hummus and avocado 112
  raspberry dipping sauce 184
  various, with breadsticks 70

E-numbers 11, 28
eating out 38
eczema 28
eggs 10, 12-14, 18-21, 25, 42
  bacon and egg scramble 57

bacon eggy bread 155
baked 158
in baked custard 84
boiled egg with soldiers 155
in cheese frittata 77
egg mayonnaise fingers 113
eggy raisin bread 57
fried, with fried bread 152
in ham omelette 58
in kedgeree 152
in pink meringues 138
poached, with muffin 105
poached, with fried parsley
    potatoes 126
poached, with soldiers 106
with potato salad, olives and
    tomato 126
scrambled 54
scrambled, with Cheddar 59
in soufflé baked potatoes 159
energy 10, 49, 96, 97
B vitamins and 19
carbohydrates and 17
sugars and 17, 30
for vegetarian toddlers 25
epilepsy 31
European Union (EU), food
    additive laws 28
Eve's pudding 182

fats 10, 16, 22, 31, 97, 118
fibre 10, 13, 17, 25
fish 12, 19, 21
baked, in tomato sauce 116
frozen fillets 43
grilled white fish with pesto 78
in kedgeree 152
oily 13-4, 18, 20, 155, 156, 160
quick lemon with broccoli 76
tinned 41
fishcakes 80
fish fingers 31
Jane's fish finger pie 111
with potato wedges 175
flapjacks, chocolate-dipped 189
flavourings, artificial 28, 33
folic acid 19
food
    additives 28, 30-1, 33, 145
    allergies see allergies
    "children's foods" 29
    convenience foods 31, 145
    to avoid 30-3, 97
    fortified 13-4, 18-20, 25
    freshness 28
    genetically modified (GM) 27
    intolerances 11
    organic 23, 27
    preparation and cooking 36
    processed 10-1, 28-9, 31, 33,
        49, 118
    purity 27-9
formula milk 22-4
freezers, useful foods 43
fromage frais 33
fruit
    citrus 13, 19, 25
    dried 13-4, 19, 25, 41, 71, 96,
        145, 153
    for the freezer 43

fresh 145, 166
frozen yogurt with fruit 88
fruit jelly with fresh fruits 88
fruit salads 84, 102, 107
grilled 183
juices 10, 13
kebabs 185
little fruit puddings 134
nutrient sources 15, 18, 20-1
pancetta-wrapped 189
with raspberry sauce 184
raspberry muffins 56
stewed apple 59
stewed fruit compote 45
stewed fruit with custard 185
warm fruit compote 89

garlic butter, with chicken 126
genetically modified foods 27
gnocchi
    with leeks and cheese sauce 60
    with tomato sauce 112
granola 31, 153
    in yogurt cereal sundae 105
grapes
    filled with cream cheese 71
    in fruit salad 84, 107
growth problems 26
guacamole, with ham 64

haddock
    with bacon and spinach 122
    in kedgeree 152
    smoked haddock soup 128
ham
    and cheese croissant 102
    with guacamole 64
    and mushroom sauce 79
    omelette 58
    and pineapple pizza 65
    with pineapple 71
    in pinwheel sandwiches 93
herbs
    carrot and coriander soup 162
    chicken withcheese 74
    chicken with mushrooms 122
    courgettes and rosemary
        pasta 160
    fried parsley potatoes 126
    herb scones 69
    herby potato cakes 110
    herby roast chicken 171
    lamb chops in herb crust 170
    parsley and garlic butter 126
    sausage and fennel pasta 111
    tomato, mozzarella and basil
        on ciabatta 161
honey 25, 30
    and banana sandwich 112
    with apple and bread 71
    with rice and soy 125
    in warm fruit salad 107
    with yogurt and raisins 136
hummus and avocado dip 112
hyperactivity 11, 28, 30, 145

ice-creams and sorbets 33
    banana ice 89
    banana, toffee ice-cream 132
    fast berry ice-cream 184

home-made ice-cream with
    fresh fruits 166
ice lollies 167
Malteser, caramel ice-cream 186
orange and passion-fruit
    sorbet 137
raspberry yogurt ice 180
immune system 19, 22
iron 13, 49
    absorption 13, 25, 31
    vegan, vegetarian diets 13, 25

jellies
    bicycle pump 138
    fruit jelly with fresh fruits 88

kebabs
    fruit kebabs 185
    lamb kebabs with mango 68
kedgeree 152
kipper, grilled 155
kitchen 35, 36, 96
kiwi fruit
    in an egg cup 118
    salad with pear and melon 107
koftas, lamb 168
korma, vegetable 165

labelling 28-9, 30-1, 33
lamb
    chop with beans, carrots and
        potatoes 174
    chops in herb crust 170
    grilled, with minty mash 79
    kebabs, with mango 68
    koftas 168
    burgers with lemony beans 179
    with a minty sauce 63
    in shepherd's pie 165
    with spices and apricots 83
    stew variants 114, 130
leek
    chicken and leek pie 131
    with gnocchi and cheese 60
lentils 12, 14
    and root vegetable stew 178
    with sausages 173
liver 18, 19
lunches 10
    1-2 years 60-9
    2-3 years 108-17
    3-4 years 156-65

macaroni bacon and cheese 117
mackerel, smoked paté 156
magnesium, tea and 31
mangoes 20
    and banana smoothie 54
    dried, with Brazil nuts 166
    with lamb kebabs 68
    smoothie 154
    with sticky chicken 108
    and strawberries with oats 59
margarine, fortified 18, 20, 25
marinades
    marinated chicken 120
    sticky salmon 168
marmite
    and cheese straws 90
    toast with chunky salad 113

mayonnaise, egg mayonnaise
    fingers 113
meal planners
    1-2 years 52-3
    2-3 years 100-1
    3-4 years 148-9
    how to build 7
mealtimes 35, 36-9
    participation in family meals
        37, 97, 144-5
    problems 99
    refusing to eat 51, 99
meat 12, 16, 20, 97
    liver 18, 19
    processed 31
    red meat 13, 14, 19, 21
    see also meats by name
meatballs, in tomato sauce 128
melon
    with cereal bar 167
    in fruit salads 84, 102, 107
meringues, pink 138
milk 12, 22-4, 25, 97
    allergies 11, 23
    banana milk 118
    calcium and 14, 22
    milk 10-1, 16, 18, 2-3
    follow-on milk 22
    full-fat 16, 18-23, 97
    goat's 23
    organic 23
    sheep's 23
milkshakes 145
    with berries 155
    coconut 107
mineral supplements 23
miso 25
mood swings 31, 49
moussaka-stuffed aubergine 80
muesli 12, 31-2, 104
    with blueberries 118
    with raspberries 156
muesli bars 145
    in crunchy yogurt 156
muffins,
    with poached egg 105
    quick muffin pizzas 110
    raspberry muffins 56
mushroom
    with beef stew 176
    chicken with herby 122
    on a doorstep 107
    with fried bread 59
    with garlic-stuffed bread 127
    and ham sauce 79
    rich mushroom stew 68
    stuffed, in chicken breast 78

nectarine crumble 137
nervous system 19
noodles 25, 41
    with peanut sauce 156
    with peanuts 160
nut butters 12, 25, 30
    with rice cakes 71
nutrients required per day
    chart 6-7
nutrition 9-21
    vegetarian and vegan
        toddlers 12-14, 19, 24, 25

nuts 12, 13, 14, 16, 17, 19-21,
    25, 33, 41, 96, 97
    allergies 11, 12, 33
    apple and hazelnut bread 116
    Brazils and dried mango 166
    , chicken and apple salad 113

oatcakes with cheese 119
oats 12, 25
    toasted, with strawberries and
        mango 59
obesity 26
oils 16, 20, 97
olive oil 16, 20
olives
    in chicken and bean stew 178
    cottage cheese and olive
        bagel 161
    with lamb stew 114
    with potato salad, tomato
        and egg 126
onion, and potato tortilla 108
orange
    and passion-fruit sorbet 137
    , squash and carrot soup 66
osteoporosis 14

pancakes
    blueberry and buttermilk 150
    corn 72
pancetta-wrapped fruit 189
parsley 25
    bacon and parsley bread 54
parsnips, and carrot mash with
    pork chop 126
passion-fruit
    and orange sorbet 137
    and pineapple smoothie 106
    quick trifle 136
pasta 10, 12, 17, 25, 41
    with avocado and tuna 64
    banana pasta 136
    with carrots and chicken 124
    with cheese and sweetcorn 64
    cheesy pasta bake 83
    courgette cream cheese 170
    courgette and rosemary 160
    with grated carrot 112
    lasagne 69
    macaroni bacon and cheese 117
    with mushroom and ham 79
    penne with chicken and
        broccoli 127
    with prawns in sauce 175
    with tomato chicken 159
    and roast veg bake 164
    sausage and fennel 111
    spaghetti with peas 65
    tomato and chicken 77
    tortelloni with cauliflower and
        cheese 174
pasta sauces, ready-made 30
pastries
    banana and chocolate 150
    filo parcels 89
    ham and cheese croissant 102
    jam tarts 92
    marmite cheese straws 90
    quick jam tarts with fruit 184
    sausage and apple pastry 72

paté
  smoked mackerel 156
  with toast 119
pawpaw, dried, peach and 137
peaches
  with dried pawpaw 137
  and banana smoothie 119
peanut butter 30, 42
  with warm pitta bread 70
peanuts 19, 33
  noodles with peanut sauce 156
  with noodles 160
pear
  , apple, banana smoothie 58
  and blueberry crisp 183
  malt loaf with butter and 118
  and pineapple dipped in
    chocolate 185
  with rice pudding 86
  salad, kiwi and melon 107
  and sesame yogurt 88
peas 14
  and bacon soup 114
  buttered with spaghetti 65
  with Thai green chicken 171
peppers, red, with with broccoli,
  chickpeas and bacon 175
pesto 42
  baked potatoes with tuna 63
  chicken 60
  with grilled white fish 78
  with new potatoes, bacon 161
phosphorus 21
pies
  apple 87
  creamy chicken and leek 131
  Jane's fish finger 111
  shepherd's 165
pineapple
  in fruit salad 107
  and ham pizza 65
  with ham 71
  and passion-fruit smoothie 106
  and pear in chocolate 185
pitta bread
  with cottage cheese 78, 166
  warm, with peanut butter 70
pizza 32, 176
  pineapple and ham 65
  quick muffin pizzas 110
plaice, with a tomato sauce 75
plums, and custard 137
popcorn 167
pork
  chop with parsnip and carrot
    mash 126
  chops with cheesy mash 124
  stir-fried, with greens 173
porridge 10, 17, 56
potatoes 17, 19, 21, 25
  cheesy mash with pork 124
  chips 30, 32
  fried parsley potatoes with
    poached egg 126
  herby potato cakes with
    bacon 110
  jacket potato and coleslaw 78
  with lamb chop, beans and
    carrots 174
  minty mash with lamb 79

new potatoes, avocado 125
new potatoes with bacon and
  pesto 161
new potatoes wrapped in
  bacon 79
and onion tortilla 108
pesto-baked with tuna 63
salad with olives, tomato and
  egg 126
in shepherd's pie 165
souffléd baked 159
wedges 32
wedges with fish fingers 175
prawns, garlic prawns in white
  sauce with pasta 175
preservatives 28, 33
protein 12, 49
  meal planning 10
  sources 12, 22
  vegan and vegetarian 12, 25
prunes
  with Ready Brek 58
  with rice pudding 136
puddings
  1-2 years 84-9
  2-3 years 132-7
  3-4 years 180-5
pulses 10, 12, 14, 17, 21, 25, 41-2
pumpkin seeds 21
pumpkin stew 82
purées, apple 71

quiches, easy mini quiches 162

raisins
  with frozen satsumas 167
  with yogurt and honey 136
raspberries
  dipping sauce 184
  fresh, with muesli 154
  muffins 56
  yogurt ice 180
  in yogurt and cereal sundae 105
restaurant menus 38
rhubarb
  and berries 137
  crisp 86
riboflavin see vitamins, B2
rice 10, 12, 25, 41
  almond rice 89
  anything goes rice 74
  with apricots and feta 161
  baby rice 17
  with baked chicken 76
  baked with squash 75
  banana and vanilla risotto 182
  brown rice 17, 97
  with chicken and bacon 65
  with honey and soy 125
  pudding with pears 86
  pudding with prunes 136
  with Thai-spiced veg 120
  with tuna and sweetcorn 113
rice cakes, with nut butter 71
routines 50, 98, 146

salads
  calcium source 14
  chicken, apple and nut 113
  couscous salad with tuna 62

marmite toast with salad 113
potato salad with olives,
  tomato and egg 126
salmon
  with steamed vegetables 127
  sticky salmon 168
salt 28, 30
sandwiches
  banana and honey 112
  pinwheel 93
sardine and tomato toast 160
satsumas
  frozen, with raisins 167
sauces
  cheese 60
  chocolate 135
  minty with chicken 65
  minty with lamb 63
  mushroom and ham 79
  peanut 156
  ready-made pasta sauces 30
  tomato 44
  white 45, 175
  yogurt 102
sausages 31
  and apple pastry 72
  and fennel pasta 111
  piggies in blankets 141
  with lentils 173
  quick sausage and beans 82
  sausage stew 127
  toad in the hole 123
scones
  with apple 119
  apricot 104
  banana 87
  herb 69
seeds 12, 16, 20, 21, 25
self-feeding 96
sesame seeds 12, 14
  cheese sesame biscuits 93
  sesame snap, with yogurt and
    pears 88
shopping 35, 36, 144
sleep 50, 98, 146
smoothies 31, 145
  apple, pear and banana 58
  mango 154
  mango and banana 54
  peach and banana 119
  pineapple and passion-fruit 106
snacks
  B vitamins and 19
  crunchy vitamin C 15
  eating problems and 166
  healthy 33, 146
  quick bites 70-1, 118-19, 166-7
  routines 50
  salt and 30
  sugary 10
  to maintain energy 37, 49
sorbets see ice-creams
soups
  carrot and coriander 162
  chickpea and bacon 164
  creamy tomato 66
  pea and bacon 114
  smoked haddock 128
  squash, carrot and orange 66
  sweetcorn and coconut 117

soya beans 12
soya drink 23-4, 25
soya products 12, 23-4, 25
spaghetti, with peas 65
spices, with lamb, apricots 83
spinach 14, 20
  with haddock and bacon 122
squash
  with baked rice 75
  squash, carrot, orange soup 66
starch 17, 28-9
stews
  beef, with mushrooms 176
  chicken, olive and bean 178
  lamb 114, 130
  lentil and root vegetable 178
  Mediterranean bean 158
  pumpkin 82
  rich mushroom 68
  sausage 127
  vegetable 158
stir-fries
  marinated chicken 120
  pork with greens 173
stock
  low-salt chicken 43
  no-salt vegetable 44
storecupboard recipes 44-5
strawberries
  with mangoes and oats 59
  vanilla strawberry cakes 186
sugars 17, 30, 32, 145
  labelling and 28-9, 30-1
sunflower oil 16
sunflower seeds 12
sunlight, vitamin D 20, 23, 25, 145
suppers 10
  1-2 years 72-83
  2-3 years 120-31
  3-4 years 168-79
sweet potatoes 20
sweetcorn 17
  with cheese and pasta 64
  corn with butter 167
  corn pancakes 72
  and coconut chowder 117
  with tuna and rice 113
sweeteners, artificial 28, 30-1
sweets 32
symbols, explained 6

tahini 25
tannins 13, 25, 31
tea 13, 31
tea breads and fruit loaves
  banana/apricot tea bread 140
  fruit tea loaf 134
  malt loaf with butter/pear 118
  raisin bread 57, 71, 107
  toasted fruit bun 107
teeth
  nutrients 14, 20, 97
  tooth decay 17, 30, 145
toast
  baked beans/cheese on 175
  marmite with salad 113
  with paté 119
  raisin with apple 71, 107
  sardine and tomato 160
  snacks 58

tofu 12, 13, 25
tomatoes 20, 29
  creamy tomato soup 66
  on ciabatta 161
  with potato salad/egg 126
  quick tomato chicken 159
  with roast chicken 174
  sardine/tomato toast 160
  and chicken pasta 77
  with tuna, beans, lettuce 79
trouble shooting
  1-2 years 51
  2-3 years 99
  3-4 years 147
tuna
  with beans/tomato 79
  with couscous salad 62
  with pasta and avocado 64
  and pesto baked potatoes 63
  with rice and sweetcorn 113
turkey 14

vanilla
  and banana risotto 182
  strawberry cakes 186
vegan and vegetarian 12, 25
  milk alternatives 24
  protein for 25
vegetable extracts 28
vitamins and minerals 13-4, 25
vitamin supps 19, 25, 97, 145
vitamins 97
  A/betacarotene 16, 18, 22
  B group 19, 22
  B₁ (thiamine) 19
  B₂ (riboflavin) 19, 22, 25
  B₃ (niacin) 19
  B₅ (pantothenic acid) 19
  B₆ (pyrdoxine) 19
  B₁₂ (cyanocobalamin) 19, 25
  C 13, 15, 25
  D 16, 20, 22-3, 25, 145
  E 16, 20, 22
  folic acid 19
  K 16
  supplements 19, 21, 23, 25,
    97, 145

water see boiled water
watercress 14, 20
wheat products 12, 25
  allergies 11, 26
  fortified 14, 19, 20
wheatgerm 14, 19, 20

yeast extract 19, 21, 25
yogurt 20, 30, 33, 42, 97
  with banana 89, 106
  with berry compote 88
  and cereal sundae 105
  crunchy 156
  with dried fruit compote 71
  frozen with fresh fruit 88
  fruit salad with sauce 102
  with honey and raisins 136
  lemon 184
  pear and sesame 88
  raspberry yogurt ice 180

zinc 14, 22, 25